Vital Truth

Vital Truth

The Convictions of the Christian Community

Nigel G. Wright

CASCADE *Books* • Eugene, Oregon

VITAL TRUTH
The Convictions of the Christian Community

Copyright © 2015 Nigel G. Wright. All rights reserved. Except for brief quotations in critical publications or reviews, no part of this book may be reproduced in any manner without prior written permission from the publisher. Write: Permissions, Wipf and Stock Publishers, 199 W. 8th Ave., Suite 3, Eugene, OR 97401.

Cascade Books
An Imprint of Wipf and Stock Publishers
199 W. 8th Ave., Suite 3
Eugene, OR 97401

www.wipfandstock.com

ISBN 13: 978-1-4982-2574-8

Cataloguing-in-Publication Data

Wright, Nigel, 1949–

Vital truth : the convictions of the Christian community / Nigel G. Wright

viii + 262 p. ; 23 cm. Includes bibliographical references.

ISBN 13: 978-1-4982-2574-8

1. Theology, Doctrinal. I. Title.

BT75.3 W754 2015

Manufactured in the U.S.A.   10/13/2015

Revised Standard Version of the Bible. Copyright 1952 [2nd ed., 1971] by the Division of Christian Education of the National Council of the Churches of Christ in the United States of America. Used by permission. All rights reserved.

New Revised Standard Version of the Bible, copyright 1989, Division of Christian Education of the National Council of the Churches of Christ in the United States of America. Used by permission. All rights reserved.

Scripture quotations marked (NIV) are taken from the Holy Bible, New International Version®, NIV®. Copyright © 1973, 1978, 1984, 2011 by Biblica, Inc.™ Used by permission of Zondervan. All rights reserved worldwide. www.zondervan.com The "NIV" and "New International Version" are trademarks registered in the United States Patent and Trademark Office by Biblica, Inc.™

Dedicated to Miriam, with love

Contents

Introduction | 1
1. The Community of the Risen Lord | 9
2. The God of Jesus Christ: The Personal God | 24
3. The God of Jesus Christ: The Relational God | 37
4. Christology | 49
5. Jesus Christ, Savior of the World | 62
6. Human Dignity and Depravity | 75
7. God's Original Creation | 89
8. God's New Creation | 99
9. God's Spirit in Creation and in Christ | 110
10. God's Spirit in the Church and in Christians | 119
11. God's Gracious Election | 131
12. The Powers of Darkness and Their Defeat | 143
13. Future Hope: The Restoration of All Things | 154
14. Future Hope: Heaven and Hell, Death and Judgment | 167
15. The Way of Jesus Christ | 179
16. The Word of God and the Words of God | 191
17. The Goodness of God and the World's Suffering | 205
18. Humanity's Spiritual Quest | 217
19. The Credibility of Christianity: Advocates and Apologists | 229
20. Communities of Salt and Light | 243

APPENDIX 1: The Apostles' Creed | 257
APPENDIX 2: The Nicene Creed | 259

Bibliography and Suggested Further Reading | 261

Introduction

THE APPEARANCE, SPREAD, IMPACT, and survival of the Christian faith is one of the greatest and most remarkable facts of human history. Whether in accepting it or countering it, no one can deny the influence of Christianity, the most numerous of the religious communities, upon the shape of the world we inhabit. However else it may find expression, the essential nature of this tenacious faith is that it is congregational. It exists in hundreds of thousands of congregations and gatherings in a multitude of cultures and contexts across the globe. They take different forms and have many ways of worshiping and of governing themselves, but they exist and they continue to proliferate.

The congregation is an idea taken from the practice of the Judaism out of which the Christian faith originally emerged. For some centuries, probably beginning with the forced sixth-century exile of many Jews to Babylon and the subsequent destruction of Solomon's Temple, Jewish believers had begun to gather in local synagogues, community meeting places for study, fellowship, and prayer. When the centre of Jewish worship in the Temple of Jerusalem was once more destroyed in 70 AD, Judaism was able to survive because in the exile it had already pioneered the synagogue as a focus for its worship. Here the people gathered, the Scriptures were studied, and the law interpreted. It is clear enough that Jesus was in regular attendance at the synagogue in his village, and when the time came he made the local synagogue the place to announce the beginning of his own ministry (Luke 4:16–21). Synagogues were central to the community, used for schooling and education and as social centers, as well as places for worship.

CHRISTIAN COMMUNITIES

When Christianity came into being, the synagogue provided a natural example of how Christians might form their own faith communities (although for a surprisingly long time believers in Jesus managed to maintain links to the synagogue itself). They formed their own assemblies, congregations, or communities, which became the primary social expression of their life together. Although since that time the word "church" has come to refer to just about any institution, denomination, or organizational form that has somehow sprung from Christian roots, actually "church" primarily refers to the gatherings through which Christian believers learn, share, worship, and evangelize together. The congregation is the true and proper form of the church. According to Peter Brain, an Australian bishop:

> Local churches are the place where the church is visible and functional. Local assemblies constitute the church.... The week-by-week meetings of local Christians are the place where the Great Commandment, of serving love between Christians, can be visible for all to experience and observe. It is also the place from which the Great Commission can be obeyed, supported and its resultant disciples nurtured. The rubber hits the road in local church congregations. Not only is it the place where Christians meet each other, and where Christians are trained to meet the world, but where the world can meet Christ. It is an exciting but difficult place to be.[1]

Any institutional form that does not emerge from and serve vibrant, creative, and faith-filled congregations is doomed to become moribund and obstructive. The health of congregational life is paramount. The local church is indeed the salvation of the world.

Yet Peter Brain's comment is that congregations can also be difficult places to be. There may be many reasons for this—when people begin to relate genuinely and honestly there are challenges enough. But congregations continually face the danger of erosion, both from without and within. Life as we now live it can drain away the resources that are needed to maintain active and effective congregational life. The world of work imposes heavy burdens upon people's time and emotional energies. Leisure opportunities provide numerous distractions from building up a faith community. Raising a well-educated, well-rounded family requires the investment of both time and attention. None of these things are of themselves wrong, but they are demanding and can sap the extra resources that congregations need to sustain themselves. In addition, the generally skeptical and unbelieving atmosphere in which believers have to live out their discipleship can have a corrosive effect on their confidence and motivations. There are few external forces that are hospitable to the building of congregations. Yet it is

---

1. Brain, *Going the Distance*, 216.

the erosion of forces from within that are more concerning. When church members lose a familiarity with the biblical sources of their faith, or have never gained it in the first place, congregational life becomes detached from the very wellsprings that will give it life in times good and bad. And when they are unsure about their convictions, about what it is they believe and why it is they believe it, then the very reasons for being in the church in the first place are undermined. It is just these convictions that this book sets out to explore and to affirm.

CHRISTIAN CONVICTIONS

Although many Christians have been brought up in the faith and so are in the debt of previous generations in particular ways, essentially the Christian faith is not something that can simply be inherited. It has to be embraced by each person on the grounds of personal conviction. It has been said that "God has no grandchildren," and this is what is meant. If people are to believe, they should believe for themselves, not to satisfy someone else. This means that they should be persuaded on their own account that the Christian faith is true: they should be convinced, even if, as is inevitable, the depth of their conviction might waver from time to time. My preference in this volume is to refer to "the Christian community" as another way of speaking about the church or the churches. The language is used interchangeably. Convictions, although personally held, are also community constructs. The knowledge we have we share with others. In fact, knowledge of any kind is only really possible within a group of people who share certain assumptions, common starting points, and rules of logic, usually unspoken but sometimes quite explicit, about what can count as "true" and "false" or "plausible" and "implausible." Christian communities, like all others, function in this way. Those of us who come to believe rarely arrive at that point without the influence of and engagement with a Christian community that has preceded us. What makes its message persuasive to us is that people, apparently ordinary, normal, and intelligent people, do believe these things. It is the sincerity and quality of their conviction that makes them attractive. Convictions are therefore heartfelt beliefs about the way the world is, about the significance of Jesus Christ, and about the reality of the God in whom he placed his trust. It is my intention in this book to describe and explore what lies behind these convictions and to offer them for the continuing commitment of the Christian community.

Christian communities that lose or weaken their convictions are in danger either of ceasing to exist or of degenerating into something that is less than a church. Where there are no convictions to counter them, a community will be swamped by whatever happen to be the conventional or fashionable beliefs of the wider society. If all a church is seeking to do is reflect back to society what it already believes and accepts then it truly has no reason to exist. It offers nothing that cannot be found elsewhere, probably in a better form. But the churches actually exist to say something surprising and unheard of. Where conviction is lacking, so will be the power to convert or to transform others. Make no mistake, the church is in the business of converting men and women to Christ; but an unconvinced church will be an unconvincing church, unable to bring anybody to the point of decision. Convictions carry with them a sense of urgency and the need to act in the light of their content. For churches to be what they are called to be, therefore, the light of clarity and conviction needs to shine brightly. This emphatically does not mean that church members should be expected simply to parrot the party line. Nothing would be more destructive! Rather, they are to be drawn into an engagement with the community's convictions that enables them to understand them, grasp them, and internalize them so that they become a part of themselves, and then to express them with a generous spirit that is both open-hearted and open-minded towards others.

AIMS AND OBJECTIVES

In offering this book for reflection and study I do not imagine that it will answer to the needs of every person found within the Christian community. We all have gifts and abilities that differ. We also possess varying kinds of intelligence. Experience suggests that not all have the same level of interest in, or aptitude and patience for, matters doctrinal and theological. This is entirely understandable, although it would be widely agreed that every church member requires a fundamental grasp of basic beliefs. What is essential however is that in every church community there should be a critical mass of people who have a deeper aptitude for doctrinal thinking (in distinction from equally necessary other forms of thinking) and who are willing to give themselves to the hard brain-work of engaging with the community's beliefs. There is no doubt that this is a demanding task. I have in mind that this book may prove useful for individuals who, having gained a foundational knowledge of their faith, now wish to deepen and extend their understanding, either for the sheer joy of doing so or to increase their usefulness to their own communities. Equally it might be used to inform the teaching or the preaching of pastors and others whose responsibility it is to shape the faith of their communities.

I have deliberately sought to avoid excessive complexity, while not sacrificing content, and to make the twenty chapters that follow relatively short. Because the book is intended for regular church members rather than academics, I have chosen to keep the number of external references or citations as few as possible, using them only when there is a direct quotation from another source. The books cited are listed in the bibliography, which also contains some titles for further reading. I am, of course, profoundly indebted to many thinkers and theologians who have influenced my own thoughts at many points, even to the extent of using or echoing words and phrases that come directly from them. Some readers may recognize these even though I give no references. I here acknowledge my many debts. Conversely, because our convictions emerge from the biblical sources, I have made reference and quoted relatively freely from the Scriptures and have sought to embody their witness within the argument of each chapter. Unless otherwise indicated, citations are taken from the New Revised Standard Version (NRSV). Different translations, the King James Bible, the Revised Standard Version, and the New International Version, are used when, in my judgment, they illuminate the point more effectively, and sometimes the reference is to the alternative translation contained in the notes, or margin, of one of the versions cited. Further biblical texts are referred to in order to substantiate the arguments from other sources, and readers are encouraged to follow these up and consider how they may be relevant. Readers will certainly notice, and I trust forgive, a high degree of repetition of some arguments in the chapters that follow. Though this may lack in literary elegance it will hopefully serve to reinforce some of the thought forms that are introduced here. In addition, it will be noticed that some significant verses keep re-occurring since, like diamonds, they have many facets. This should be taken as testimony to their centrality in identifying Christian convictions.

CLARITY OF THOUGHT

Stating Christian convictions involves weighing and articulating the intellectual content of the Christian faith in a way that is ordered, connected, clear, and faithful to the Christ who is at the heart of our discipleship. Christian teachings, or doctrines, are derived from the biblical witness that gives us access to the story of salvation as it is being worked out through the people of Israel and the early Christian community. In the Bible itself the project of summarizing and stating what is at the heart of faith is already under way and occurs with the intent to offer back to God the glory that is God's due (as examples see Deuteronomy 26:5–11, "A wandering Aramean was my ancestor," and the words of Ezra in Nehemiah 9:6–38, "You are the LORD, you alone"). In the New Testament the elements of basic statements of conviction can be found in verses such as 1 Corinthians 12:3; 15:3–11, and Philippians 2:5–11, words that some believe had already developed either into songs shared in the communities or poetic forms that could be committed to memory by the baptized. The New Testament refers to an emerging "standard of sound teaching" (2 Tim 1:13–4), intended as a summary of apostolic testimony. In turn, this was to develop into what was known in the post-apostolic age as the "rule of faith" and then, as the churches stabilized and became established, into the Apostles' Creed (included here as Appendix 1) and, from 325 AD, the Nicene Creed, regarded today as the ecumenically agreed statement of normative Christian faith (Appendix 2). Such creedal statements, while remaining secondary to Scripture, can be understood as guides as to how to read those Scriptures and prompts as to how they should be understood and what should not be overlooked.

In formulating their convictions the churches always have in mind the biblical sources of their faith, the interpretations of those sources by previous generations of the Christian community all the way back to the apostles themselves, and the ways in which contemporary thinking about the world is likely to confirm or conflict with those convictions. The Christian faith is, after all, like a conversation that has been going on for a long time. Whenever present-day Christians take a Bible in their hands, sing a hymn, or recite the creed in worship, they are implicitly acknowledging the ways in which they are dependent on previous generations who handed the faith on to them in the first place. None of us invents the conversation as though from the beginning: we insert ourselves into one that has long preceded us. We should be willing to listen with humility to the wisdom of our mothers and fathers in the faith.

Although all Christian convictions are important, it is wise and possible to discriminate between those that are absolutely core to the identity of the faith and those that are not. To this end they can be classified as dogmas, doctrines, and opinions. The words "dogmas" and "doctrines" essentially mean the same thing—the principles, teachings, and tenets of the faith. But the word "dogma" is used to refer to teachings that are absolutely at the core, such that were they no longer to be believed, the Christian faith would lose its identity and become something else, a reformed form of Judaism, for instance. Roughly speaking, the church's dogmas correspond with the Apostles' and Nicene Creeds. It is expected that all Christians across the board share these beliefs. Doctrines are convictions that are of high importance but where there might be legitimate differences and disagreements, the kinds for instance that give rise to distinct denominations within the

Christian spectrum. In other words, there are truths that are non-negotiable and define what it means to be Christian; and then there are truths that are negotiable and that determine what kind of Christian we might be. Opinions (more strictly "theological" opinions) are where there is an accepted right of personal judgment in matters that are neither at the core of the faith nor determined by church doctrine. When opinions are made into dogmas friction and divisions will inevitably occur. Conversely, where dogmas are only regarded as opinions then the churches would lack conviction and resilience and would probably cease to exist. For the sake of the well-being of the churches, their preservation in both truth and unity, distinguishing between what is essential and non-negotiable and what is not, is an important part of shared conversation and life. This book seeks to honor these distinctions and to work within them.

GRACE AND TRUTH

Holding firm convictions, and caring deeply about them, is not without risk. Whereas it tends to be people who hold convictions who get things done, being able to persist in times of discouragement and to press forward despite opposition, it might also be the case that those of strong conviction can be over-forceful, both in expressing and pursuing what they believe, to the point of over-riding or compelling others. "Conviction politicians," for instance, are not always appreciated; but then those without convictions are regarded as unprincipled. Similarly the very word "dogma," that we have used, might for some have connotations of "dogmatic," the inability to see or to value contrary points of view. Yet the heart of all Christian convictions is that Jesus Christ, God's Son, is the supreme gift of God and the highest example of what it means to be truly human. Christ was "full of grace and truth" (John 1:14), the perfect expression of truth humanly embodied in a compassionate and forgiving life. It is not enough therefore to have right beliefs ("orthodoxy"). These must be combined with right attitudes and living ("orthopraxis") if they are to be congruent with the one who is the "way, the truth, and the life" (John 14:6). This books seeks to follow the way of "generous orthodoxy," fully and gladly espousing normative Christian convictions and, for that very reason, holding those convictions in ways that are open to truth wherever it be found and seeking "peace, goodwill among people" (Luke 2:14 margin).

The starting point for this book, both in the way it is set out and the beliefs it contains, is the resurrection of Jesus Christ without which there would be no convictions of which to speak.[2]

---

2. I am grateful to Wipf & Stock/Cascade, and in particular their UK editor, Dr. Robin Parry, for allowing this book to see the light of day. Accordingly the text follows the spelling and punctuation conventions of American English.

1

The Community of the Risen Lord

THE CHRISTIAN COMMUNITY EXISTS because of certain convictions that both define and motivate it. Chief among these is the firm belief that Jesus of Nazareth, acclaimed by his first followers as the Messiah and Savior of Israel, died on a Roman cross, rose again, and is now present in the midst of those communities that meet in his name. So crucial is this belief to Christians that were it not true, or if it could be demonstrated to be false, the whole project of the Christian church would be shown to be illusory. On the other hand, if it is indeed true then it is the most important truth that human beings could possibly know, revolutionizing as it does all accepted ways of thinking. The Christian faith stands or falls with the resurrection.

The church as we know it today has grown out of that initial community of disciples that Jesus gathered during his lifetime to be formed by his presence and teaching and to share in his mission to the world. Jesus himself, and his community with him, was in large measure, some would say almost exclusively, the product of the long story of the Jewish people in whom the God of Israel had sought to find a "royal priesthood, a holy nation" that would live in the world, to the benefit of the whole, as a "paradigm nation," an ordered people living with supreme reference to God and exemplifying as a consequence what it meant in a particular land and era to live for the glory of God (Exod 19:1–6). Continuing and extending this story, the gospel of Jesus and the community of disciples became the possession not of Israel alone but of the whole earth, and continue to spread astonishingly to cultures and places far removed from their Palestinian starting place. Their common theme and message remains the same: Jesus the Messiah is alive and continues to take form for us within the church. The church is the body of Christ, not in the sense that it is without fault, as Jesus was, but in that it is the place above all places where Jesus can be found. Embodied existence has many delights and joys, but it means most obviously that we know where to find someone. Locate their body (with which they are inextricably involved) and there you will find him or her. Similarly, the body of Christ makes Jesus locatable within the complexities of modern life. The risen Christ is in the midst of his church. There he continues to take form. There he continues to be Emmanuel, "God with us" (Matt 1:23).

CHRIST PRESENT IN THE CHURCH

How are we to understand this presence of Christ in the church? It is certainly the case that churches exist to sustain the memory of Jesus. They ensure that his memory will not perish from the earth, and this is to the benefit not only of Christian believers but of all others as well. That company of non-Christians, whether non-believers or other-believers, which nonetheless reveres Jesus as teacher, or supreme exemplar of the good, humane life and is grateful for him, only has access to him because there is an enduring community that has kept the memory of Jesus alive and offered that memory to the world. His memory lives in the writings that Christians have produced and now revere as Scripture, and that they preserve through translation, publication, and constant reiteration in their services of worship and liturgies. His memory lives through the church's rites and practices focused in baptism and the breaking of bread by means of which the church recalls and perpetuates events and realities embedded in the life of Jesus himself and prescribed by him. His memory lives in the testimony and witness of people for whom the light of Christ illuminates their present living, who are inspired both to live and to live well on the basis of what he taught. The power of living memory should not be underestimated.

Yet important and indispensable though memory is, when we refer to the resurrection we are talking about more than memory. To say that Christ is "risen" constitutes an infinitely more radical claim. It might be true enough to say that the resurrection of Jesus is a way of insisting that the "spirit" or the "values" of Jesus did not perish with him but live on in the community that reveres him. It might also be true after a fashion to say that for as long as the memory of Jesus persists he cannot be said to be dead. But though true, neither of these constructs would be enough to address the reality of the resurrection. The resurrection claim is that by the power of God something happened to Jesus before it ever happened in the minds of those who became his witnesses. By the power of God the whole of Jesus' identity, body and soul, was brought through death into the life of the new age, the life of God itself, and he appeared for a period of time in glorified form to his closest followers, and some others, to impress upon them indelibly that he had defeated death and would never succumb to it again (Acts 1:3). When, for good reasons, these bodily appearances ceased, the risen Christ continued to be with his disciples in the Spirit, who is the form of his enduring presence today. By the Spirit of God (of whom more later), the risen Christ is in the midst of those communities of faith that look to him and keep his memory alive and believe that in so doing they share in the life of one who lives not just metaphorically or by force of human imagination, but truly and actually.

Christian communities live by this conviction and without it would lose their very reason for being. Yet it is not their only conviction. It acts like the hub of a wheel from which multiple spokes extend. Because Christ is risen many things follow. Christ inspires a whole way of thinking that has come to reshape for Christians their interpretation of the Jewish Scriptures and religion, resulting in a distinctive faith-position that has proven to be imaginative, persuasive, adaptable, and transformative for two thousand years, and that continues to grow and make its impact today. These convictions are rooted in the history of Jesus of Nazareth as his story is told in the documents that now comprise the New Testament. Attention needs to be paid therefore at the beginning of this exploration to the Jesus of history, the Jewish carpenter and unaccredited rabbi from Nazareth, and to the accounts of the resurrection that are so fundamental to the Christian testimony.

THE JESUS OF HISTORY

There are a few people, a very few, who claim that Jesus never lived and that he is a character of imaginative fiction. There are others who believe that he did indeed live but that we know hardly anything about him, the Gospels being largely fabrications of his early followers. More sober historians are thoroughly skeptical about such skepticism and acknowledge that in actual fact we know a remarkable amount. Jesus is firmly located in datable and reliable history. Doubt about his existence is arguably not motivated by a desire to uncover objective history so much as by bias against him and the faith that stems from him.

The following sets out a number of secure facts about the Jesus of history that it is possible to affirm, whether a person is a Christian or not:

- Jesus was born around the year 4 BC, near the time of the death of Herod the Great;
- He spent his childhood and early adult years in Nazareth, a Galilean village;
- He was baptized by John the Baptist;
- He called disciples;
- He taught in the towns, villages, and countryside of Galilee (apparently not the cities);
- He preached "the kingdom of God,"
- About the year 30 he went to Jerusalem for Passover;
- He created a disturbance in the Temple area;
- He had a final meal with his disciples;
- He was arrested and interrogated by the Jewish authorities, specifically the high priest;
- He was executed on the orders of the Roman prefect, Pontius Pilate.

To which we may add the equally secure facts about the aftermath of his life:

- His disciples at first fled;
- They saw him (in what sense will be explored further below) after his death;
- As a consequence, they believed that he would return to found the kingdom;
- They formed a community to await his return and sought to win others to faith in him as God's Messiah. This community is what we now call the church.[1]

These facts are as secure and certain as any other historical facts, and perhaps more so given that compelling evidence for many events we take for granted is not always to be found. Together they mean that the basic outline of the life of Jesus that is presented to us in the Gospels, Matthew, Mark, Luke, and John is reliable and dependable—contrary to what some people sometimes claim (often not historians, and usually with an ideological axe to grind). It is important for Christians that the basic shape of Jesus' life and career should be confirmed in this way since the Christian faith, unlike some other world religions, depends upon certain things, like Christ's death and resurrection, actually having happened. Christian conviction is rooted

---

1. Based upon Sanders, *The Historical Figure of Jesus*, 10–11.

in history. Historical evidence is therefore important in attesting some basic facts.

JESUS IN HIS CONTEXT

As time and scholarship have developed, we have come to understand a great deal more about the world in which Jesus lived and which formed the background to his life. The Jewish historian Geza Vermes has demonstrated in a series of books (the clearest of which is *Jesus the Jew*) that the picture we have of Jesus in the Gospels fits remarkably well with what we now know of his context from other places. Vermes demonstrates from contemporary sources how Galilee, the home province of Jesus in the north of Israel and bordering the Gentile nations, was a location for non-rabbinical and anti-establishment Judaism. We have knowledge of other charismatic, itinerant rabbis from the first century who were also exorcists and healers not dissimilar to Jesus, such as Hanina ben-Dosa and Honi the Circle-Drawer. Like Jesus, such men attracted disciples, taught wisdom, and performed wonders; they evoked devotion and lived on in the memory of their followers once they were dead, with shrines being erected to them. Honorific titles such as "lord" and "son of God" were applied to them by their devotees. Whereas some might at first feel that the existence of such parallel figures to Jesus reduces his uniqueness, what it in fact does is to confirm and authenticate the picture of Jesus that is presented in the Gospels. The New Testament itself hints that there were others who did some of the things that Jesus did, not only John the Baptist, but others who cast out demons (Luke 9:49–50) or had messianic pretensions (Acts 5:33–39). Judaism at the time of Jesus was very much in flux and was capable of throwing up all kinds of variations, yet the most significant thing to note is that the figures we have mentioned have all but been forgotten, except by historians who research largely inaccessible texts, whereas Jesus of Nazareth has become the central figure in a global religion—the world's largest religious tradition. This remarkable fact, that a carpenter and wandering rabbi from a minority ethnic group in a small province of the Empire has achieved global status, cries out for some kind of explanation. How has this happened? What is it that Jesus had that the others did not?

First of all, in answering this question, we are able to point to the *quantity* of what Jesus taught. By contrast, we have only a few isolated sayings from figures such as Honi and Hanina. The New Testament gives to us a surprising amount of information concerning Jesus' life and teaching, such as his unsurpassed parables, the Sermon on the Mount, his prophetic and compassionate acts of healing and deliverance, his friends and followers, his controversies with establishment figures, the events of his public ministry, and above all of his final week and of his trial, death, and resurrection. Together these accounts supply a rich and powerful narrative that has gripped the imagination of people across the world, from all kinds of cultures, countries, and conditions. Whatever else might be said, the story of Jesus is one of the greatest stories ever told. For that reason it has proved to be exceptionally attractive and persuasive from the beginning until now.

Secondly, this leads us to affirm the *quality* of what Jesus taught. Jesus was a creative interpreter of the Jewish heritage. Although a faithful son of Israel, he was able to take his heritage and its Scriptures and both affirm and develop the direction in which they were tending. Recent Jewish scholarship is at pains to stress how well Jesus reflects the best and most advanced in Jewish thought of his day, which, as we have already indicated, was passing through a time of creative ferment. It is clear that Jesus brought both a distinctive message and a special kind of genius to his preaching and communication. The parables he told, such as the stories of the Prodigal Son and the Good Samaritan, are outstanding forms of communication and have become part of the common heritage of the human race as a whole, not simply of Christians. However, the assumption that Jesus taught in parables in order to illustrate his message and make it clear is only partly correct. He saw himself fulfilling the words in Isaiah addressed to the people of Israel, "You will indeed listen, but never understand, and you will indeed look, but never perceive" (Matt 13:14, Isa 6:9–10). Many of the parables of Jesus are enigmatic, such that to understand them the hearers needed to have a good disposition, a willingness in advance to understand and be taught: "For to those who have, more will be given, and they will have an abundance" (Matt 13:12). This is highly sophisticated. Moreover, it is reported that Jesus "taught them as one having authority, and not as their scribes" (Matt 7:29). This suggests that the authority of Jesus came not from referring to other rabbis and teachers but from within, from one who was deeply engaged with what he taught and the God from whom it came. The profound and unique relationship Jesus felt he had with the Father, "Abba," was the wellspring from which his teaching came (Luke 10:21–22).

Thirdly, we might draw attention to the *content* of what Jesus taught. Jesus proclaimed the kingdom, the reign of God, the coming of God, and understood himself to be the very agent of God's coming. God's kingdom is that realm where God's will is done, God's justice is upheld, and God's peace is known. Its coming was foretold by the prophets and eagerly awaited in the future, but according to Jesus it was even now present. God's kingdom was both "now" and "not yet." The Spirit of God was active in the works of healing and deliverance that Jesus ministered: "But if it is by the finger of God that I cast out the demons, then the kingdom of God has come to you" (Luke 11:20). Because the coming of God to help and deliver God's people was near, Jesus called upon his fellow Israelites to repent and make themselves ready. The message of Jesus was therefore about an imminent transformation, about something that was happening in history according to the purpose of God which would fulfill the expectations of the Old Testament prophets and introduce something radically new. Particularly to be noticed here is the way Jesus identified himself with Israel's God and saw the coming of God in his own person and deeds: "All things have been handed over to me by my Father; and no one knows who the Son is except the Father; or who the Father is except the Son and anyone to whom the Son chooses to reveal him" (Luke 10:22). If the kingdom of God is the coming of God's own self to reign and if that coming of God is taking place in and through Jesus, Jesus is to be closely identified with God, and so the foundation is laid for the followers of Jesus later to speak of him as the Son of God.

Finally, and supremely, Jesus has been remembered whereas other charismatic teachers of his day have been forgotten because of the *confirmation* of what Jesus taught. God's confirmation of Jesus was his resurrection from the dead. This is seen as God's vindication of Jesus in face of the fact that the authorities and powers of his day rejected him and what he stood for, and put him to death. The resurrection was God's rejection of the human rejection of Jesus. Being raised from the dead makes a difference to whether or not you are remembered. This is to understate the case. Being risen, Jesus' life and mission could now be interpreted backwards in the light of the resurrection. Who he was, what he did, what he said, everything about him, could now be looked upon with new eyes and new depth. We noted the historical fact that titles such as "Lord" and "son of God" were used of some charismatic figures of Jesus' era, supporting the Gospel account of such and similar titles being applied to Jesus in his lifetime. Now, in the light shed retrospectively by the resurrection such terms acquire new depths of meaning and become the basis of the "Christology" of the New Testament, the activity of explaining the true and full identity of Jesus of Nazareth as the Son of God. He truly is the Lord. Without the resurrection Jesus would have fallen into obscurity, as did so many others, and been more or less forgotten. He was remembered because he was raised and being raised his importance could not be denied. The memory of Jesus became too powerful to be discarded.

THE RESURRECTION OF JESUS AS THE CHRIST

That Jesus has been remembered, more than this, that he has been embraced and honored by so many people for so very long without a sign, globally speaking, that devotion to him is diminishing, is itself testimony to the truth of the resurrection since without it, it is problematic to explain why Jesus should have been so remembered. Yet the fact is that according to our regular human experience people are not raised from the dead. This salient fact is, of course, the whole point: that Jesus was raised when no others are is what distinguishes him. It is essential therefore for Christians to stand on firm ground when they make the enormous and extraordinary claim that Jesus is risen from the dead. Although the great majority of Christians wish to assert this fact because of their experience of encounter with Christ in conversion, worship, and prayer, experiences that can be intensely real and personal, such claims remain nonetheless subjective and in principle beyond objective testing. It is necessary therefore to support them by more objective arguments and evidence. After all, the Christian claim is that something has actually happened in history that affects us all. If it could be shown that nothing actually happened or that a more credible alternative explanation is available, in other words, if the resurrection claim could be falsified, then Christians would need to retract their claim and think again about the meaning of their religion. We need therefore to demonstrate that the claim to a resurrection is soundly based. It is not that the historical event of the resurrection can be historically proved (though some people claim this). Rather it is about demonstrating that the burden of evidence points in the direction of Jesus truly being raised and that this claim is the most persuasive explanation of the relevant evidence. On this basis Christians are justified in placing their faith in Christ not as an act of blind faith but of reasonable and warranted trust.

First of all we need to reflect upon what the resurrection does or does not imply. It certainly implies that something happened to the dead Jesus. Something happened to Jesus once dead before anything ever happened to his disciples. The resurrection is not about the rebirth of hope within the hearts of the disconsolate disciples, nor is it about a decision on their part to keep the movement going and the memory of Jesus alive. All these things were consequences of what first of all happened to Jesus. The disciples were broken and disillusioned until it became clear that Jesus was indeed alive.

Secondly, we should be clear that the resurrection does not mean that the dead body of Jesus was restored to the condition it had before he died—this would be a resuscitation rather than a resurrection. Resuscitations are well within the bounds of common experience. It is recorded that in this sense Jesus himself raised people from the dead (for instance, Lazarus in John 11). Those so raised would one day die again and for good. But resurrection is an event of a different order. It means that the body of Jesus was raised into a new dimension of existence having been transformed from its mortal condition into immortality. Jesus' body was "glorified" (Luke 24:26, Phil 3:21 margin), that is, taken up into the quality of life that is God's own and raised beyond the possibility of dying again. In this sense the resurrection should be seen as a happening in history whereby the future life, the life of the world to come, was already found within the present. Jewish belief was that in the fullness of time all would be raised from the dead to face judgment, the "general resurrection," but Christians claimed that here and now it had happened to Jesus. It was in this glorified form that Jesus then appeared to his disciples, which probably explains some aspects of his appearances, such as passing through locked doors. In the resurrection Jesus was identifiably himself, bearing in his body the scars of his crucifixion and speaking with the same voice (John 20:16, 26–29). Yet he was also mysteriously transformed, still present in the body, but a different kind of body, a "glorious" body. It should be clear then that the resurrection was an event of a different order. Although it happened in history and made its impact it cannot properly be defined as a "historical event" as such since it did not arise by cause and effect out of what had gone before. Rather it was a unique act of God in history, introducing something completely new, which for that very reason holds open the possibility of new life for all.

Although the resurrection itself cannot finally be proved and requires an openness to God and divine possibility before it is likely to be embraced, there is something that can indeed be taken as cast-iron history with a confidence that matches or exceeds any other historical event. This is that *the disciples of Jesus firmly believed that he had been raised from the dead*. Even if they were mistaken, the fact that they believed as they did is supported by all the evidence that we have and is itself the explanation for their subsequent actions in spreading the message, always at the cost of suffering and frequently of their own lives. But if they did believe this the question clearly follows: why did they do so and act upon their belief with such boldness? The most persuasive answer is that they were eye-witnesses, that Jesus actually was raised from the dead and appeared to them so that there was for them overwhelming proof that he was alive. This confidence is clearly seen, for instance, in a passage such as 1 John 1:1–2: "We declare to you what was from the beginning, what we have heard, what we have seen with our eyes, what we have looked at and touched with our hands, concerning the word of life—this life was revealed, and we have seen it and testify to it, and declare to you the eternal life that was with the Father and was revealed to us."

Although the New Testament certainly shows a degree of development in the ways in which Jesus was understood, and we shall explore these in due course, it is entirely mistaken to believe that the high view the disciples held of Jesus was something that simply developed slowly over time. This is a common assumption that skeptics advance: the claim they make is that Jesus began as an ordinary Jewish teacher, but over a lengthy period of time he was gradually raised in the imagination of his followers to higher and higher status until he became for them God incarnate. All the evidence suggests, however, that this was not the case. To the contrary, it was from the very beginning, within a very short time, even days, of his death, that they ascribed such high status to Jesus in calling him "Lord." "God has made him both Lord and Messiah, this Jesus whom you crucified" (Acts 2:36). All of this points to an abrupt and startling event by which Jesus moved from the humiliation of death on a Roman cross to exaltation at God's right hand. The transition from Jewish carpenter to divine Lord and Son of God was not gradual but immediate and a consequence of the astonishing exaltation of Jesus in the resurrection.

EVIDENCE FOR THE RESURRECTION

It is time then to review the evidence for the resurrection. Some basic facts are worth stating.

- Jesus died a shameful death. Death on a cross was a very cruel form of execution and was regarded by Jewish people as particularly accursed. Crucifixions were common under Roman occupation and Jesus was one of very many whose lives were taken in this way. That Jesus met his end on a cross is beyond doubt and few question it. It is not the kind of event that anyone would invent to promote their favored teacher or create a new religion. Jesus was crucified on the Friday of the Passover feast in or around the year 30 AD.

- He was given an honorable burial. The bodies of the crucified were often left to rot or alternatively were disposed of by being deposited in a pit. Some believed this happened to Jesus, though there is nothing to suggest this in the Gospel sources. However, everything we know about those who attract deep devotion in their lives suggests that their followers seek to care for their bodies after death. Exactly this happened after the execution of Jesus' predecessor, John the Baptist (Mark 6:29). It is more likely therefore that the body of Jesus was treated with respect by his followers. The Gospel record is that Joseph of Arimathea, a prominent person and a secret follower of Jesus, asked

- for the body of Jesus and along with the female followers and relatives of Jesus ensured that he was properly buried with appropriate dignity.
- The tomb was then found empty. For this to be discovered the location of Jesus' tomb had to be known, as indicated in the previous point. On the third day (counting Friday and Sunday as whole days and after the Sabbath was over), when those closest to Jesus came to complete the burial preparations (which had been rushed because of the onset of the Jewish Sabbath at dusk on the Friday), the tomb was found to be empty. Of itself this did not imply that he had been raised and the first, and natural, assumption was that someone had removed his body (John 20:15).
- Jesus was seen alive by his closest disciples, who became convinced that he had "risen." It was the repeated appearances of Jesus after his death that persuaded the disciples that he had indeed been raised. This was the explanation for the tomb being empty, which itself implied that the resurrection involved the raising of the body of Jesus and not his "spirit" only.
- Those disciples were transformed by their encounter. Having scattered after the death of Jesus for fear of their own lives they were now gathered together once more. Some of them, such as Peter, Mary Magdalene, and James the brother of Jesus, experienced individual encounters with Jesus, others encountered him within a group. The clearest and earliest witness to this comes not from the Gospels (which were written later), but from the apostle Paul who wrote, "he appeared to Cephas [Peter], then to the twelve. Then he appeared to more than five hundred brothers and sisters at one time, most of whom are still alive, though some have died. Then he appeared to James, then to all the apostles. Last of all, as to someone untimely born, he appeared also to me" (1 Cor 15:5–8). These words were written less than twenty years after the resurrection. But the literary form of this section and the use of Peter's Aramaic name "Cephas" indicate that Paul was citing a tradition that was handed on to him when he was converted, just a few years after the resurrection itself. This takes us very close to the event.
- The disciples of Jesus were to pay a huge price for their conviction including in many cases martyrdom. People are prepared to die for what they believe in, but not for what they know to be untrue or themselves have fabricated. As has been said, therefore, the fact that they truly believed Jesus had risen must be taken as a solid historical fact. The most

convincing explanation of this fact is that he had indeed been raised and they were witnesses of his appearances (Acts 10:34–43).

- The resurrection supplied the energy that carried the Christian faith into the Roman Empire and the world. It is worth pondering how a faith centered in a Jewish carpenter from Nazareth in Galilee whose life came to an end in shameful crucifixion could have undergone such an astonishing trajectory. This unlikely occurrence is hard to countenance without concluding that some remarkable event assisted it on its way. The resurrection, and the energy and conviction it supplied, is that event. Other explanations are either lacking or inadequate to explain it.

ARGUMENTS AGAINST THE RESURRECTION

Arguments against the resurrection are often more difficult to believe than the resurrection itself because they are based on speculation rather than evidence. They often border on historical fiction. It is certainly the case that alternative hypotheses aplenty have been suggested, conspiracy on the part of the disciples being one and probably the first approach. It was put about by the Jewish authorities that the disciples stole Jesus' body by night (Matt 28:11–15). This sees the resurrection as a fraud perpetrated by the disciples. Indirectly, and ironically, this is actually evidence that the tomb was indeed empty, and so in fact ends up substantiating the fact of the empty tomb. However, it fails to explain why the disciples should go on to preach the resurrection so heroically and to pay for it with persecution and their lives. Other hypotheses see the resurrection accounts as being based on some kind of mistake. These include the possibility that the wrong tomb was visited by the women on the morning of the resurrection; that Jesus did not actually die on the cross but had his place taken by another, Simon of Cyrene being the most obvious candidate (Luke 23:26); that Jesus was on the cross but did not actually die and then revived once he was in the cool of the tomb, only to escape from it and convince people he had conquered death. Given that each of these scenarios could easily have been uncovered and disproved at the time, and the resurrection therefore falsified, they do not command much credibility, let alone explain how the world's most prominent and ennobling religion could be based either on a mistake or a conspiracy.

While these wilder theories are easy to dismiss, Christians need to be aware of some weightier objections to their claim. It may be objected that after two thousand years it is impossible to recapture what actually did happen after the death of Jesus and that agnosticism is the best policy. There is currently a greater willingness to accept that religious experiences are a recurring fact of human psychology through the ages. Even today religious experiences, such as visions and apparently extra-sensory perceptions, can be recorded and documented, but not necessarily explained. The fact that we do not yet understand this dimension of the human subconscious, the argument runs, should not lead us to abandon the assumption that it might with time be explained "naturally" and without reference to God. It is known for instance that "bereavement visions" sometimes occur in which one who has recently died reappears, or is thought to do so, in a highly vivid way, sometimes in a way involving touch as well as speech, to the living. Reported visions of the Virgin Mary are a parallel example of this and can be both intense and repeated. Neither is there available to us any way of adjudicating whether those who bear witness to these experiences are actually seeing a real, though deceased person, or undergoing a psychologically induced phenomenon that is simply an illusion, though one that feels real. The distinction here is between visions that are "viewer-dependent" or "viewer-independent." The unconvinced and skeptical might therefore acknowledge that the first disciples underwent some hard-to-define religious experience or bereavement vision that sincerely convinced them that Christ had risen. They then objectified this in a series of resurrection narratives, both to capture their experiences and to develop a kind of apologetic to answer objections to their claim, for instance in showing how it was not true that the disciples removed the body. In its turn this might explain for the skeptic why the resurrection accounts differ from each other in details, though not in their main claim, and why after the down-to-earth and historically convincing account of the crucifixion the accounts of the resurrection apparently assumed a much more unhistorical form, with accounts of earthquakes, angels, and stones being rolled away. It is true that the borderline between a vision of a person who is truly living beyond death and that contains tactile elements, and that of a person actually raised from death, but appearing only to his faithful followers (Acts 10:39–41), begins to seem quite slender. However, the account of the empty tomb and the disappearance of the body of Jesus are testimony that the early witnesses clearly meant us to understand that something happened to the *body* of Jesus and not just his spirit. If we are relying on the available evidence this must be given considerable weight.

The arguments are set out here for the sake of honesty. If Christians are to believe in the resurrection it must be in the face of some strong objections to it. Honesty requires this. These arguments against, however, remain mere hypotheses and suppositions that are suggested without evidence and are to be contrasted with the evidential nature of the claim to resurrection. Human psychology is difficult enough to interpret in the present, let alone after an interval of two thousand years and in the case of people to whom we have no direct access, so speculative psychological theories are at a disadvantage and tend to fall apart when probed more deeply. The lack of evidence of a historical kind is surely significant, especially in an age when all manner of claims are meant to be "evidence-based." Having rehearsed the arguments against, the Christian is entitled to feel that they still fall short of adequately explaining the dramatic and pivotal events that took place after the crucifixion and to which the original eye-witnesses were soberly committed. The fact that their experiences were repeated, corporate, and multiply attested counts against their being "explained" in these ways.

THE RISEN CHRIST

After his death on the cross the original followers of Jesus were persuaded that he had risen from the dead and that once more he was present with them. The appearances of Jesus as the conqueror of death were of limited duration for a good reason. They made it clear that not just anybody could now claim to be an authenticated witness to the resurrection, but only those who had been with him "from the beginning" (Acts 1:21–26). The only exception to this was the apostle Paul, who, as we know, had to struggle to establish his position among the primary witnesses. It is their testimony that constitutes the normative version of the Christian faith that we here endeavor to set out. Yet through the Spirit Christ is present in the midst of those faith-communities that embrace and trust him and believe that he has been raised from the dead. This is both the starting point and the central point for our understanding of Christian convictions, the hub at the centre of the wheel from which all the spokes ultimately derive.

GUIDING CRITERIA

In investigating the truth of Christian convictions there are several criteria that need to be applied. One concerns the *coherence* of what is claimed: in other words, do Christian convictions make sense in themselves or are they internally self-contradictory or without sense? A second criterion is that of *correspondence*: do they describe reality as it actually is or are they out of kilter with what is experienced of the world around us, or indeed, the spiritual realm that in a Christian worldview is discernible beyond it? The third criterion is that of *congruence*: do our convictions resonate with what we know of God in Jesus Christ, who is risen from the dead and is found within our communities? Are we being true to Christ, faithful to what he taught and enacted, or do we miss the mark? At this point we need to pay particular attention to the fact that the resurrection is the resurrection of the historical Jesus. The Jesus of history did not become lost in the resurrected Jesus as though we can regard his earthly life as now unnecessary, swallowed up in the glory of the exalted one. To the contrary, the life of Jesus is given new meaning and prominence precisely because he is the one who is marked out by God. Everything he did and said is to be given our fullest attention. These criteria, but especially the last, will guide us as we attempt to think *Christianly* about the convictions that uphold us and make us what we are.

As has been indicated, for the sake of simplicity of presentation it is not the intention in this book to refer to other literature except on rare occasions. However, a significant and explicit quotation directly relevant to our theme is available in the writings of an ancient Jewish historian contemporary with the early church. This is Flavius Josephus (37 AD—post 100 AD), who wrote in his history of the Jewish people:

> At this time there was a wise man who was called Jesus. And his conduct was good, and he was known to be virtuous. And many people from among the Jews and the other nations became his disciples. Pilate condemned him to be crucified and to die. And those who had become his disciples, did not abandon his discipleship. They reported that he had appeared to them three days after his crucifixion and that he was alive; accordingly, he was thought to be the Messiah (the Christ) concerning whom the prophets have recounted wonders. And the people of the Christians, named after him, have not disappeared till this day. (*Antiquities of the Jewish People* 18:63–64).

Much debate has surrounded this passage in Josephus' *Antiquities of the Jewish People*. The general belief is that the Greek version of this text has been interpolated by a later Christian scribe adding in some more affirmative and Christian-biased statements about Jesus. However, the quotation above is from the less well known and more recently discovered Arabic version, which shows no signs of interpolation: The translation in this form is taken from the Jewish scholar David Flusser.[2] This summary by a near contemporary of Jesus' life, death, and claimed resurrection, but one who was not himself a believer, is both significant and accurate. No Christian would wish to disagree with it.

---

2. Flusser, *The Sage from Galilee*, 147–48.

2

The God of Jesus Christ
The Personal God

IF WE ARE PERSUADED that Christ has risen from the dead and is present in his church then we are immediately confronted with the reality of God. The life of Jesus makes no sense without reference to God. The word "God" is itself problematic since it could refer to whatever we wish to make the word mean: it is a "floating signifier." Before we can truly say we believe in God we need to make the term specific. What understanding of God do we invest in that simple word? Since Jesus was Jewish and emerged from the long story of the Jewish people, we can assert that Jesus believed in the God of Israel, the God of Abraham, Isaac, and Jacob, the God of the unfolding revelation of the Hebrew Scriptures in which he was nurtured and whose faith he shared. Not only did Jesus believe in this God, he was confident that he knew this God personally and intimately, addressing the Holy One as "Abba, Father" (Mark 14:35; Luke 10:21) and so using the language of family intimacy and love. In time we shall examine what it means to call Jesus the "Son of God," but for the moment we recognize that as God's Son Jesus found in the God of Israel his Father and his Lord. By derivation we may say that Christians believe in the God of Israel as they have come to understand him in the light of a Messiah who died and was raised. To this understanding we shall return.

THE GOD OF ISRAEL

To believe in the God of Israel is foundational. The Bible begins with the strong statement that, "In the beginning God created the heavens and the earth" (Gen 1:1 NIV). It all begins with God. The narrative of creation that then follows certainly has much to say about creation, but even more about God the creator. This early chapter is a confession of faith in Israel's God and by its nature it excludes a variety of alternative beliefs that are still commonly found in the religious experience of humankind. By grasping what is not implied or intended by this chapter of the Bible we can approach more confidently its positive witness. For instance, the chapter excludes:

- *Polytheism*, the belief that there is a variety of gods, perhaps many gods, each of which is responsible for some aspect of creation's life, for instance, the god of the sea, or of the mountains, or of war, or of love, or of particular tribes and nations. The list can be extended. Ancient religions, including those of Greece and Rome and of the Nordic nations, paid homage to many gods who were often thought to be capricious or imagined as human beings writ large. The gods needed to be kept favorable and so were propitiated through gifts and sacrifices. By contrast, for Israel there was one God who was the sole source of everything that is, who ruled over the creation and who gave unity and integration to it and, potentially, to its peoples. This is called "monotheism" and is a view shared by Jews, Muslims, Christians, and some others, though the differences between these approaches are important to note. Also excluded is:

- *Pantheism*, the belief that the word "God" is a way of speaking of the totality of creation, that God is the "world-spirit," the spirituality created by the life-force of all things. God therefore has no existence or reality apart from the things that exist. We are entitled to feel a sense of transcendent wonder when we observe the immensity of the universe and are belittled by it. Equally we should reverence the creation, treating it as something holy and inviolable and living in harmony with it. It can be seen that in an age of ecological concern pantheism has achieved a new relevance for many people and has come to undergird a new sense of responsibility for the world around us and on which we ourselves depend. By contrast the biblical view understands God to be other than the world, its creator, but not part of that which is created. God transcends the world. If the world were subtracted God would still be and would still be God. The creation therefore is not to be worshiped, but it is to be valued, enjoyed, appreciated, and honored precisely because it is the creation of a good and holy God. The faith of Israel also excludes:

- *Dualism*, the belief that there are and possibly always have been two equal and opposite realities in the world, one good and one evil, that are eternally opposed to each other and in continual conflict. This is the belief of an ancient religion such as Zoroastrianism. It has the merit of accounting for the phenomena that we see in the world around as creative and discreative, constructive and destructive forces struggle with each other persistently. But it is ruled out by the biblical narrative, which insists that there has been a beginning to all things and that God is supreme over all, existing before creation began. There is indeed a conflict between good and evil and we live in the midst of it, yet this is not eternal, but temporary, and will finally come to an end. Then we can exclude:

- *Paganism*, the extension of pantheism that offers worship to created things such as the sun and the moon, to trees and places, and finds divine spirits to inhabit specific objects or aspects of the creation. This is a religion that venerates nature and finds healing in being in harmony with it whilst also seeking to control it and its forces. One form of it goes under the name of Wicca and understands itself to be benign, earthy, and beneficial in its approach. Yet in contrast, the Genesis narrative sees sun, moon, and stars not as divinities, but as objects that God has hung in the sky to define seasons, years, days, and night (1:14–19). They are useful, indeed necessary. They are emphatically not divine, but simply have their origin in the one God. The biblical faith also excludes:

- *Atheism*, the belief that there is no God, and that it is probably pointless to ask where the world comes from or what meaning it has since such questions are beyond us and are unlikely to yield an answer. Rather, the world is just there, without explanation, and it is up to us to get on with life without the illusion of there being any more to it than we can see. Atheism considers itself to be a noble belief since it forces us back on our own resources, having to do the best we can with what we have without seeking for a help that will never come. Religion, on this view, belongs to humankind's infancy or adolescence and should be discarded in favor of a harsher but more adult perspective. We are on our own and this life is all there is. By contrast, the biblical witness asserts that we are not on our own, that there is something, indeed someone, behind the world; that it has an origin and therefore it also has a purpose and a direction, a reason for existing that it is in fact possible to know and embrace. This something is God.

THE BIBLICAL VISION OF GOD

By excluding certain possibilities we are in a better position to understand the positive nature of belief in Israel's God. The Christian God equates to none of the above. It is entirely reasonable to believe in God. The creation of which we are a part is amenable to investigation. It can be studied scientifically and found to have its own rationality and logic. It can be understood mathematically to have its own order and patterns, and it is the human mind that is capable of doing all these things. The reason for this is that the world itself is the product of Mind, the mind of God. Because the world is not itself God but is created by God to be other than God's own self, there is no sacrilege involved in penetrating creation's secrets. The world is there to be understood and when we investigate it we are thinking God's thoughts after God's own self. Belief in a God who is the origin of all things is not only instinctive, such that when we see the intricacies and beauties of creation we are moved to worship its creator, it is also rational. It is reasonable to believe this. To infer from the reality of the world that the world is not just "there" but has come from somewhere or someone, that there is some supreme power or presence beyond it as well as within it, is an entirely rational point of view. It also seems to be hard-wired into human brains. The universe has not come into existence without a cause and to claim this is not illogical. Furthermore, such an understanding helps us to live within the world as those who have reverence for the gift of life, who instinctively wish to give thanks for it to something or someone, who believe that there is a direction and a purpose to creation, and who can make sense of it because they believe that within the reality of all things there is a coherent reason for being that is deeply satisfying, emotionally, intellectually, and aesthetically.

God is not an extension of the world, as though God were subject to the same conditions and characteristics that limit it. Where the world is finite, God is infinite. If it is time-bound, God is eternal. Where the world has an origin and a beginning, God has no origin or beginning beyond God's self, but rather is his own origin and being, having existence from within God's own life. Where the world passes away, God does not pass away, but is eternal and everlasting, not subject to the passage of time, but Lord over it. To say of God, as people often do, that God "exists" falls short of capturing the ultimate nature of God's own being. God does not exist as one being among others. This would be to reduce God to our own size. Rather God is fullness of being, Being-itself, the very possibility of anything's existing. There is nothing higher than, greater than, more ultimate than, fuller than, wiser than, more beautiful than the God who breathes life into everything that exists. God is both the source of life and the one who breathes life into creation on a moment by moment basis. "In him we live and move and have our being" (Acts 17:28). In relation to the world God is free. God does not depend upon the world in order to be God. God is free and without limitation. God has complete power over the world and is present to every part of it at the same time. The world lies open to God's gaze and there is nothing that lies hidden or unknown to God. God is supreme and is to be worshiped as such by all things since when God is so acknowledged and honored then reality is recognized as it should be and all things find their rightful place. A world in which God would be truly worshiped would be one in which perfect peace prevailed and in which in true harmony everything discovered itself and its place in relation to its creator.

All of the above statements can be derived from the vision of God that is presented to us progressively within the Bible. In particular, there are two understandings of God that are determinative for understanding the God of Israel in whom Jesus believed. The first is found in Exodus 3. In this passage the greatest leader and teacher of Israel, Moses, encounters God in a strange form. In the desert he sees a bush burning, but not being consumed by the fire. His attention is seized by what he sees and he finds himself being spoken to by God. God identifies himself as "the God of your father, the God of Abraham, the God of Isaac, and the God of Jacob" (v. 6). This God commissions Moses to return to Egypt, where the people of Israel are suffering, and to lead them out of captivity into freedom in "a good and broad land, a land flowing with milk and honey" (v. 8). Moses is to be a freedom fighter. In the course of their dialog Moses dares to ask God's name and receives the reply "I AM WHO I AM" (v. 14). This is to be God's identity, and it is in connection with this revelation that the name of God is identified in the religion of Israel and in Judaism past and present. God is known by the name "Yahweh," a name considered by Jewish believers to be so holy that it cannot be spoken aloud. Instead, the title "Adonai" or "LORD" is used as a spoken alternative. The divine self-declaration can be variously translated, for instance as "I will be what I will be." The revelation of God's name here is crucial for understanding the Jewish and the Christian vision of God. It indicates that who and what God is, is a mystery. Who God is, is to be discovered as we relate to God and as God makes God's own self known to us progressively as our own devotion grows and increases. God's identity would be made known to Israel in all the events that were to follow on from Moses' initial encounter with God in this way. God is not to be known through philosophical, abstract argument or enquiry, but through concrete, existential, historical encounters in which God is present, revealing himself as the One Who Is.

One Jewish thinker (Martin Buber) has described the crucial difference between I-It knowledge and I-Thou knowledge. I-It knowledge applies when we subject an object to scrutiny in an objective or scientific way. We are examining it as a thing that is over against us, and our personal engagement with it is minimal. It is subject-to-object knowledge. However, this is not the way we come to know other people, especially those who are closest and most important to us. Neither is it the way we know God. This requires I-Thou knowledge, personal encounter, not with an object but with another subject, so that personal knowing requires subject-to-subject engagement. This takes us beyond the realms of scientific or philosophical knowledge into personal knowledge, the most significant and interesting knowledge of all. This is the kind of knowledge that bears fruit in knowing God, as indeed it does in knowing each other. The God of Israel who reveals the name of I Am Who I Am is to be known through personal encounter and engagement, and this is the nature of the meaning of faith. Faith is not opposed to knowledge but is a way of knowing, a reasonable trust in another subject who is personal, progressive, challenging, and all-absorbing. Neither is it opposed to the human capacity and responsibility for the exercise of reasoning powers; but it does insist that we follow reason as far as it can go only to peer into the mystery that lies beyond it and that can only be known through personal knowledge. This is the way Jesus knew the God he called Father and in divine, spiritual things it must be our path of knowing also.

The second highly significant passage is found in Exodus 34:6–7 and also concerns Moses. Here at a crucial time of divine revelation Moses is engaged intensely with God. In order that Moses may truly know God's presence the Lord says that he will "pass before" Moses. But God's glory is so overwhelming that neither Moses nor anyone else is able to see God's face, "for no one shall see me and live" (33:20). Moses is allowed to glimpse God's back as God passes by. In doing so the Lord proclaims the following words:

> The LORD, the LORD,
> A God merciful and gracious,
> Slow to anger,
> And abounding in steadfast love and faithfulness,
> Keeping steadfast love for the thousandth generation,
> Yet by no means clearing the guilty,
> But visiting the iniquity of the parents upon the children
> And the children's children,
> To the third and fourth generation.

So important are these words in the unfolding story of Israel that they are closely echoed on at least eight other occasions throughout the Hebrew Scriptures (as examples, see Exod 20:5–6; Num 14:18; Neh 9:17; Pss 86:15; 103:8; 145:8; Joel 2:13; Jonah 4:2). They are significant because they reveal the moral character of Israel's God. God is merciful and gracious and deals with people kindly and compassionately. Yahweh is a God of steadfast love who remains true to promises made and commitments given and may be relied upon utterly. Indeed God "abounds" in steadfast love. This is overwhelmingly who and what God is, more so than any other way we may choose to characterize God's own self. Indeed, the steadfast love and faithfulness of God is being displayed in all that Moses is being called to do since God is in the process of liberating the people of Israel, long since chosen for God's purposes, from slavery in Egypt for a new life in the promised land. Moreover, God is "slow to anger." Anger is not God's preferred emotion or stance and it takes a great deal to move God to this point. God's anger is always just and not vindictive wrath. But none of this means that Israel's God is a "soft touch" who will allow people to live any way they choose with impunity. "Wrath" is what happens when the darkness of human behavior encounters the pure light of the holy God who "is light and in him is no darkness at all" (1 John 1:5); yet the divine wrath is shot through with the divine compassion for a humanity that is bound to sin. It is because of God's steadfast love and its passion that God can be moved to anger. Indeed it is because of the wrath of God that mortals may count on justice prevailing in the earth. There is a reckoning. God will "by no means clear the guilty," but will call them to account. Those who read these words often wonder about the justice of "visiting the iniquity of the parents on the children and the children's children to the third and the fourth generation." Later texts make it clear that God holds people accountable for their own sin, not that of the parents, and vice versa (Ezek 18:19–32; Jer 31:30). But God's characteristic way of judging is by handing people over to the consequences of their own chosen actions so that they may reap what they have sown (Rom 1:18–32), and when this happens the consequences of wrongdoing affect more people than simply the wrongdoer. The third and fourth generation are those of grandchildren and great-grandchildren and indicate that when people live wrongly others share in the fallout from these actions. Yet this is to be contrasted with the "thousand generations" to which God shows steadfast love and so the divine anger is shown to be minimal compared to the immensity of the divine compassion.

With these words we begin to come to grips with the vision of God with which the biblical record presents us. God is a mystery far beyond our capacity to grasp or understand, but those who have faith in God come to know God progressively as this God is disclosed in time. God shows steadfast love and faithfulness. This same God is overwhelmingly glorious such that humans cannot look upon God's face and live. And God is also fierce, resisting the proud and the wrongdoer. In these two Exodus texts foundations are laid for the vision of God to which Israel bears witness and that Jesus of Nazareth embraced as his own understanding. As the early Christians articulated their faith they followed in the footsteps of Israel and of Jesus in affirming that "God is love, and those who abide in love abide in God, and God abides in them" (1 John 4:16). When this God is moved to anger and to wrath by wrongdoing it is not an abdication of love but an expression of it. This wrath is not irrational and *vindictive* anger but wrath that is *just*, the appropriate divine response to everything that negates and corrupts life, and that upholds righteousness. Even human beings are moved to anger when there are things and people about which we care. If we did not love we would be apathetic and disinterested not angry. But the wrath of God is inconsiderable by comparison with God's love. "For a brief moment I abandoned you, but with great compassion I will gather you. In overflowing wrath for a moment I hid my face from you, but with everlasting love I will have compassion on you, says the LORD, your Redeemer" (Isa 54:7–8).

THE LANGUAGE OF PERSONHOOD

What should by now be clear is that when Israel, Jesus, and Christians at large think and speak of God they are using personal language to do so. God is some*one*, not some*thing*. This is not to say that impersonal images are not also used as a way of expressing the immensity of God. The images of water, fire, wind, and spirit are all used to say something about God. God is likened to a rock and a fortress (Ps 18:2). But supremely God is understood to be intensely personal, and so thinking about this God is best done through the language of personal encounter rather than by means of abstract philosophy. This is the kind of faith to which the biblical narratives bear witness as the personal God encounters Abraham, Moses, the prophets, and Jesus. They speak to us out of this engagement with God founded upon personal experience. In due course we shall learn to call this "revelation." The Christian faith is a witness to divine revelation.

Understanding God as personal cannot be too highly emphasized, but needs to be done with a degree of care. Although it was not included in the range of alternative understandings of God that are excluded by the theological narrative of Genesis 1, there is a further option that needs to be addressed. This is the idea that God is impersonal, an ultimate and final spiritual reality that lies behind the world that we see and that yet does not have the character of personhood. On this understanding, found for example in Buddhism, the object of spiritual searching is to merge with this final reality by progressing beyond our own sense of personhood, attachment, and particularity so that we are lost in harmony with this ultimate reality. Personal existence is an illusion, a constructed self that is to be given up, a form of small-mindedness that needs to be transcended. Disciplined meditation and detachment from the world are the means by which this is done. In the current world, this form of spirituality is on the rise and is sometimes considered to be more sophisticated than Christianity precisely because it goes beyond personal identity. Personal language for God is thought to be immature and primitive by comparison with an approach that allows for mysticism and spiritual discipline of a more undefined and, reputedly, less limited kind.

The Christian vision of God is indeed far removed from this, although it must be conceded that sometimes, by speaking of God as personal, some Christian discourse runs the danger of trivializing and diminishing the one who ultimately is beyond our power to describe. We can speak of God as though God were just another being among other beings, though a bit bigger, rather than Being-Itself, the very ground and possibility of being. Despite this concession, however, personal language of God is not at all to be surrendered, but used properly and appropriately.

It is true that the biblical witness uses anthropomorphic language of God, that is, language whose meaning we can grasp because we know what it means from our personal and inter-personal experience. God is said to speak, to act, to choose, to regret, to be moved to compassion and to anger, to respond, to feel, to forgive, to challenge, and to reflect many other emotions belonging to the human range of experiences. It can be thought at this point that we are projecting human images on to the divine and indeed, since such analogical language is inevitably drawn from our humanity, this is what we are doing. It is how language about God *has* to work if it is to have any meaning for us, and it is justified in that God's own self-revelation comes to us supremely in the form of Jesus Christ, God's Son, who is said to be the "reflection of God's glory and the exact imprint of God's being" (Heb 1:3). Yet this is not intended to suggest that God is simply an enlarged version of ourselves. To the contrary, we should understand what is happening here the opposite way round. God does not reflect us; we reflect God. God is the maximally personal ultimate reality. We are made in God's image, not the other way round (Gen 1:26–28). Human beings are small pin-pricks of light reflecting the immense glory of the creator, who can also be called Father. It is, of course, not that God is male or female, but personal language is necessary in identifying the ultimate personal reality. God transcends gender, but gender in its male or female form is a sliver of reflection of the divine reality in which everything good about or motherhood or fatherhood finds its ultimate personal expression. Both Old and New Testament apply female analogies to God: "Can a woman forget her nursing-child, or show no compassion for the child of her womb? Even these may forget, yet I will not forget you" (Isa 49:15). "Jerusalem, Jerusalem, the city that kills the prophets and stones those who are sent to it! How often have I desired to gather your children together as a hen gathers her brood under her wings, and you were not willing!" (Luke 13:34). To speak of the God of Jesus Christ as the "Motherly Father" is entirely appropriate.

Far from it being the case of the personal being an inferior way of imaging the divine, it is in fact the highest form of imagination. This is because personhood, even in its human form, is the fullest, most complex, and most beautiful reality known to us. Consider the facts about the human brain. "There are a hundred trillion synapses in a human brain; the number of possible ways of connecting them is greater than the number of atoms in the universe. A higher level of organization and a greater richness of experience occurs in a human being than in a thousand lifeless galaxies. It is human beings, after all, that reach out to understand that cosmic immensity"[1] The brain is the most complex organism, and it is on the platform of such complexity that human personhood can be formed and supported. As persons we are able to learn and grow, to relate and to love, to create and to shape, to imagine and to design. To image God simply as some overwhelming force or power of an impersonal nature falls far short of what becomes possible once we begin to think of God in personal terms. Supremely, it is only a personal reality that is able to love and it is in love that we all find our personal fulfillment. To depersonalize God would be to abolish love in favor of indifference. An impersonal God would be a cold, uncaring, unfeeling reality that could neither give love nor receive it, and this is the precise opposite of the God who encounters us in revelation. No apologies need therefore be made for Christian belief in a personal God in whose image human beings are made, and no other conception comes near to capturing its possibilities. It is just such a God who is able to feel for us, to have compassion and mercy on us, to hear and respond to our prayers, to engage with us in the adventure of life, to rejoice over us, to forgive us when we do wrong, to guide us when we need to be guided and set us on a straight path—should we, that is, set ourselves to seek after God and relate to God as an I relates to a Thou.

---

1. Barbour, *Religion in an Age of Science*, 147. See also Fergusson, *The Cosmos and the Creator*, 73.

PERSONHOOD AND PURPOSE

A further aspect of the necessity of personal language is that it requires us to think in terms of divine intention and purpose. There is a purpose that underlies the creation and its direction and that gives us the decisive clue to the meaning of life. If there is no God there is no final purpose or meaning to the universe or anything within it. Things simply exist without any context of meaning, a perspective that atheists can often be heard to articulate. If this is so then any firm foundation for ethical living is, to say the least, under threat, since how we should live cannot be disentangled from the purpose of our living in the first place. Human beings cannot live, and cannot live well, without something to live for. Absent God, this means we are left to create our own meaning, which is exactly what most people do, locating their motivation for life in love of family and friends, a career or a cause. There is in principle nothing wrong with these subsidiary purposes and they too are necessary for a productive and enriching life. However, they achieve their maximum value when they themselves are subject to yet higher purposes. Without this larger framework, the subsidiary meanings we manufacture risk becoming idols that are ultimately destructive. There is a difference between finding meaning *in* life by constructing our own goals and finding the meaning *of* life. It is when these perspectives coincide, when we are learning to live in harmony with the meaning *of* life that we are most likely to flourish and achieve our full potential. For there to be a meaning to life we need a personal creator who supplies the purpose that undergirds everything else and calls the world to move towards its own fulfillment within that purpose.

The purposes of God might be expressed in many ways and some of them will find their way into these pages. It is difficult however to imagine a fuller and more complete statement than that found in Ephesians 1:8–10: "With all wisdom and insight [God] has made known to us the mystery of his will, according to his good pleasure that he set forth in Christ, as a plan for the fullness of time, to gather up all things in him, things in heaven and things on earth." Implied in this statement is the recognition that although the world and everything in it is God's creation, it is currently fractured and alienated. God's purpose is universal and all-embracing: to restore all things to unity through, in, and under Jesus the Christ so that peace and harmony might be restored to the ultimate degree. This is what is made known in the Christ who has come to us and who has been raised from the dead as the initial and promising fulfillment of that final reality.

THE PERSONAL GOD CREATES SPACE FOR THE WORLD

Finally, in this section something needs to be said about God's self-limitation. In relation to the world and universe God knows all, sees all, is present to all, and in the divine freedom has power over all. This is what is traditionally recognized in the language of omnipotence, omniscience, and omnipresence. These are not simply abstract terms, but express the ways in which God is related to the concrete realities of existence. Space and time lie open before God and God is free in relation to them, not bound or limited by any power other than God's own self. If there were such a power God would not be God, but as it is, sovereignty and lordship belong to God. Although nothing can set a limit to God, God chooses and wills to set a limit to God's own self, retracting the divine omnipotence so to speak. This happens in order to "make room" for creation, for a reality that stands over against God as a relatively independent sphere that has its own integrity, intelligence, and agency. This is an act of creative love and it creates the possibility of responsive love in return.

It is not that creation could ever be wholly independent of God since it depends for its origin and its moment-by-moment continuance on the love and grace of its creator. But even while holding it in being, God grants it freedom to be itself as that which is not-God, yet which has its own space and time, the capacity to develop, to grow, and in the case of species to multiply and to realize the inherent potential they have been given. The divine self-limitation is freely chosen and self-determined and owes itself to the will of God to overflow with love, summoning a reality other than God's own self into being that may be embraced by that love. God confers upon this creation agency, the capacity to decide, to act, and to self-determine, and the fuller and more complete God's creatures are in terms of intelligence and imagination the greater is this capacity for agency. Divine self-limitation is not the abdication of omnipotence but its expression, its realization in another, more indirect form. God works *with* creation, not just *on* creation. Omnipotence might now be conceived as *omni-competence*, God's capacity to bear with creation, to endure with it, especially its human dimension, and to weave its often contrary decisions and actions into a providential purpose that will in the fullness of time turn all things to their final purpose and therefore to good. It is this divine self-limitation that makes the story of the world and the human race as we know it a possibility. It also locates the reality of prayer as a yearning on the part of the creature to be at one with and to further the purposes of the personal creator. When we pray we align ourselves with God's own being and purpose and join with God and the creation itself in willing the triumph of God's kingdom and the healing of all creation (Rom 8:22–25). Prayer is personal engagement with the personal reality at the heart of all things and its desire is to further both the present and the final coming of God's reign of peace and justice. For this reason Jesus said: "Pray then in this way: Our Father in heaven, hallowed be your name. Your kingdom come, your will be done, on earth as it is in heaven" (Matt 6:9–10).

3

The God of Jesus Christ
The Relational God

THERE REMAINS MORE TO be said about how we are to think of the God known by and made known to us in Jesus Christ. The Christian faith, we have said, is the faith of Israel as this is now to be interpreted in the light of a Messiah who has suffered, has died, and has risen. Its roots are both ancient and deep in the traditions of the Hebrews and radically new in the insights it has derived from this tradition. It is first of all the continuance of the story that has unfolded in the history of Israel as this is witnessed to by the Hebrew Scriptures. But in Christ revolutionary new and surprising understandings of God are made known and stretch our imagination. The various forms of Christianity and of modern Judaism have common origins in the story of Israel but have taken divergent paths in the way they understand the one God whose worship they share. Whereas Judaism has maintained its focus on the first five books of the Bible (the "Torah") and has sought to extend and elaborate their message into the various ages to meet the challenges through which it has lived, the Christian faith places its focus on Jesus, the Risen Lord, and sees him as the embodiment of the truth, the key to interpreting the Hebrew Scriptures, both affirming them as true revelation of God and modifying them in new directions. Nowhere is this more evidently the case than in the ways Christians have come to experience and think about the God of Israel and of all the world.

Most of what was said about God in the last chapter was drawn from the Hebrew Scriptures and can be said to be shared with Judaism. There is one God who is holy, steadfast in love, sovereign, gracious, and above all personal. This God has called the people of Israel to be a particular means of revelation, but has purposes in which all human beings are called to share and will finally bring these purposes to fulfillment. Yet Christians wish to affirm that although there is one true God, the oneness of God is to be understood not as "singularity," but as unity and communion in diversity: God has three ways of being God, as Father, Son, and Spirit. God is therefore relational. This understanding is a unique form of monotheism, different from both Judaism and Islam, and is the result not of abstract philosophizing about God or of mathematical speculation but of following carefully the unfolding story of Israel, Jesus, and the church as it is contained in the Bible. It is an understanding that is widely prepared for in the history of Israel and of divine revelation and that comes into clearer focus and expression in the New Testament. In what God does, we discover who God is. God's being is disclosed in God's action. In the light of God's presence in Jesus and then in the Holy Spirit, Christians find they must speak of God as both one and three, yet without separating these two ideas. This is known as the doctrine of the Trinity, but it is important to note that the word "Trinity" does not itself appear in Scripture. The doctrine is an attempt to express in words the whole Christian experience of salvation and of prayer as these have become clear through revelation.

VISIONS OF GOD

When thinking about God most people come to the subject with some kind of preconceived idea about what they mean by the word. They then either believe in or decline to believe in the idea that is in their mind. This is not, however, a good way to proceed. Although there is an instinct in human beings to believe in and seek after something beyond ourselves, to look for "God," because they are finite and limited they are not actually qualified to define what God is. Only God can do this about God's own self. If humans are to know anything of God it can only be on the basis of God's self-disclosure or self-revelation. As we shall see, it is precisely the belief in God's self-revelation that enables Christians to begin to talk about God. This revelation is witnessed to in the Scriptures through the unfolding story of Israel's history, supremely in the person and life of Jesus Christ, and then in the continuing work of the Holy Spirit in world and church. The following verse has already been referred to and will recur in this book: "All things have been handed over to me by my Father, and no one knows who the Son is except the Father, or who the Father is except the Son and anyone to whom the Son chooses to reveal him" (Luke 10:22). In addition, we read:

"The Father and I are one" (John 10:30). "Whoever has seen me has seen the Father" (John 14:9). For Christians, the truth about God appears at its clearest and most accessible in Jesus Christ. This means that to think well about God we need to do so with the closest reference to Jesus, who has been authenticated by the resurrection as the "faithful witness" and the "true witness" (Rev 1:5; 3:14). This certainly applies to what is believed about the moral character of God. God is Christ-like. At deeper levels it must also apply to the very being of God. How are we to think about God in the light of what Jesus shows us of the nature and being of God? Truly Christian thinking is the kind that asks and answers these questions in the light and the presence of Christ himself.

DIVINE THREENESS

It would be a mistake to imagine that the Christian understanding of God as one and yet three first emerged in the New Testament and was unknown before then. Rather, the New Testament draws from and develops latent materials in the Hebrew Scriptures and gives new expression to them. One way of thinking of this is that what is concealed in the Old Testament is revealed in the New. The sub-text of the Hebrew Scriptures is brought more explicitly to the surface in the New Testament. God is clearly understood to be one: "I am the Lord and there is no other; besides me there is no god" (Isa 45:5). Yet throughout the revelation to Israel there is also a degree of complexity or fullness within this one God. In Genesis 1 God creates all things, but does so by speaking out the creative word, and God's Spirit is said to hover over the waters (Gen 1:2 NIV). Immediately we are introduced, therefore, to ways in which God's being and power are extended into the world and become effective. This idea—that God is beyond the world but at the same time able to project God's own self into it—is one we encounter in various ways. Apparently God is able to take form for human beings in different ways at different times. In the revelation of God given to Abraham God appears to him in Genesis 18 in the form of three mysterious visitors. Initially they are presented as three men whom Abraham receives hospitably. As the narrative proceeds they are referred to as the Lord (v. 13, v. 20, v. 22). They can, seemingly, separate, and two of them are referred to as "angels" (19:1). In chapter 19 the language fluctuates between angels, men, and the Lord. This is a confusing incident and is certainly intended to be mysterious, as God is mysterious. What it suggests, however, is that God is able to make God's own self known under different forms, some of which appear as "alter egos," or different ways in which God is God's own self.

This impression is further strengthened in Genesis 32 when Jacob is said to wrestle with another mysterious "man" (vv. 24-25) in an experience that will change his life. After the experience, the man blesses Jacob (v. 29) but declines to reveal his name. Jacob believes himself to have seen God face to face and so names the place Peniel, which means "face of God" (v. 30). Frequent references are also made in the history of Israel to the "angel of the Lord" by means of which God accompanies, protects, and guides the people. Although seemingly other than the Lord, this angel is nonetheless closely associated with God, so much so that God's name is said to be "in him" (e.g., Exod 23:20-21). In a related way, there are frequent references to the glory or Shekinah of God. The Shekinah is God's glorious presence dwelling among the people whom God makes his own (Exod 29:45-46). The glory of God is God's own glory, but in some way can be extended out from God's own being (Exod 16:7-10). When Moses has a revelation of God, God allows his glory to pass by him, even though Moses is not allowed to glimpse God's face (Exod 33:17-23). God's glory therefore appears to be a bridge between human beings in their finite existence and the transcendence of God. God is beyond us, yet also with us. The same can be said about other extensions of God's being: God's Word, through which the world is created; God's Wisdom, by means of which it is fashioned and that is itself personified into something alongside God but other than God (Prov 8:22-31), and God's Spirit (Pss 104:30, 139:7).

Far from it being the case that belief in Jesus as the Son of God is a departure from the faith of the Hebrew Scriptures, we are now able to see how that faith of Israel prepared the way for understanding Jesus as the incarnation of God. Nowhere is this clearer than in Daniel 7, which contains a vision of God as the Ancient of Days and of one "like a son of man" (vv. 13-14) to whom God gives, "dominion and glory and kingship, that all peoples, nations, and languages should serve him. His dominion is an everlasting dominion that shall not pass away, and his kingship is one that shall never be destroyed." Here we are presented with one who is both divine ("coming with the clouds of heaven" is a sign of this) and in human form, who fulfils God's purpose and is given sovereignty. It becomes clear that the seeds of later Christian belief in the incarnation and the Trinity were already present in Judaism and would come to flower in Christianity. It is no surprise in the light of Daniel's vision that Jesus referred to himself repeatedly as the "Son of Man," and in so doing was drawing upon the Jewish traditions and Scriptures to identify himself.

It seems then that, according to the Hebrew Scriptures, the God who is one nevertheless projects or extends himself in a variety of ways and takes form within the world for its benefit and to become available to human beings. None of this compromises the sovereign power of God, but rather demonstrates it. We are to think of God as possessing fullness of being and infinite potential, to whom nothing is impossible in fulfilling the good and gracious divine purpose. This prepares us for the momentous next step that we find taking place in Jesus. The God who is free and able to take form in a variety of ways takes form definitively in the person and life of Jesus of Nazareth. In Jesus God becomes incarnate, taking a human identity and nature as the means by which God is to be made known within history to human beings. The one who pre-existed the incarnation as God's Word and Wisdom and who was both present as such at the creation, and the very means of creation coming to be, then became a human being (John 1:3, 14). Because human beings are made in the image of God, it is appropriate that God's highest self-manifestation should take place in becoming a human being as Jesus of Nazareth without ceasing to be all that God ever was and shall be. This is the radical Christian claim and it transforms our understanding of the nature and being of God. The Christian faith is still the faith of Israel, but now interpreted by means of the Messiah who suffered, died, and has risen. In addition then to the moral claim that God reflects Christ and so is Christ-like, there is the additional claim that God's being is such that it is possible for this God to extend God's own self into the world and take the form of a humble human being (Phil 2:6–11).

THE APOSTOLIC WITNESS

The New Testament passage which is clearest and most explicit about this is John 1, sometimes known as the Prologue to John's Gospel. Of the four Gospels that we have, John is the most reflective. The other three ("Synoptic") Gospels are more narrative based. They tell the story of Jesus, each in its own way, and bit by bit they lead the reader to question who Jesus may have been and to give their answers. By contrast John's Gospel is up-front and personal. The Prologue confronts us with the highest theological statements about Jesus before then going on to tell us his story. We read about Jesus therefore with a clear impression in our minds about who he is. John 1:1 echoes the opening words of the Bible in Genesis 1 because in Jesus a whole new world is opening up. It describes him as the "Word." This itself is reminiscent of Genesis 1 in which the divine word is the means by which God created the world. For John, the Word that is Jesus was "in the beginning" with God, suggesting that the Word is eternal as God is eternal. The Word was with or alongside God and was himself God. These words echo what Proverbs 8 says about the Wisdom through which God has made the world: "The Lord created me at the beginning of his work, the first of his acts of long ago" (v. 22). At the same time, John goes beyond these words in that the Word to which he refers was not created, but, being God, uncreated and eternal. This is clear from John 1:3, which says, "All things came into being through him, and without him not one thing came into being." In other words, everything without exception that has been created and come into being did so through Christ the Word. Christ existed prior to any created thing as one who is eternal and uncreated. He is God in that he shares with the Father everything that belongs to divinity. But the one through whom all things were created then entered into the creation itself to become the means of its re-creation and renewal.

The crucial words reflecting the truth upon which the whole of the Christian faith is grounded are then found in John 1:14: "The Word became flesh and lived among us, and we have seen his glory, the glory as of a father's only son, full of grace and truth." If the first words of the Prologue have been about what the Word was eternally (he was with God and he was God), these further words refer to what the Word became: the Word *became* flesh. In other words, something happened, something took place that signified a change, both for God and the world. The one through whom the world was made actually became part of that world as a human being reflecting the image of God. If it is the case that the worlds were made through the Word, then here is that same Word being born into the world in order to do a new work of creation or of re-creation. The Word has come among us as a finite and limited human being (all of which is implied by the word "flesh") as an extension and fulfillment of the divine purpose. This is by no means a denial of the divine glory and power, but the opposite: God's glory is shown in divine humility and God's power in achieving the divine purpose even through weakness. Christ does not so much lay aside divine power and glory as manifest them in an unheard of and surprising form.

The claim that God in Christ has become incarnate is of course profoundly radical, so much so that it is offensive to other monotheistic faiths. Far from it contradicting, however, the faith embodied in the Hebrew Scriptures, we can see here that it is a development of that faith and an extension of beliefs about the divine nature that were already contained there. This belief places Jesus of Nazareth, the Messiah, at the very heart of Christian thinking. He is the decisive clue as to the being and nature of God. All that is taught in the Hebrew Scriptures may be readily received, but is now to be interpreted in the light of the one who counts as the highest revelation and manifestation of God. God has come to dwell in the midst of us in the form of a human being whom God has raised up and sent. The incarnation is an event in space and time, a becoming that can in principle be dated. Indeed, for many, history is divided into BC and AD, before and after Christ. John goes on to say "we have seen his glory, the glory as of a father's only son." The event, then, is one that has been witnessed and found to be life-transforming. In Jesus, people have seen the glory of the Father precisely because Jesus is the revelation of the Father. Behind this language we find references to the tabernacle and the temple by means of which the God of Israel came into the midst of the people of Israel. As God's glory or Shekinah dwelt among the people in the shrine that God had commanded them to make, first in its form as a tabernacle then as a temple, so now that central dwelling place is located in a human being who becomes the place of meeting, reconciliation, and encounter between God and humanity.

John 1 can also be seen to stress the key role that Christ now plays in our knowledge of God and of the world. He might be thought of as the key that unlocks the greatest mysteries of life. If he is the Word of God, and if words are used to express, communicate, and to clarify, then he may be said to unlock the mystery of God: "No one has ever seen God. It is God's only Son, who is close to the Father's heart, who has made him known" (v. 18). Christ is the supreme revelation of the Father. And if he is also the one through whom all things that exist have come into being, he can further be said to unlock the mysteries of the universe. Human beings are able through their scientific abilities to work out how it is that creation functions, but it is only by means of revelation that we are able to know why it is that creation exists in the first place, why there is something and not nothing. Christ is the one who manifests the purpose of creation, namely to exist in and for communion with God in the same way that Christ is in communion with the Father. This is the purpose that undergirds all things. It may also be said that as God in Christ has embraced a human existence and identity, so it is that he is able to reveal to us the true nature of what it is to be human and what it means to live a good and fulfilled human life. Finally, in view of the words of John, "But to all who received him, who believed in his name, he gave power to become children of God" (v. 12), we can also say that Christ is the key that unlocks the mystery of salvation and new life for those who turn to him. He through whom all things were made is eminently qualified to be the means of all things being made new.

THE UNFOLDING REVELATION

So far we have shown that a Christian understanding of God unfolds as the revelation to which the Bible bears witness progresses. In the Hebrew Scriptures we become aware of the deeply personal God of Israel whose being is full of potential for us. We noticed God's ability to extend God's own self into the world and to take form. Supremely God has taken form in the human being Jesus of Nazareth, in what we call the "incarnation," the event of God's becoming human without ever ceasing to be what God has always and will always be. This is the key event of history. The one who became incarnate is the Word or Son of God and this says something highly significant about the being of God. It is not that the one God has now simply assumed a new appearance, as though God had donned a different mask. If God has been making God's own self known to us as God truly is within himself, then the distinction between the Father (whom we identify with the God of Israel) and the Son, who became incarnate, is one that exists within God's own being and has always done so. This is where we begin to speak of the "tri-unity" of God, God's "three-ness in oneness." Shortly we shall go on to talk of the Spirit, who provides the third perspective on the triune being of God. For the time being we note that these ideas, like all Christian understanding, arise out of a sense of encounter with God, first with the Father, then with the Son, and then with the Spirit. We speak of God in these ways because this is how we encounter God in revelation, not for the sake of a speculative exercise. The Hebrews, descended at first from Abraham and led and instructed by Moses, experienced the presence of God in their midst as one who was near to them: "For what other great nation has a god so near to it as the LORD our God is whenever we call to him?" (Deut 4:7). Their belief in God was founded upon the presence of God among and for them. For the first Christians, Jesus the Messiah was "Emmanuel, God with us" (Matt 1:23), the one in whom a new quality and depth of the divine presence was made known to them. God came to be present and encountered therefore in a further way that they were unable to deny and yet that expanded their understanding of who God was and what God could do. God was still the God of Israel, but now also the Father of our Lord Jesus Christ (2 Cor 1:3) and the God who raised Jesus from the dead (Acts 5:30).

Christian understanding of God was further enriched by the coming of the Holy Spirit on the day of Pentecost (Acts 2). Jesus having completed his work and returned to the Father from whom he came, God poured out the Holy Spirit, calling the church into being and empowering it for its work of worldwide witness and mission. The Spirit represents the third way in which God is to be understood. Father and Son are present and active in the world by means of the Holy Spirit, and this Spirit is not known by means of abstract speculation but in dynamic encounter. The Spirit is like the wind. The wind is invisible, but is universally active. The Spirit can blow as a gentle breeze or as a mighty hurricane force. It was as "the rush of a violent wind" (Acts 2:2) that the Spirit fell on the gathered disciples at Pentecost.

This coming was predicted by Jesus who described the Spirit as "another Advocate, to be with you for ever" (John 14:16). The force of these words is that the Spirit is "another of the same kind as Jesus." In other words, if Jesus as the Son of God shares divine nature and being with the Father, then the Spirit shares divine being and nature with both the Father and the Son. When we encounter the Holy Spirit we encounter God's own self, active and present in the world.

TRI-UNITY AND PERSONHOOD

To be clear, it needs to be said that it is not a case of the Son or the Spirit having come into existence in the course of the unfolding revelation. Because each shares in the being of God, each has always existed, from everlasting. Rather, the eternal existence of Father, Son, and Spirit has become known to us in the course of revelation in history, so our vision of God, as not only the personal God but the relational God, has expanded. We mean by this that Father, Son, and Spirit have shared in an eternal communion of the closest kind. The nature of this communion is glimpsed in Jesus' prayer to the Father in John 17, that the believers, "may all be one. As you, Father, are in me and I am in you" (v. 21). In fact, here we have further insight into what it means to speak of God as "personal." It is not possible to have personhood without relationship. On the human level each of us becomes a person by means of the relationships in which we are formed and held and by which we are located. In turn this reflects the divine life. The Father cannot be Father without the Son. This is an eternal reality, and since the Holy Spirit is in particular associated with the bonds of fellowship (2 Cor 13:14), it is reasonable to speak of the Spirit as the bond of communion between the Father and the Son.

The concept of God as Trinity therefore is not meant to be a speculative idea derived from abstruse mathematical theory, but as the summary and safeguard of a narrative, the narrative of unfolding revelation of the divine name and nature. It is entirely the case that the word "Trinity" does not appear in the Bible, and for this reason must always have a secondary status, but this does not mean that it cannot serve as a faithful way of summarizing the truth about God that is found there. It serves as an aid to our interpretation of the Bible. Although the word as such does not appear, there is to the Bible as a whole, and the New Testament in particular, a "deep structure" that has a trinitarian shape. Examples of this include the birth narrative, which depicts the Father's action in sending the Spirit to conceive in Mary's womb the one who is the Son of God and Immanuel

(Matt 1:18–25); the baptism of Jesus at which the Father's voice proclaims, "This is my Son, whom I love; with him I am well pleased," while the Spirit of God descends and rests on Jesus like a dove (Matt 3:16–17); the worship life of Jesus in which "full of joy through the Holy Spirit" he says, "I praise you, Father, Lord of heaven and earth" (Luke 10:21); the final commission of Jesus to his disciples in which the tells them to "go and make disciples of all nations, baptizing them in the name of the Father and of the Son and of the Holy Spirit" (Matt 28:19); the divine blessing that runs, "The grace of the Lord Jesus Christ, the love of God, and the communion of the Holy Spirit be with all of you" (2 Cor 13:13); the shape of Ephesians 1, which begins with praise to the "God and Father of our Lord Jesus Christ" (v. 3), moves on to speak of the redemption and forgiveness we have through Christ's blood (v. 7), and ends with speaking of the way we have the "seal of the promised Holy Spirit" (v. 13); and the blessing of grace and peace "from him who is and who was and who is to come, and from the seven spirits who are before his throne, and from Jesus Christ, the faithful witness, the firstborn of the dead, and the ruler of the kings of the earth" spoken of in Revelation 1:4–5 (the expression "seven spirits" here is a way of speaking of the one but "sevenfold Spirit" of God).

Together, verses like these, and many others, lay down a structure to the biblical narrative according to which all things come to us from the Father through the Son and by the Spirit so that in the fullness of time all things may be gathered back by the Spirit through the Son to the Father. Although Son and Spirit share in the divine being, the Father is sometimes especially referred to as "God" since the Father is the fountain and origin of deity from whom the Son is eternally begotten (John 3:16) and the Spirit proceeds (John 14:26; Acts 2:33). If this is the shape of revelation, it is also the shape of both personal salvation and prayer. It is through the Son and by the Spirit that we must come to the Father. In other the words, the Spirit of God draws us to the Son of God who is the way to the Father (John 14:6) and whose saving work enables us to draw near. Similarly, when we pray, it is in the Spirit (Eph 6:18) and in the name of the Son that we pray to the Father (John 15:16). To repeat: this is the way God has shown us God's own self in the revelation given to us. If God is truly revealed in history as God is, then this must reflect the way God is and always has been in eternity. God's self-manifestation is not a mask or pretence assumed for a temporary purpose, but a true revelation of God's own being. We conclude therefore that from all eternity God has been within God's own self Father, Son, and Spirit, a communion of persons within the one being of God, fully personal, fully relational, and fully one, each divine person worthy of worship and honor.

God is therefore the relational God. At the heart of the universe there are personhood, relationship, and community and these provide key themes for understanding the nature of our existence. For instance, human beings made in the image of God are created for community, not solitary existence, and it is by means of community that they become fully personal and realize their God-given potential. Human community and human flourishing work together for the common good. Within this community there is the community of men and women providing complementarity in their difference. However, human community itself depends upon the community of creation, which provides the essential environment and habitat within which human beings may live. Human beings have been created in order that they may share in the life of the divine community, having access to the Father through the Son by the Spirit, and it is the restoration of this communion to human beings and a lost and fractured world that constitutes salvation or "eternal life" (John 17:3).

DIVINE RELIABILITY

Before leaving this section there is one more point to be made about the trinitarian, relational vision that has been outlined. It concerns the reliability and the commitment of God within the work of divine creation and redemption. It is God, the whole of God, who is committed to creation, revelation, and salvation. Father, Son, and Spirit have their part in bringing creation into being, therefore we can be assured that the divine commitment to preserve and one day renew the earth is full and complete. The divine purpose for creation will not be neglected or forsaken, but God will complete that which has been begun. When it comes to revelation, the fact that "God has spoken to us by a Son" who, as one who shares the divine nature and is the "reflection of God's glory and the exact imprint of God's very being" (Heb 1:1–4), means that we have an accurate and truthful revelation of God. There is no hidden God behind the God revealed in Jesus, one who is somehow different from what is revealed. Because of the divinity of Christ we are able to be sure of the Christ-likeness of the divinity. We are able to say that we know who God is and what God is like because in Jesus we see God's own self. It takes God to reveal God—no other medium is adequate to the task, and such a revelation we have in Jesus Christ who is no less than God's own Son. Furthermore, in the work of bringing salvation to a lost world it is God's own self who secures this salvation through the Son and by the Spirit. The incarnation has a purpose, which is the reconciliation of human beings to God, and beyond this the reconciliation of all things.

This is achieved in history through Christ's saving work and is worked out in the life of the church and its individual members by means of the Spirit acting within the human heart. It might be said therefore that nothing is more certain and secure than a work to which Father, Son, and Spirit are indissolubly committed.

4

Christology

CHRISTOLOGY IS THE STUDY of the person of Christ, the full exposition of who Christ is. It should be clear that we have already said a great deal on this topic, and rightly so if the Risen Lord does indeed occupy the key and central place in the convictions of the Christian community. In chapter 1 we gave attention to Jesus as an historical figure and to the claim that he is risen from the dead, and so singled out by God as the one who is to be listened to above all others. This was our starting point. In the following two chapters we considered how we are to understand the personal and relational God in the light of Christ's knowledge, function, and teaching. In the course of this much more was said about Christ and we began to see in him the very incarnation of the Word or Son of God, one who had been with the Father "in the beginning" and who became a human being with the identity of Jesus of Nazareth. In this chapter there is a degree of repetition of some of the points already made and these will serve to reinforce the arguments so far employed.

CHRISTOLOGIES FROM ABOVE AND BELOW

It can be repeated here that when we read Matthew, Mark, Luke, and John, they chose to follow different paths in telling their story. John commences his Gospel with the prologue and paints a magnificent picture of the cosmic Christ, the key to the mysteries of the universe. He then goes on to tell the story of the historical Jesus, but in such a way that the glory of God keeps shining through Jesus' words and actions. By starting with who Jesus was in eternity before entering into time, John is following a route sometimes known as a "Christology from above," beginning with Christ's eternal identity and then moving to his incarnation as a human being. By contrast Matthew, Mark, and Luke take a different route. They begin with the historical Jesus and the questions he posed for his first disciples about who he really was. Gradually they came to understand more about him until at the end of their Gospels they had (more or less) grasped his identity. This is sometimes called a "Christology from below." So far we have followed a mixture of these two approaches, but in the last chapter the emphasis was on a Christology from above. In the present chapter the intention is to focus on a Christology from below and to use this as a way of testing and amplifying what has already been said about Christ.

Whether from above or from below, Christology aims to tell the truth about Christ. The two approaches are complementary and address the subject from two different perspectives. Christology from above is concerned with the "order of being," that is to say, the Son of God has always existed and precedes earthly time and so it is appropriate to follow the order of the way things are in how we explain who he is. Christology from below by contrast follows the "order of knowing" in that, however things may be in logical or chronological order, the way we human beings have come to know about them is through the historical figure of Jesus. We begin therefore with Jesus of Nazareth. To all intents and purposes this is the way we have come to know what we do know of Christ and his incarnation. Martin Luther explained it helpfully like this: "The Scriptures begin very gently and leads us on to Christ as to a man, and then to one who is Lord over all creatures, and after that to one who is God. So do I enter delightfully, and learn to know God. . . . We must begin from below, and after that come upwards."[1]

BEGINNING WITH JESUS

We are presented, then, with a Jewish male of mature but still young years, aged about thirty (Luke 3:23), living in the relatively unknown and insignificant town of Nazareth, in Galilee, the northern province of the land of Israel, which we also call Palestine. He was a devout and practicing Jew, born into a pious Jewish family that nonetheless had few associations with the more established forms of Jewish religion that were associated with the temple of Jerusalem, with the aristocratic high-priestly families, and with the religious grouping of the Sadducees that represented them. The family of Jesus stood in the tradition of biblical Judaism. The Judaism of Jesus' day

1. www.biblicalstudies.org.uk/pdf/asw/captive/captive-to-the-word_16.pdf.

was a more fluid affair than we might imagine, capable of expressing itself in a wide variety of ways. Jesus had been educated in the standard Jewish way, relatively advanced for its day and age, and was able to read the Scriptures in the synagogue where he was in regular attendance at the Sabbath day meetings. Along with his family he attended where possible, the Festivals of Weeks, Passover, and Tabernacles in Jerusalem held three times a year.

Although close to the burgeoning and Roman-influenced city of Sepphoris, Nazareth in particular and Galilee in general were not well regarded within the southern Jewish community of Judea. For one thing, Galilee bordered the Gentile territories to the north, east, and west and so was suspected of ethnic compromise. Furthermore, it was close to Samaria, where a heretical form of Judaism was practiced by tribes whose ethnic Jewish inheritance was suspect. For another thing, Nazareth had no historical pedigree, was not mentioned in the Hebrew Scriptures, and was a relatively new town. It is possible, though far from certain, that it was founded by members of the royal family returning from exile in Babylon, since its name is cognate with the Hebrew word for "branch," a word applied to descendants of the royal family. This could explain why Joseph, who was of the house of David (Luke 1:27), was living there while also having continuing connections with Bethlehem, David's town (Luke 2:4). The royal connection was not necessarily prestigious, given that the royal family were associated with Israel's failure and the deportations to Babylon. At any rate, neither Nazareth nor Galilee were prestigious places (John 7:40–44, 52) and nothing good was expected to come from there: "Can anything good come out of Nazareth?" (John 1:46).

By trade Jesus was a *teknon* (think of "technician"), a carpenter or builder (Mark 6:3), as was his father (Matt 13:55), and so he occupied a recognized and high status role within workaday Jewish society. Although we imagine a carpenter laboring at his bench, Jesus' work would also have taken him around the region working on buildings, tools, agricultural implements, and boats, leading to his removing, once his ministry began, to Capernaum on the north-west shore of the sea of Galilee, where much of his early ministry was to take place (Matt 4:13). It is probable he also worked in Sepphoris, being large, under construction, and close to Nazareth. As he traveled to find and deliver work, Jesus would have had opportunity to observe the country and its people, and to take note of nature and of the economic condition of the people, which observations later found their way into his parables and preaching. Perhaps much of this was gestating throughout the hidden period of his life, before the years of his public ministry, and concerning which we know little. It is probable that in addition to reading Hebrew, Jesus was bilingual in Aramaic and Greek, the former being the language of his own people (a form of Hebrew) and the latter the trade language of the ancient world, and Galilee was very close to significant trade routes. Jesus himself left no writings to his followers though he clearly sought to imprint his oral teachings on their minds.

All of this is worth rehearsing to fix one essential point in our minds: Jesus was unambiguously and typically a human being of his day and age, subject to similar needs, desires, and pressures as ourselves. It is clearly stated that "he had to become like his brothers and sisters in every respect" and that "we have one who in every respect has been tested as we are, yet without sin" (Heb 2:17; 4:15). This certainly included the capacity to suffer. Like us, Jesus had to learn what it means to be human. "Although he was a Son, he learned obedience through what he suffered" (Heb 5:8). It is a great failing when we ignore the implications of Christ's real humanity. It is necessary for our salvation that Jesus should have come to where we are, sharing in the same kind of humanity we have. Attempts to ring-fence Jesus from being fully human are mistaken. Not only would Jesus have had to learn obedience to his parents and to God (Luke 2:51–52), he would have needed to learn in every other sphere of his life. It is not necessary to imagine that he was good at everything he did. Perhaps he was not the world's most skilled carpenter and not everything to which he turned his hand was a perfect product. Christians imagine that because Jesus was "perfect" he would never have failed at anything. But real human beings are not perfect in this way: they are limited, finite, incomplete, unskilled in multiple areas. They know what they need to know and have limited understanding of most things in the world. To say the same of Jesus is not to detract from his glory, but to add to it, since his glory consists in his willingness to humble himself for the sake of humanity: he "emptied himself, taking the form of a slave, being born in human likeness" (Phil 2:6–7). Jesus was not God pretending to be human. He was altogether human and this is a cardinal conviction of the Christian community, although its implications are often overlooked. There is nothing intrinsically dishonorable about being human. Limitation and finitude are not sinful failures, but belong to the dignity of being creatures. Human beings are created by God and in God's own image. Their dignity is enhanced beyond measure by the participation of God's own Son in their condition.

JESUS' MINISTRY

What we must go on to say about Jesus however is that, unlike all other human beings, he was without sin. By contrast with Adam and Eve, who represent us all and in whom we see ourselves, when presented with temptation, even in extreme form, he did not follow the path of self-exaltation and disobedience (Luke 4:1–13). For this reason he could later be described as the "last Adam" (1 Cor 15:45), the ultimate human being. Expressed positively, Jesus lived in the love of God, loving the Father with all his heart, soul, mind, and strength, and his neighbor as himself. This was the basis of his life and his first priority (Matt 22:34–40). This is where he may truly be said to be "complete" or "perfect." Similarly, whatever understanding Jesus may or may not have had about mathematics, astronomy, astrophysics, or global politics, he had a true and redeeming knowledge of God. "All things have been handed over to me by my Father, and no-one knows who the Son is except the Father, or who the Father is except the Son and anyone to whom the Son chooses to reveal him" (Luke 10:22). Such knowledge is the greatest kind of all. It is what the Old Testament describes as "the fear of the Lord," which is "the beginning of wisdom" (Ps 111:10; Prov 1:7).

It is as a teacher and preacher therefore that Christ began to make his mark upon his world. Although educated in none of the rabbinic schools that were emerging before and during his lifetime, and so without formal training or credentials, he showed profound insight from the earliest days into Israel's Scriptures and faith. In the only solid glimpse we have into Jesus' life between his birth and his baptism, he was found in the temple in Jerusalem at the age of twelve (the age of Jewish adulthood) listening to the teachers, asking and answering questions: "And all who heard him were amazed at his understanding and his answers" (Luke 2:47). Jesus followed in the footsteps of another remarkable preacher, John the Baptist, and was apparently related to him. He was baptized by John and so identified himself with those who were repenting and preparing for the coming of God's kingdom. This event marked the commencement of his own ministry (Matt 3:13; Luke 3:21–22). Jesus, like John, preached the coming of God's kingdom and called people to a change of life and acceptance of his message (Mark 1:14–15). That message was reinforced, by acts of healing and deliverance, which does not seem to have been the case with John the Baptist.

As a teacher, preacher, wonder-worker, and exorcist, Jesus' fame began to spread and he attracted crowds from which he began to choose disciples to be the companions whom he could train and who would work with him (Mark 3:13–19). These did not in the first instance include close members of his own family, who seem to have feared for his mental health (Mark 3:21). However, after the resurrection they were to reappear as significant church leaders (Acts 1:14). Up to this point Jesus might have been identified both as a charismatic rabbi and as a prophet, and he may even have understood himself in this way. It is certainly how his followers came to regard him: for them Jesus of Nazareth was "a prophet mighty in deed and word before God and all the people" (Luke 24:19). After a poor reception in his own town he proclaimed, "Truly I tell you, no prophet is accepted in the prophet's home town" (Luke 4:24). Yet as a teacher of the faith people were already beginning to notice in him a different quality: "They were astounded at his teaching, for he taught them as one having authority, and not as the scribes" (Mark 1:22). Jesus himself was aware of this greater quality. In reference to himself he said, "[The Queen of the South] . . . came from the ends of the earth to listen to the wisdom of Solomon, and see, something greater than Solomon is here!" (Matt 12:42).

It was this "something more" that raised further questions about Jesus. On witnessing him still a storm on the Sea of Galilee his disciples asked, "What sort of man is this, that even the winds and the sea obey him?" (Matt 8:27). In a breakthrough moment when Jesus was asking them what they made of him, Peter the fisherman (and the leading figure among the disciples) had a moment of inspiration: "You are the Messiah, the Son of the Living God" (Matt 16:16). The Jewish people were expecting a kingly figure who would lead their people, liberate them from oppression, and complete the renewal of the nation. In the tradition of Israel, kings, priests, and prophets were all anointed with oil, literally or figuratively, to signify their appointment. At his baptism Jesus had been anointed by the Spirit and a voice from heaven had declared, "This is my Son, the Beloved, with whom I am well pleased" (Matt 3:17). Significantly, Jesus never directly claimed to be the Messiah, although he accepted the title when it was applied to him by others, as in the incident with Peter. He showed remarkable reticence about the word, specifically telling his disciples not to tell anyone that he was the Messiah (Matt 16:20). This is sometimes spoken of as "the messianic secret." The reasons for Jesus' caution are clear: he was not the kind of Messiah that most people were expecting. He was not a warlord or a warrior or a political leader. The powers from which he came to set people free were spiritual before they were political. He had not come to cause others to suffer, but to suffer himself, not to shed blood, but to allow his own blood to be shed, and by doing all this completely to redefine what it meant to be the Messiah. To bring such a redefinition to pass Jesus needed to live the full course of his life, yield to death on a cross, and trust for God's confirmation in the resurrection before it could be done. Yet do this he did, as the non-violent, self-giving Messiah of God.

TITLES AND THE PERSON OF CHRIST

Other words and titles emerge here to elucidate further the mystery of Christ's person. He is referred to as God's "son." To begin with, this title had no greater meaning than that contained in the word "Messiah." Israel's kings were sometimes referred to as God's son (Ps 2:7), indicating the favored relationship the king had with God. It may be that in Peter's confession this was what was intended: "You are the Messiah, the Son of the Living God." It was a word, however, that was capable of considerable further expansion. Jesus was deeply conscious of an intimate relationship with the Father, signified in the Jewish family word "Abba." He believed himself to share that relationship with God in a uniquely intense way (Luke 10:22). This is the language he used in the Garden of Gethsemane, where we have deeply moving insights into the nature of his suffering (Mark 14:36). In John's Gospel the term is frequently used to indicate a relationship with the Father that stemmed back into eternity, pre-existing the historical career of Jesus (John 1:18; 3:16–21). It seems that while this word was used in Jesus' lifetime to indicate his closeness to the Father, after the resurrection new reservoirs of meaning were found in it in signifying an eternal relationship to the Father as one who was "in the beginning with God" and "close to the Father's heart" (John 1:2, 18).

The mystery of Christ's person that is captured by the language of sonship was evoked not only by the titles applied to Christ, but by the assumptions and convictions that shaped his actions. Whereas the ancient prophetic formula was expressed in the words, "Thus says the Lord" by those who spoke on God's behalf, Jesus, a prophet and more than a prophet, repeatedly used the striking formula, "You have heard that it was said . . . but *I* say to you" (Matt 5:21–22, 27–28, 33–34, 38–39, etc.). In other words, in interpreting the divine instruction contained in the Hebrew Scriptures, Jesus claimed to speak as though he himself had divine authority to do so. His own authority is placed alongside and even on occasion against Scripture (John 8:1–11—although it is widely considered that this passage does not belong to the original edition of John's Gospel), and regarded as equal if not greater than it. Similarly Jesus claimed for himself the power to forgive sins. In a striking incident early in his career, a paralyzed man was brought to him. Jesus forgave his sins. The scribes around him considered this a form of blasphemy: "Who can forgive sins but God alone?" To show that "the Son of Man has authority on earth to forgive sins," Jesus healed the man, who then went out in front of them (Mark 2:1–12). Here Jesus claimed to do that which would properly be done in the temple in Jerusalem, where atonement was made for sins through the offering of prescribed sacrifices.

In effect, he was setting himself up alongside the temple as an alternative place and means of forgiveness. If not a blasphemous act, this was certainly an audacious one, one that set himself alongside God as the forgiver of sins. At the very least Jesus saw himself acting as God's agent in this regard. In the interpretation of Jesus' disciples however there was more than this. Jesus had come from the Father as the very incarnation of the divine Word.

Also significant in their interpretation of Jesus was the use of the title "Lord," in Greek *Kurios*. This was also an elastic word that at a basic level could be used simply as a title of respect, meaning "sir." At its fullest level it was the word used in the Greek translation of the Hebrew Scriptures, the Septuagint, to render the very name of God. Jews would not pronounce the name of Yahweh, but would substitute the word *Adonai*, Lord, for it when reading the Scriptures. The Greek *Kurios* translates *Adonai* and therefore *Yahweh*. The word is applied to Jesus at its more basic levels on numerous occasions (as examples: Matt 8:2, 6, 8, 21, 25), but as with other terms it accrued meaning, especially after the resurrection. The resurrection proclaimed Jesus to be "both Lord and Messiah" (Acts 2:36), and therefore worthy of honor, submission, and obedience, and so creating the title "the Lord Jesus Christ" (Acts 11:17 and many other places). Jesus is here being placed decisively on the divine side of the divine-human distinction, following the trend we have seen in the Gospels. "Yet for us there is one God, the Father, from whom are all things and for whom we exist, and one Lord, Jesus Christ, through whom are all things and through whom we exist" (1 Cor 8:6).

The clearest passage to affirm the divine lordship of Christ is in Philippians 2. Having traced the downward trajectory by which the one who shared "equality with God" humbled himself, took the form of a servant, and gave himself up to death, this passage asserts that "God also highly exalted him and gave him the name that is above every name, so that at the name of Jesus every knee should bend, in heaven and earth and under the earth, and every tongue should confess that Jesus Christ is Lord, to the glory of God the Father" (vv. 9–11). Christians are rightly accustomed to viewing the name of Jesus as the name above every other name, but this is not the thrust of the passage. The name above every other name is the name "Lord," Kyrios, Adonai, or Yahweh, and this is the name that is attributed *to Jesus* at the climax of this passage. Jesus has divine status because he is the incarnation of the Word that was with God in the beginning. In the light of this, many biblical passages can be more clearly understood. When John the Baptist, the forerunner to Jesus, understood his vocation to "prepare the way of the Lord, make his paths straight" (Matt 3:3, compare Isa 40:3), he was doing just that, preparing the way for *God's* coming *in Jesus*. When Malachi prophesied that the "Lord whom you seek will suddenly come to his temple" (Mal 3:1), this can be found fulfilled in Jesus' own coming to the temple. When Isaiah described the Lord of Hosts as "a rock one stumbles over" (Isa 8:14), the apostle Paul found this fulfilled in Jesus the rock (Rom 9:32–33). When in the Acts of the Apostles it can speak of God purchasing the church "with *his own* blood" (20:28 margin), it is absolutely identifying God with the incarnate Christ. The writings of the New Testament came to identify Jesus with the creation of the universe (John 1:1–3,) with salvation, and with final judgment (2 Cor 5:10), all of which are divine activities and prerogatives. They are able to speak of finding "the light of the knowledge of the glory of God in the face of Jesus Christ," who is the very image of God (2 Cor 4: 4, 6). All of this was said by witnesses to Christ who emerged from biblical Judaism in which the unity of God was most emphatically believed and defended: "I am the LORD, that is my name; my glory I give to no other, nor my praise to idols" (Isa 42:8). Yet that glory is given to Christ and leads almost inevitably to the designation of Christ as "God manifest in the flesh" (1 Tim 3:16 KJV).

THE DIVINITY OF CHRIST

It is by the cumulative process outlined above that from the beginning the Christian church has been persuaded of the divinity or deity of Christ, that is, that the Son of God incarnate as Jesus of Nazareth shares divine nature with the Father and the Spirit. It is sometimes objected that when Jesus came he came preaching the kingdom of God as his message whereas Christians preach not the kingdom, but Christ himself. But there is no real contradiction here. Christ did indeed preach the coming of God's kingdom (Mark 1:14–15), but also that the kingdom had come in his own person and actions: "But if it is by the finger of God that I cast out the demons, then the kingdom of God has come to you" (Luke 11:20). The kingdom is in fact God's own reign among human beings and if Jesus is the agent of that reign then it is in him that God is present, thus identifying Jesus with God's own self. To preach Christ is to preach the kingdom. Although the New Testament is reticent about making the bald statement that "Jesus is God," there are points where it comes very close to doing just that. Hebrews 1:8 is a salient example: "But of the Son he says, 'Your throne, O God, is for ever and ever, and the righteous scepter is the scepter of your kingdom.'" Romans 9:5 is a further example: "To them (the Jews) belong the patriarchs, and from them, according to the flesh, comes the Messiah, who is over all, God blessed for ever. Amen."

Although we have so far given an account of how in the New Testament the identity of Jesus Christ as the Son of God came to be realized and articulated, there is another dimension that captures the same truths in an existential rather than an intellectual way. This is found in the way in which Christ is not only honored as a significant human being, but offered the kind of worship that is only properly given to God's own self. These incidents and insights are to be understood against the background of a strictly monotheistic religious culture in which the first commandment in the Ten Commandments insisted, "I am the Lord your God, who brought you out of the land of Egypt, out of the house of slavery; you shall have no other gods before me" (Exod 20:2). To offer worship to any other than the Lord God was seen as a form of blasphemy, and yet Jesus is offered worship freely. This begins in the birth narratives where the magi (wise men) are portrayed as kneeling down to the infant Christ, paying him "homage" (Matt 2:11—or in the NIV "worship") and offering gifts of gold, frankincense, and myrrh. It is seen in the startling words of the apostle Thomas on encountering the risen Christ, "My Lord and my God" (John 20:28). It is clearly to be seen in the book of Revelation in the vision that portrays Christ as the sacrificial Lamb who now shares the very throne of God and receives the unambiguous adoration of creation expressed in precisely the same language as worship for the Father: "To him who sits on the throne and to the Lamb be praise and honor and glory and power for ever and ever!" (Rev 5:11–14). The fact that Jesus received such worship indicates the implicit assumption that he was worthy of it and that it was right and true to offer it to him, because in this human being God's own self had been made incarnate.

In this context it is appropriate to note the importance of the ascension of Christ. Described in Acts 1, this incident, however we may imagine it taking place, is full of meaning. It indicates the termination of Christ's presence on earth and the commencement of a new stage in the history of salvation to be put into effect when the Spirit has come (Acts 1:4). It brings to an end the resurrection appearances in the period immediately following Christ's death and reappearance. It places Christ beyond the power of human beings to control or manipulate according to their whims, desires, or interests. It signifies the physical absence of Christ from the world, but also his transition to that position from which he can carry forward the next phase of the divine purpose for creation. Most importantly, it shows how we are to think of Christ as one who is now exalted to the highest place, who is worthy of supreme honor and praise, and who is continuing to rule until his own return (Acts 1:11; 2:33). It is not that in the ascension Christ became something he had never been before; rather, he was revealed to be what he has always been. He is now doubly worthy of worship because of his divine origin and for all that he has achieved by his incarnation, death, and resurrection.

The ability and desire not solely to honor Christ as a wonderful and outstanding human being, but to worship him as the exalted Lord who has come from and returned to the Father is what distinguishes true Christian faith. "Jesus is Lord!" is the primal confession of Christian conviction (1 Cor 12:3). Worship of Christ is an implicit Christology that places him on the side of God and that identifies him fully with God. If this were not so it would be entirely wrong to worship Jesus. In this light we can see that the one we call Jesus of Nazareth pre-existed his earthly incarnation as the Son of God and the Word of God who was "with God in the beginning" (John 1:1), who "was in the form of God" before humbling himself (Phil 2:6), through whom all things were created, visible and invisible (Col 1:16). He became a creature, but did not at the same time cease to be the eternal, uncreated Word (John 1:14). As one who shares the very nature of God as God, therefore, he is to be described as the eternal Son whose being is as much without beginning as are the Father and the Spirit.

FROM WOMB TO TOMB

All this said, it is fitting that the earthly life of Christ as described to us in the Gospels is framed between two miracles or signs that we may describe as the "miracle of the womb" and the "miracle of the tomb." At the end of Jesus' life he was marked out, as we have seen, by the miracle or the sign of the resurrection, "declared to be the Son of God with power according to the Spirit of holiness [the Holy Spirit] by resurrection from the dead, Jesus Christ our Lord" (Rom 1:4). An Old Testament verse clearly significant for the first Christians was Psalm 118:22: "The stone that the builders rejected has become the chief cornerstone" (cited in the New Testament in Matt 21:42; Mark 12:10; Luke 20:17; Acts 4:11; and 1 Pet 2:7). The idea is that the builders had rejected a stone because it did not fit their building plan, but that now by the action of God it has become the "capstone," the final stone that fits perfectly and holds the whole edifice together (the Greek term, "head of the corner," can apply to both the first stone and the last stone to be used). The resurrection is God's verdict on Jesus, the prophet who did not "fit" his contemporaries. Yet his birth also was marked by a remarkable sign, that of the virginal conception, which declares that although Jesus was born of a woman, a Jewish woman (Gal 4:4), and although Joseph was to all intents and purposes his earthly father, having named him at his birth in the way that traditionally acknowledged him as his own (Matt 1:25), Jesus was conceived in Mary's womb by God's Spirit as she willingly gave herself to God for this purpose.

The virginal conception is not an attempt to explain how Jesus was both fully divine and fully human. It is rather a sign of the mystery of God's work in the Son of God's assuming a fully human identity by the Spirit. This defies human explanation, but is entirely within God's power to accomplish. Something completely new has happened that may rightly be seen as an act of new creation. As the Spirit hovered over the waters of creation at the beginning (Gen 1:2 NIV) so now the same Spirit overshadowed Mary (Matt 1:20; Luke 1:35) to work something new. Jesus is not finally the product of the human race, not even of the most devout Jewish flesh, but a gift from God without whom we would be bereft of salvation. Jesus Christ is the great Godsend, God's gracious intervention in the affairs of human beings, God's renewal of the human race from within by means of God's coming to our aid in the most intimate and profound way it is possible to imagine.

In working out its Christology the Christian community has needed to avoid various wrong turnings along the way. We identify three of these here. The first was the idea that because he lived a holy and obedient life, the prophet Jesus of Nazareth was adopted by God as God's own Son and given divine honor. The adoption of Christ is variously to be imagined as taking place either in the resurrection (Rom 1:4) or at his baptism (Matt 3:17) or at his birth (Matt 1:18). This position rejects the idea that Christ was pre-existent, that he was with God prior to his earthly career. A second proposition was that Christ did exist prior to his birth, but in the form of an angel or semi-divine figure or "second god" that was itself created by God at some point in the long distant past. This figure then assumed flesh in the incarnation, but though divine in some sense was not God as God is God. A third opinion was that Christ was fully and completely God, so much so that his divinity overwhelmed his humanity, replacing the human soul in such a way that although he appeared to be human he was not fully human as are other humans. In their zeal to assert the divinity of Christ some Christians neglected to celebrate his full humanity and so undermined the delicate balance that properly exists in affirming two things simultaneously, Christ's identity as truly God and truly human.

These three ideas were all clearly and decisively rejected by the Christian community in favor of the confident conviction that Christ was *both fully divine and fully human*. Both aspects of this affirmation are important. He is to be honored, in the words of the Nicene Creed (Appendix 2), as the eternal Son, "God from God, Light from Light, true God from true God, begotten not made, being of one substance [or nature] with the Father," but also was made incarnate for our sakes and for our salvation. This is the crucial Christological insight to which the Christian community joyfully holds fast and its implications are both radical and life-generating.

5

Jesus Christ, Savior of the World

AN EARLY CHRISTIAN SYMBOL was that of the fish. Perhaps this has something to do with Christ's first followers including a number of fishermen, but its larger significance lies in the fact that the letters of *ichthus*, the Greek word for fish, can be made to stand for *Jesus Christ, Son of God, Savior.* Having explored the person of Christ, we need now to examine more closely the Christian community's conviction that Jesus Christ is the world's savior and that he saves eternally each person who looks to him in that capacity. To call Jesus a "savior" is to imply that human beings are in need of salvation and that they are individually and collectively unable to deliver themselves from the condition in which they find themselves. They need help from another source, from beyond themselves, from someone who is able to do for them and in them what they are incapable of doing for themselves. Christ is given to us for this purpose and all that we have considered concerning his person and identity indicates how Christ is qualified to save. Because of who he is he can do what he does. Conversely, what he does reveals who he is. Only he is able to save in the way he does, and in this he is unique.

SALVATION BY PARTICIPATION

Essentially, Christ saves us by participating in our human condition and lifting us out of it. It is for this reason that he is both fully divine and fully human. Christ participates in our human existence as God's own Son acting as and on behalf of the one God, but also as a real human being acting for and behalf of the human race. In this way he can be the mediator between

God and humanity: "For there is one God; there is also one mediator between God and humankind, Christ Jesus, himself human" (1 Tim 2:5). A simple "mission statement" that Jesus himself offered us is Luke 19:10, "For the Son of Man came to seek out and to save the lost." To find what has been lost, in this case human beings and all they have forfeited through their sin and failure, Christ has come from God seeking us, and to seek us means to come to where we are. To find anything that is lost requires going to where it actually is. In the incarnation and all that has flowed from it, Christ has come into our humanity in order to reverse our situation, to redeem what has been lost. It is important here to understand that Christ has not come to us in a special and protected kind of human nature: "For we do not have a high priest who is unable to sympathize with our weaknesses, but we have one who in every respect has been tested as we are, yet without sin" (Heb 4:15). As a human being Christ had to fight the same fights as us all, the difference being that where we are prone to lose he has decisively won (Luke 4:1–13). Christ is qualified to save us because he has not allowed himself to be ensnared by the sin and failure that characterizes the rest of us. The New Testament draws a contrast between the first Adam, who represents us all in his turning away from God, and the "last Adam," who has been and done everything the first Adam refused to be and do (Rom 5:18–19). Christ stands on solid ground from where he is able to lift us up. In Christ God is active to save and deliver, but the price to be paid for this is God's own participation through the Son in the life, suffering, and death of humankind. Salvation is costly and not easily accomplished, yet by participating in our human existence in Christ, God has imparted forgiveness and enabled reconciliation with God's own self.

It is possible to think of God's work in Christ as the conversion of the human race, the turning back to God of those who had gone astray and wandered into the far country. By the Spirit through whom Christ was conceived in Mary's womb and by whom he was sanctified and empowered in his life, God has assumed a human identity and turned it radically and completely to God's own self in order to provide in Christ the "pioneer of salvation" (Heb 2:10). In this way, Jesus stands as the "last Adam" (1 Cor 15:45), or "the ultimate man," the complete and full embodiment and exemplar for both men and women of what it means to be human. In Christ God is renewing humankind from within, taking the old and making it new by a process of regeneration. God does not abolish the old, but renews and restores it until it bears the divine image as it was always intended to do. To abolish the old would mean God forsaking the divine purpose in creating the world in the first place, but God wills to persist with that original purpose by making a new creation out of the old creation. There is both continuity and innovation: "So if anyone is in Christ, there is a new creation: everything old has passed away; see, everything has become new!" (2 Cor 5:17). Through this person as the world's savior, God is now redeeming lost humanity as people turn to Christ and find a new life and a new way in him. God's participation in our humanity gives us a means of access to this new life and gives us a way of understanding the loving purpose that lies behind the incarnation: "I came that they might have life, and have it abundantly" (John 10:10).

A further way of expressing this is to see Christ as one who saves through liberating those who are captives: "The Son of God was revealed for this purpose, to destroy the works of the devil" (1 John 3:8). Understood in this way, Christ saves through overcoming the powers that hold human beings in their grasp, the tyrants of sin, guilt, death, hell, and the devil, against all of which human beings are helpless, but from which through Christ they may be set free, because he has overcome them all and is able to bring others into his victory. The work of Jesus might then be likened to the work of a skilled mountain guide who first of all crosses a forbidding mountain range himself, facing and overcoming its challenges in order that he might then be qualified to guide others safely across. Those who look to Christ to save and guide them will not be disappointed or led astray since he is "the Way, the Truth, and the Life" (John 14:6).

Within this overall perspective of a God who in Christ participates in human life, suffering, and death in order to liberate and redeem us from the powers that hold us captive, we are able to distinguish aspects of the work that Christ has done for our salvation. These may be summarized as his work as prophet, priest, and king. These three "offices" reflect the social practices of the people of Israel for whom God made provision of prophets, priests, and kings and signified their appointment either by literal anointing with oil or figurative anointing by the Spirit. As Messiah, the "anointed one," Jesus is the supreme example of each of these offices and brings salvation by speaking the word of life, offering himself as a sacrifice and ruling over lives.

CHRIST'S WORK AS PROPHET

We have already noted that Jesus was understood in prophetic terms in his lifetime and yet was much more besides. Unlike the ancient prophets, he spoke not by using the formula "Thus says the Lord," but rather by proclaiming, *"I say to you."* In other words, he spoke directly as the representative of God referring to his own authority to interpret the Hebrew Scriptures and apply them in new directions. He is like a greater Moses who systematically instructed his disciples in the ways of God and gave them a new law of righteousness and mercy. Jesus spoke with an unusual degree of personal authority. But it was not merely his speaking that communicated the will and purpose of God. His life was an enactment of the saving message he proclaimed. He forgave sins, healed the sick, liberated the oppressed, and in all of these ways made it known that he had come to save, to do for us what we could not do for ourselves. God who spoke through the prophets has now "spoken to us by a Son" (Heb 1:1-2). Jesus not only spoke the word, he was the Word (John 1:1), and for this reason every aspect of his earthly life can be considered significant as a representation of the heart and mind of God. It can be said therefore that he was the light of the world (John 8:12) and the "reflection of God's glory and the exact imprint of God's very being" (Heb 1:3).

This is saving activity in that it overcomes the spiritual darkness and ignorance that are part of humankind's predicament. It is certainly true to say that human beings have been universally aware of a sense of God and that the creation carries with it some kind of witness to the divine. For those who have eyes to see, the "heavens are telling the glory of God; and the firmament proclaims his handiwork" (Ps 19:1) and "his eternal power and divine nature, invisible though they are, have been understood and seen through the things he has made" (Rom 1:20). Yet the fact is that human beings do not have eyes to see what ought to be obvious and either through deliberate choice or inherited blindness turn away from the witness of creation, losing themselves in devotion to and sometimes worship of that which is not God. The revelation in creation is therefore reduced for many into a nagging question about whether God exists rather than a glorious confirmation to the effect that God does. Into this darkened world the light has come to pierce the darkness and bring illumination. Christ therefore saves by illuminating our minds as to the way things really are, enabling us to see the witness to God in creation and most of all the supreme and central witness to God's love and righteousness that Christ himself is. Those who look to him and allow his light to shine into their lives will find themselves being stirred and changed by the "grace and truth" that he represents (John 1:17).

Jesus himself said, "You will know the truth and the truth will set you free" (John 8:32). He is the truth embodied, the truth incarnated in a single person (John 14:6). Therefore, he lifts us out of our condition of ignorance and distorted thinking. He enlightens us to the truth about God, the world, the future, and ourselves (Eph 1:18). Whereas many people seek for enlightenment and believe they have found it in one place or another, one religious figure or another, the Christian community is persuaded that light is to be found above all in Jesus Christ and that the revelation that comes through him outshines all other lights in its intensity and power. They do not deny that there is light elsewhere, but believe that the light of Christ enables us to test it and recognize it as such. They are also persuaded that this light can never finally be overcome, but will outlast all other realities: "The light shines in the darkness and the darkness did not overcome it" (John 1:5).

The prophetic ministry of Jesus points us to him as our teacher, master, and guide in all matters of faith and conduct. He is the decisive starting point for our communities when it comes to embracing, articulating, and explaining the convictions to which we hold fast. This counts for a great deal, yet remains only one aspect of the office of the Messiah that we accord to Jesus. It can be considered a saving ministry because on our own we are unable to make out the truth. Christ comes into our lives at this point as one who can do what we ourselves cannot do, open our eyes to the reality of God and the world. This is a first step in the direction of the abundant life that the other ministries of Christ as priest and king open up for us.

CHRIST'S WORK AS PRIEST

A great deal can be said under this heading. In the religious practices of Israel priests, and in particular the high priest, played important roles. Originally descendants of Moses' brother Aaron, the priestly caste within Israel was responsible for offering sacrifices in the tabernacle and then the temple and so for maintaining the ritual purity of the people of Israel when they came to the temple to worship. Through these practices Israel maintained its sense of the presence of God in their midst. Of particular significance was the Day of Atonement, when the high priest alone was allowed to enter into the Holy of Holies, the Most Holy Place of the Jewish temple, to make atonement for the sins of all Israel by offering up the blood of a sacrificial bull (Lev 16). He was permitted to do this on one day only in the year. In this way, the high priest, assisted by the priesthood, acted as mediator between God and the people. The priests represented God to the people and the people before God. Although Jesus lived as a faithful Jew in observing the worship and festivals of Israel, showing full respect for its practices and customs, it is also certain that he saw himself offering an alternative to them. He had the authority to forgive sins, and saw himself as a temple: "'Destroy this temple, and in three days I will raise it up.' . . . But he was speaking of the temple of his body" (John 2:19-21). It is in keeping with this that his disciples were to see him as the one in whom the glory of God had come to dwell, as in the temple itself (John 1:14), and this belief was to receive more significance once the Jewish temple had been destroyed in AD 70, as Jesus predicted it would be (Mark 13:1–2).

The forms of worship prescribed for the temple depended heavily on the sacrifice of animals. Worshipers were to bring an animal to the priests, either as an act of thanksgiving or to atone for some fault, and to lay their hands on its head. In the case of a sacrifice for all the people, the elders were to do so (Lev 4:15), and to offer it up to God through the shedding of its blood. The underlying belief within the sacrificial system was that an animal's life was in its blood: "For the life of the flesh is in the blood; and I have given it to you for making atonement for your lives on the altar" (Lev 17:11). By releasing the animal's blood and the life that was in it, the life of those who had identified with the animal by laying on hands was deemed to be purged and cleansed. The animal's life was offered on behalf and in the place of that of the worshipers. Two important things need to be noted here, however. The first was that the sacrifice was deemed invalid if it were not an expression of the repentance and contrition of the person offering it (Amos 5:21–24). This suggests that the real sacrifices God looked for were to do with the heart, of which the ritual offering of a sacrifice was meant to be a sign: "The sacrifice acceptable to God is a broken spirit; a broken and contrite heart, O God, you will not despise" (Ps 51:17). Ritual acts are of no value if they are not signs of the right inner disposition, and what truly reconciles us to God is heartfelt repentance. Secondly, sacrifices were valid within the Israelite religious system and were intended to maintain the ritual purity of those who took part in that system. They could not of themselves take away the pollution of real sins. They may cleanse from unintentional sins, but were powerless to cover the guilt of those sins that are intentional. The priest "takes the blood that he offers for himself and for the sins committed unintentionally by the people ... gifts and sacrifices are offered that cannot perfect the conscience of the worshiper" (Heb 9:6–10). The role of Israel's sacrificial system should be seen therefore as largely educative and symbolic, inculcating the right attitudes and assumptions in those who took part in it. But what really mattered was what was taking place in their hearts.

From a Christian point of view the sacrificial system was intended to prepare the way for a greater reality that was yet to come: the appearance of Jesus as a priestly figure in whom the purposes of God were focused and who would act on behalf of humanity in making atonement for sin. For this reason the book of Hebrews can speak of Jesus as the true high priest who would offer his own life, allowing his own blood to be shed as the one true sacrifice made once for all that can truly take away sins: "But as it is, he has appeared once for all at the end of the age to remove sin by the sacrifice of himself" (Heb 8:1; 9:26). Christ therefore is both high priest and sacrifice in the making of atonement. Christ offered his own blood, symbolizing his life poured out for humankind, and in so doing made atonement for sin, cleansing those who repent of their sins, turn to him as their Savior, and place their trust in him and what he has done for them. As God has come to participate in the person of the Son in the human story, with all its tragedy and pain, so this same Christ is the one through and by whom we may draw near to the Father to receive forgiveness and acceptance. All of this is by the gift and grace of the Father and it is the way to enter into life.

Because the cross is absolutely crucial for Christian faith it is necessary to understand its profound mysteries as well as we are able. Here God was in Christ reconciling the world to himself (2 Cor 5:18–19) and doing so by going as far into the depths of human experience as it is possible to go. God did this to demonstrate and prove love for humankind and before we for our part gave any thought to God. It was "while we were still sinners" that "Christ died for us" (Rom 5:8). Christ has journeyed into our human story in the incarnation. This has taken him into the realities of human suffering and even into death itself and into what lies beyond death. All of this has been for us and "for our sins" (1 Cor 15:3). He himself likened his death to a ransom, a price that needed to be paid in order to liberate those who are captive (Mark 10:45; 1 Tim 2:6). This was an act of sheer grace in that not only was it not deserved by us, it was the exact opposite of what we deserved, namely condemnation and rejection. "For our sake [God] made him to be sin who knew no sin, so that in him we might become the righteousness of God" (2 Cor 5:21). The death of Christ needs to be seen as a willing act on the part of Christ, one he could easily have avoided yet which he endured because it was necessary for our sakes to do so. It is the culmination of a whole life in which he gave himself in self-sacrifice for humankind. It was anticipated in his baptism because just as he had no need to repent of sins but underwent baptism in order to identify with sinful and lost humanity, so he embraced the cross, not for his own sake, but for ours. And just as in baptism he was overwhelmed by the waters so in his death he was overwhelmed by death itself as he "tasted death" for everyone (Heb 2:9).

Christ died for us, as our representative and in our place. What he did on the cross was undertaken for all Israel and all people everywhere. In it Jesus was including us in what he did so that we can genuinely claim that we have died on the cross with him and "in him." Jesus was doubly qualified to die as our representative. First of all we have seen that he was the Word of God made incarnate, that Word through whom all things were created in the first place. Because all things were made through him and were and are dependent on him, he is able to act on behalf of us all. What he did and does makes its impact upon us all because we have derived our life from him in the very beginning. This is why Colossians 1:19–20 can read: "For in him all the fullness of God was pleased to dwell, and through him God was pleased to reconcile to himself all things, whether on earth or in heaven, by making peace through the blood of his cross." Christ's death upon the cross, his self-offering to make atonement for sin on our behalf, is not only universal in the sense that Christ died for all people, it is cosmic in that the whole of creation is affected by it. This can only be because the whole of creation depends for its life on the Word that was with God in the beginning. Secondly, because Christ has lived a fully righteous, God-centered, and God-loving life he has qualified himself to draw near to God as a representative of all human beings. This is why the contrast between the first Adam and the last Adam can be made. Adam represents humankind as its head and stands for the disobedience of all people. Christ is a new and last Adam (Rom 5:15–21) whose righteousness before God enables him to act as our representative in "making intercession" for sinners: "Yet he bore the sin of many, and made intercession for the transgressors"; "All we like sheep have gone astray; we have all turned to our own way, and the LORD has laid on him the iniquity of us all" (Isa 53:12, 6). What Christ did was therefore done for our sakes and in our place. It is as though he has come into the world and gradually displaced human beings in their place before God, edging them on one side, in order that in their place he might speak and pray and die for them.

Christ has made atonement for a sinful and lost world in offering himself as a sacrifice. It was by the express plan and purpose of God that he has done this and as an expression of God's love that wills to reconcile humanity, and the world, to God's own self. We have stressed that Christ saves by means of participation. He has not only participated in our life and lived the righteous life that we have failed to do, offering to God the gift of obedience and devotion, but has also participated in our death, so taking upon himself the "wages of sin" that we have earned (Rom 6:23). When human beings sin they unlock the consequences of that sin and these lead to death, namely estrangement from God and the spiritual death that follows from it. In the Genesis narrative God warned Adam and Eve that "you shall die" (Gen 3:2) if they disobeyed God by eating of the fruit of the tree of the knowledge of good and evil. All of this points to the fact that to live in defiance of God leads to alienation from God and loss of God's life. When Jesus came it was to bear this self-imposed fate as though it were his own. When God judges human beings God chooses to do so by giving us over to the consequences of our own actions (Rom 1:24, 26, 28). This is what we have already indicated to be God's just "wrath," God's steadfast resistance to and rejection of that which runs against God's nature and will. We may rightly say therefore that on the cross Jesus endured in our place the wrath of God in that he bore the consequences of our own sin. In so doing he acknowledged on our behalf the righteousness of God's judgment and in offering the whole of his own, obedient life back to God in place of our disobedience he transformed the cross into an act of atonement, that is, of recognition of the holy will and judgment of God leading in him to forgiveness and reconciliation to the Father.

In saying this it would be wrong to imagine that God the Father was angry with the Son. Christ was and always will be God's beloved Son with whom he is well pleased (Matt 3:17). What Christ did was done in our place. It would certainly be accurate to say that God's anger is directed towards rebellious and slothful human beings who have vandalized the peace of God's creation. The Bible gives ample evidence of such divine hostility. However, divine anger is an aspect of divine love: it is because God loves that God cares enough to be angry. God's concern with the world is more like that of a "lover's quarrel" than the hostility of an enemy, although, of course, we can indeed make ourselves into God's enemies. It could be understood as God's "wounded love." It is also unhelpful to imagine that on the cross Christ is in some way appeasing or placating the Father, as though God needed to be "brought round." The cross is not about God dealing with God's own anger. It is rather a revelation that from eternity, in God's own self, mercy has triumphed over wrath, anger has been put away and our hostility towards God has been absorbed by God's own self. For this reason, in love God has purposed to provide a place in space, time, and history where atonement is made and to which human beings can come to find help in time of need (Heb 4:16), to be reconciled to God. That place is the cross. The cross of Christ is the enactment in time of that which has been true from all eternity—that God wills to forgive. This eternal reality has become a once-for-all event in time at the cross. To claim that Christ is "the Lamb who was slain from the creation of the world" (Rev 13:8 NIV) is to say that forgiveness has always been possible, that it did not suddenly become possible once Christ had died, as though this had brought about a change in God. What has changed is that now there is a particular place to which we may come, a place of atonement and a "mercy seat" (Exod 25:17; 1 John 2:2; 4:10), at which by placing our whole reliance on what Christ has done there for us by God's provision and trusting in his work on our behalf we may enter into forgiveness.

Properly understood there can be no complete forgiveness without repentance. Once wronged, people might proclaim themselves willing to forgive, but forgiveness can only flow where offenders recognize their fault and ask to be forgiven. At the cross, leaning on the atoning work of Christ, we are able to do this because through him we are able to acknowledge the extent of our failure and sin, and if there is anything lacking in our own act of repentance it is completed by Christ's "full, perfect, and sufficient sacrifice, oblation and satisfaction" (*Book of Common Prayer*). God forgives, but it is necessary that God should for the sake of justice do so in a way that is satisfactory, that is, in a way that does not overlook or make light of the reality of sin. By bearing God's judgment on the cross in our place and acknowledging that it is just, righteous, and true, Christ has enabled us to be forgiven in way that does not pass over sin, as though it did not matter. In the cross therefore it is proven both that God is "righteous and that he justifies the one who has faith in Jesus" (Rom 3:26). God forgives, but in a way that blends both justice and mercy, grace and truth, and that extends forgiveness and new life to human beings while satisfying the divine integrity in not overlooking or minimizing sin. This is not a question of God inflicting violence on the Son, but of God absorbing and overcoming violence in the Son.

What is clear here is that God's forgiveness is costly. If the Bible portrays God creating the world with relative ease (God speaks and the worlds spring into being), the redemption of that world is at infinite cost, the cost of suffering and death on the cross. God's grace is not cheap grace and neither should it be imagined that forging forgiveness is a painless task. The full cost to God of human salvation is captured in the dying cry of Jesus recorded in Matthew 27:45–46, "My God, my God, why have you forsaken me?" In his last moments Jesus experienced what it was to undergo the total loss of God, the horror of utter God-forsakenness. It is not that the Father had permanently forsaken the Son (the resurrection reveals the opposite), but that the Son, having been given over to death and having journeyed into that far country, came to the point of bearing the utter desolation of knowing himself to be without God, to have lost sight of the Father. This is the logical end of human rejection of God. If the wages of sin is indeed death, estrangement from God, leading finally, should there be no repentance, to loss of God, then this is what Jesus endured for our sakes. It might rightly be said that Christ suffered the pains of hell on the cross—in that place he "descended into hell," the ultimate and logical outcome for those who choose to be without God. Jesus did this for us. At this point Christ is more than our representative acting on our behalf, he has become our substitute acting instead of us and displacing us. He endured something for us that we now need no longer ever know for ourselves. He underwent this for us, in our place, that we may be spared such ultimate grief. This is the full extent of the saving love of God in Christ and the ground of our deepest gratitude.

In the light of this it is appropriate at this point to touch on the possibility that God also suffers. It could be said that while the Son on the cross experienced the pain of God-forsakenness, the Father underwent the pain of bereavement. Although we should touch on such matters with great caution, to do so opens up new insights into divine compassion, God's capacity not only to sense the depth of human suffering, but also to suffer with the creation. There is no doubt that Jesus underwent immense suffering. If what we have claimed is true and the Son is the revelation of the Father then we can only conclude that what we see in the Son is also true of the Father. This takes us back into our whole understanding of God as personal. God is both intensely personal and intensely passionate. Although a traditional Christian understanding has been that God is "impassible," incapable of suffering, there are good reasons for now rejecting this belief as an alien philosophical concept, rather than a biblical one. The God of Israel is not portrayed as remote, removed, and passionless, but rather as engaged, responsive, capable of the deepest emotions of love, and, amazingly, capable of knowing pain. Isaiah 63:9 (NIV) suggests this: "In all their distress he too was distressed, and the angel of his presence saved them. In his love and mercy he redeemed them." Hosea 11:8 gives a further example: "How can I give you up, Ephraim? How can I hand you over, O Israel? How can I treat you like Admah? How can I treat you like Zeboiim? My heart recoils within me, my compassion grows warm and tender." It is possible to grieve God's Holy Spirit by our rebellion and resistance, in other words, to cause grief and pain to God (Isa 63:10; Eph 4:30).

To understand this correctly we need to qualify it. God does not suffer as do humans, since when we suffer it is largely because of forces that are greater than we are over which we have no control. Not so with God. We do not typically choose to suffer, it is involuntary. But when God suffers it is because God chooses to do so and because there is a goal that God clearly perceives that renders the suffering redemptive and creative. Furthermore, God is not destroyed by suffering, but absorbs and overcomes it in the deeper resources of love and blessedness that belong to God's nature. Yet this aspect of God's nature, the willingness to cancel sin and bring reconciling forgiveness through the costly means of the cross, inspires all the more within us the love for God that is the proper response to the cross. "In this is love, not that we loved God but that he loved us and sent his Son to be the atoning sacrifice for our sins. . . . We love because he first loved us" (1 John 4:10, 19). It is for this reason that Christians are convinced that the cross is the most powerful place on earth.

CHRIST'S WORK AS KING

According to Mark's Gospel, the first mighty act Jesus did on commencing his public ministry was to set free a man from an unclean spirit in the synagogue at Capernaum (Mark 1:21-28). This act of liberation was symbolic of what Jesus came to do in his whole ministry. He indicated this in the "Nazareth manifesto" preached in the synagogue of his home town: "The Spirit of the Lord is upon me, because he has anointed me . . . to proclaim release to the captives . . . to let the oppressed go free, to proclaim the year of the Lord's favor" (Luke 4:16-21). All of this was a manifestation of Christ's ministry as king, overcoming the oppressive powers of evil and liberating the people for God. Jesus preached the good news of the arrival of God's kingdom, or reign, to be received with repentance and faith (Mark 1:14-15) and saw himself as the agent of this kingdom. The nature miracles of Jesus draw some of their meaning from this fact: Christ stilled the storm and incidentally demonstrated his rule over the sea (Mark 4:39). It is in his power over the demons and unclean spirits that the kingly rule of Christ is, however, most keenly shown. The kingdom of God is God's action to reclaim a world that has denied God's lordship over the creation, and in particular over the people God has called to be God's particular possession. It is the end of history in the sense that it is the final goal of the whole creation and stands for the ultimate healing and peace of all creation (Matt 8:11).

The appropriate response to a king is to acknowledge his rule and submit to it. It is not hard to submit to Jesus because of who he is. Jesus is the ultimate contrast with what we imagine to be domineering and privileged earthly kingship: "Come to me, all you that are weary and are carrying heavy burdens, and I will give you rest. Take my yoke upon you, and learn from me, for I am gentle and humble in spirit and you will find rest for your souls. For my yoke is easy, and my burden is light" (Matt 11:28-30). When Jesus entered Jerusalem it was not on a war horse, the weapon of choice for kings, but on a humble donkey (Zech 9:9; Matt 21:1-11). None of this should be taken to suggest that God is weak, rather that the power of God can find expression even in and through that which in our eyes appears to be foolish or weak: "For God's foolishness is wiser than human wisdom, and God's weakness is stronger than human strength" (1 Cor 1:25). Nowhere does God's purpose, or God's agent, appear to be weaker and more defeated than in the moments of Christ's death upon the cross. Yet what appeared to be a defeat was in God's economy a significant victory. The victory consisted in the refusal of the Son of God to give in to the temptation to depart from the path of obedience, even under the greatest duress. Jesus refused to allow himself to be deflected from his vocation by the earthly powers, whether they be political, ethnic, religious, or spiritual. He had already won this victory, both in defeating the temptations that beset him throughout his life (Luke 4:1–13) and in emerging from the agonies of Gethsemane with the resolution, "yet, not what I want, but what you want" (Mark 14:36). All of this is in marked contrast to the rest of humankind, which has turned away from its vocation. In his resistance Jesus gained the ultimate victory, whatever appearances might have suggested, and this victory was then made manifest in the resurrection. By his obedience Jesus was seen to have triumphed over the powers of his day, the rulers of this age. This is well expressed in Colossians 2:13–15: "And when you were dead in trespasses and the uncircumcision of your flesh, God made you alive together with him, when he forgave us all our trespasses, erasing the record that stood against us with its legal demands. He set this aside, nailing it to the cross. He disarmed the rulers and authorities and made a public example of them, triumphing over them in it." The death of Christ is therefore a divine victory, one in which we share because it is the point at which our sins have been atoned for and cancelled, thus setting us free from any alien power that claims to have authority over us and to be able to accuse us. Instead we are now free to live under the liberating and dignifying power of God's own self.

The kingship of Jesus is proclaimed by both the resurrection and the ascension and continues still in his providential rule over history: "For he must reign until he has put all his enemies under his feet: The last enemy to be destroyed is death" (1 Cor 15:25–26). The final expectation is that Christ will be proclaimed in the fullness of time as King of kings and Lord of lords (1 Tim 6:15; Rev 19:16). Although Christ's earthly work is indeed finished and stands for ever, his work as king is as yet incomplete. We await its fulfillment and work towards it. As Christ "made intercession for sinners" in his life's work, he continues to do so even now, since it is said that he "is at the right hand of God," the place of honor, and "indeed intercedes for us" (Rom 8:34), and that "he is able for all time to save those who approach God through him, since he always lives to make intercession for them" (Heb 7:25). Having achieved human salvation through his life, death, and resurrection, he now works to ensure that this salvation comes to pass. This in no way suggests that salvation remains in doubt, but rather that the very presence of Jesus, the royal human being in heaven at the Father's right hand, is the guarantee that what he is now we one day will be. When the Word of God assumed in Jesus of Nazareth a human identity he did do not do so just for a time, not simply for the period of the incarnation, but for eternity. Jesus will never cease to be human. He has pioneered the way into the very presence of God, there to remain. God in deep and gracious humility has joined himself to humanity, and so to us, for all time.

6

Human Dignity and Depravity

To any intelligent observer of the human race it should be startlingly clear that human beings are capable of both the best and the worst, of the most outstanding works of beauty and acts of charity and at the same time the most heinous of crimes and cruelties. The human race is a contradiction within itself. The Christian faith is at its most persuasive in offering explanations for this paradox, and of all the convictions of the Christian community it is in the area of anthropology, the study of humankind, that it is at its most realistic. The conviction is that human beings are made in the image of God and yet have fallen from this vocation and high calling with disastrous consequences.

MEASURING HUMANITY

It should be noted that in this book we come to think about being human only after having spent time thinking about the incarnation of God in Christ and his saving life, death, and resurrection. There is a logic to this in that both the dignity and the depravity of God's human creatures are most clearly understood in the light of Christ, who is the key to wisdom. Jesus is the light of the world (John 8:12), not only in the sense that he reveals the truth and reality of God to us, shining light into our darkness, but also in that he reveals the truth about what it means to be human. We are persuaded that Jesus was a real human being just as we are, not a superman on the one hand or a human being merely in appearance on the other, but a real human being who lived the kind of life we all live, growing, learning, suffering, and dying on the same terms as everybody else. He was indeed a real human being, but he was also a *true* human being in the way that we are not. His humanity was humanity as it ought to be, fulfilling the vocation to love the Lord our God with heart, soul, mind, and strength, and doing so from the beginning to the end of his life without interruption. So when we look at Christ, we see one who truly reflected God, being the very image of God (Heb 1:3; Col 1:15). It is as though the image of God having been obscured in fallen humanity, God has now come to redraw that image in the person of his Son, who is the prototype of a new and restored humanity to be followed by many others (Col 3:10; Heb 2:10). He represents humanity turned once more towards God. Christ therefore is what humanity is called to be. He stands as the permanent example of what we have the potential to become and is an inspiration to all those who aspire to live good, honorable, righteous, and compassionate lives.

Yet in being all this, Jesus is also the standard by which we judge ourselves. He reveals to us how far we fall short of what we should be. Compared to him we become aware of the darkness and self-obsession that characterize our own lives. The light he brings illuminates us, but also exposes us as the failed and fallen human beings that we are. We do not do what we ought to do and we do those things that we ought not to do, and apparently we find ourselves helpless in this condition, in our best moments aspiring to what we know we ought to be, but never achieving that to which we aspire. We might say there is a gap between what we are capable of being and what we actually succeed in being. This gap is the measure of what we call "fallenness," our chronic falling short of what God call us to. This condition is universal, it is shared by the whole of the human race, Christ being the only exception to the general rule: "All have sinned and fall short of the glory of God" (Rom 3:23).

HUMAN ORIGINS

A Christian concept of what it means to be human properly begins with Christ. But on this foundation it is possible to develop our analysis by referring to the Hebrew Scriptures and in particular to the highly formative early chapters of the book of Genesis, a book that deals, as its name suggests, with "origins," the origin of creation, of sensate life, of human beings, of sin, fall, and inhumanity, of civilization and then of God's purposes of salvation, beginning with Abraham and the calling of his descendants to a particular vocation in the service of God. In the purposes of God the human race plays a central and significant role. Genesis 1 narrates God's speaking of the world into being. On the six days of creation described there God first of all established the framework within which living creatures might exist and then proceeded to populate the world. On the sixth day, as God's culminating act of creation, God purposed to create human beings:

> "Let us make humankind in our image, according to our likeness; and let them have dominion over the fish of the sea, and over the birds of the air, and over the cattle, and over all the wild animals of the earth, and over every creeping thing that creeps upon the earth." So God created humankind in his own image, in the image of God he created them; male and female he created them. God blessed them, and God said to them, "Be fruitful and multiply, and fill the earth and subdue it; and have dominion...." (Gen 1:26-28).

These words are foundational and crucial for our understanding of humankind. The creation of male and female is seen as the high point of creative work and reflects the empirical reality that human beings are the most highly developed among all the species. They belong, of course, to the organic creation and there should be no thought that being part of the animal creation is demeaning—this too is God's good creation. The uniqueness of humans, however, is seen in the fact that they are made in God's image and are therefore singled out for a particular calling and responsibility. At the very least the idea of being in the image of God suggests a quality of relationship between God and people, a relationship of call and response by which God speaks and we respond. It is this capacity for response to God, human "respondability," that might be said to be the essence of humanness, the consciousness of God, of the transcendent realm, and the personal responsibility that goes with it. Human beings may be animals, but they are also more. They have complex brains, the faculty of speech, capacity for music, humor, and imagination. They have consciences and can foresee the consequences of their actions. Uniquely among the higher animals, their facial muscles are so constructed that they are capable of expressing a multiplicity of inward emotions. They are able to go beyond their organic natures and imagine higher realities. They are more than their genes and this in turn places them in a position of great power, for good or ill, within the creation itself. It also renders them capable of seeking after God.

It should be noticed that there are in fact two creation stories and although they tell different stories they in fact point to the same realities. The Genesis 2 creation narrative does not build up to the creation of human beings on the sixth day as the pinnacle of creation. It rather starts with the creation of Adam from the dust of the ground and imagines the world of nature being formed around him. Adam has the power to name the animals and so displays a partnership with God in the work of creating and forming the earth. God then provides the woman to be his companion and equal, his counterpart as "bone of my bones and flesh of my flesh" (v. 23), and the institution of marriage follows. Once again, therefore, human beings are at the centre of the creation project, sharing with God in communion and creative partnership. The garden in which they find themselves is called "Eden," which means "bliss." This idyllic picture is an expression of God's will for his human and other creatures, that they should live together in wholesome peace and well-being. Whatever might then have followed, we can remain convinced that this continues to be God's highest purpose and desire for the world God has made.

THE IMAGE OF GOD

What does it mean, then, to have been created "in the image of God"? The word suggests a likeness to God and there are several ways we might develop this thought. In an earlier chapter we laid great stress upon the divine personhood, that God is person and not just power. Human beings are called to be like God in the sense that they too are made to be persons, to think, feel, create, respond, and act in ways that, albeit modestly, reflect the divine nature. Without in any way demeaning the rest of creation, which has its own ways of being and its own kind of intelligence, human beings stand out in their uniqueness in this regard. Only they exist as persons with this degree of depth. It is for this reason that God looks to human beings to respond to the love that God shows and to relate to God's own self responsibly and fully. It must also be claimed that the formation of persons emerges from and depends upon the capacity for relationship with other persons. We know ourselves only in the midst of a community of selves in which there is the interchange of love and mutual respect. Here it is significant that Genesis 1:27 sees our existence as "male and female" as part of the image of God. Relationality is part of the divine image, not least because this is God's own way of being, eternally united in the relations of Father, Son, and Spirit. It is our relationships that enable us to become fully personal and fully human and it is for this reason that from our birth we are integrated into a network of relations that at their best are the deepest sources of joy and well-being. We might even claim that at the heart and in the depths of the universe is the community of persons. God is such a community. The narrative of creation and redemption that forms the basic shape of the Christian faith concerns the readiness for, the loss of, and then the restoration of relationship, as we shall continue to see.

A further aspect of the divine image concerns the bestowal on human beings of "dominion" over the creation, the mandate to "fill the earth and subdue it" (1:28). This vocation also reflects God in that as the world's creator and sustainer, as its true Lord, God has intended for humanity a role within creation as stewards of what has been entrusted to them, the responsibility to nurture, direct, and enable creation in the fulfilling of its potential. It is the misuse of this God-given power that has led human beings not to tend the earth as though it were a garden, enhancing its beauty and its capacities while also benefiting from its fruits, but to exploit it for selfish purposes without regard to its own integrity and sustainability. "Dominion" refers not to the merciless exploitation of the earth's fruitfulness, but to a proper creation care that reflects God's own care for the world. Being made in the image of God is not a license to misbehave, but a call to live up to the vocation that has been divinely bestowed on God's human creatures. Those who deny the image of God in humanity will inevitably reduce the value and significance of human life.

The reality of this powerful and responsible position within creation is sadly seen as much in humanity's capacity to despoil the earth, and even in its potential to destroy it, as in its virtuous stewardship. Despite this, we are able to believe that all human beings are made in God's image, that each person and every community is to be honored as such, that in addition to the respect that should be shown to all creatures because they are made by God, human beings possess a particular value to God and that this constitutes the basis of what is sometimes called the "sanctity of life." To destroy a human being is to destroy the image of God in that person and so is not just an immoral act, but a blasphemous one. It is for this reason that in the traditions of Israel the severest of penalties were to be expected when life was illegally taken: "Whoever sheds the blood of a human, by a human shall that person's blood be shed; for in his own image God made humankind" (Gen 9:6). In the light of God's mercy it might be that societies choose not to extract this penalty, but this does not diminish the fact that it is the penalty that fits the crime.

Our existence as persons through the relationships we enjoy within the community of fellow-persons and within the community of creation grants to us a vision of human flourishing and joyful existence. In its turn this reflects God's intention clearly portrayed in the early chapters of Genesis. At each stage of this creative work God sees what God has made and pronounces it good. After the creation of human beings in God's own image God sees what he has made and pronounces it "very good" (Gen 1:31).

There is divine joy and pleasure here. God blesses the whole creation and commands it to be fruitful indicating the pleasure God takes in the gift and enjoyment of life. This vitality is reflected in the delight Adam takes in the wife God creates for him (2:23). It is further emphasized in that in the Garden of Eden God plants the tree of life and indicates that Adam and Eve might freely eat from it (2:9; 3:2). An open gate of life is therefore set before human beings and reflects God's loving purpose that they should prosper and flourish. The picture is overwhelmingly positive. Yet it is painfully obvious that the human story has not lived up to this early vision. The dignity of being made in God's image has given way to depravity. Things are not as they are supposed to be and we need to enquire as to why this is the case.

THE SPOILING OF CREATION

Before pursuing this, it will add to our understanding if we were to reflect on the best ways to understand the literature we are drawing from in Genesis 2 and 3. This is not history in the usual sense of that word. It is impossible to put a date to the events described here. When it speaks of God "walking in the garden at the time of the evening breeze" (3:8), it is clearly speaking figuratively. It can be described as "primal history" in that it deals with some fundamental realities about the human race that are of universal significance, yet that cannot be dated in time. It may be possible to understand what is written here as parable, poetry, saga, or even "myth," provided this last term is not thought to mean something that is not true, but rather a narrative that embodies what is universally and persistently true—"true myth" that serves to illuminate the truth about the whole human race. The positive things we have already derived from it are themselves of this nature as they have illuminated our human existence. The narratives here can be understood on several levels:

- They are a way of speaking of the human race as a whole. "Adam" means "humankind" and Eve is "the mother of all who live" (3:20). Together they represent the whole of the human race and in them we see the realities that are true about us all. For this reason their story is our story, and our story is theirs.

- In Adam and Eve we therefore see ourselves as individuals. As one rabbi put it: "Adam sinned and brought untimely death upon us all, and each of us has become the Adam of our own soul." Their story of a calling offered and willfully refused is also my story. The narrative's Adam and Eve were no better nor worse than the rest of us. They only did what all of us do. We cannot blame them for our fate, we are all to blame.

- All this said, logically and biologically there must have been the first human beings from whom the rest of us have descended. When and who these people were is for the geneticists and anthropologists to determine. But whoever the first humans were, they were the first to deviate from the calling given to them and set their descendants on a path that was to lead away from the original intention of life into one of spiritual death. Paul puts it like this (in a sentence he never quite completes): "Therefore, just as sin came into the world through one man, and death came through sin, and so death spread to all because all have sinned . . ." (Rom 5:12). This is what is called "original sin" and we shall return to it.

What Genesis offers us is a highly sophisticated and universally accessible analysis of what is fundamentally amiss with the human race. Called to live as the image of God exercising responsible stewardship within the creation and in interdependence with it, we have irrationally and unreasonably refused the invitation, rejected the call, and deviated from the path. "All we like sheep have gone astray; we have all turned to our own way" (Isa 53:6). When tested we have fallen and in place of heeding and obeying the word of God we have preferred to listen to other voices, the voice of temptation. We have believed the lie that we cannot depend upon what God has said to us, that God does not truly will our well-being, and we have imagined that we are ourselves gods. In the Garden of whose trees Adam and Eve could have freely eaten and lived there was one tree forbidden to them, the tree of the knowledge of good and evil (3:3). Within the imagery of Genesis 3 this tree represents the temptation to believe that we are not subject to God's will and word but are at liberty to invent for ourselves what we believe to be good or evil. It represents the fantasy that we are godlike, that we can replace God with ourselves. This is both a bizarre act and a deluded belief that leads to no good, but it rings true with our constant human desire for self-referring autonomy, with our resentment of God's legitimate authority over our lives.

The essence of human sin is therefore self-exaltation: "You will not die . . . you will be like God knowing good and evil," claims the serpent (3:5). Sin is the attempt to displace God and to insert ourselves in God's place. It is a turning away from God and God's way in favor of our own. It is the adoption of an attitude of resistance, of hardness towards God, a failure to answer God's legitimate call on our lives. Fundamentally, sin is not "sins," individual actions of wrongdoing (though it includes these). It is rather a life-posture, an orientation of our lives away from God so that we become turned in upon ourselves, self-centered and self-seeking. Although this was never intended for us, it is the default position of the human race as a whole and of the individuals within it. An examination of our own hearts can only confirm this. The outcome of sin is spiritual death in that we become estranged from the source of life in God's own self and therefore tend towards disintegration and loss. If not interrupted or renounced, this movement in the wrong direction will become our self-imposed fate, and by "fate" here we mean not something imposed externally upon us but the inevitable outcomes of a life of rejection of God, a self-imposed imprisonment. This "anatomy of sin" accords with Jesus' own understanding. In Luke 15 Jesus told three parables about lost things: a lost coin, a lost sheep, and a lost son. To be lost means to be in the wrong place or to be heading in the wrong direction. Having so described the human condition, he proclaimed that he had come "to seek out and to save what was lost" (Luke 19:10), that is, to reverse it.

The idea that we are "alienated" is not only a deeply biblical idea, it recurs frequently in modern philosophies in the intuition that human beings and societies are dislocated at a profound level. This is well illustrated in the narratives of Genesis 3. Because of their self-exaltation and rejection of divine lordship, human beings have become, first of all, alienated from God who is the ground of all being. Whereas they were created for friendship and communion with their divine parent, a communion symbolized by walking with God in the Garden, once they had fallen they begin to hide from God and to fear God (Gen 3:8). We may call this the *theological* dimension of the human dislocation and fall. It is no longer instinctive to them to live at peace with God and to seek God, but rather to keep their distance. God is no longer perceived as a life-giving and gracious companion in the adventure of life but as a spoiler. A second consequence is on the *psychological* level. In place of their being naked and unashamed (2:25), they now know themselves to be naked and are ashamed. In other words, they are no longer at peace with themselves but inwardly conflicted, sensing guilt and unable to accept themselves simply as they are. Here the human being is like a gyroscope that instead of spinning on its axis becomes eccentric, begins to wobble and to lose its momentum. At a further *sociological* level, Adam and Eve are estranged from each other. Where previously there was harmony, mutual delight, and complementarity, we now find them blaming each other, passing the buck, and vying for control (3:12). The warning comes that men will domineer over women (3:16), and so we begin the long history of the suppression of women. However, the battle between the sexes stands here for the whole range of inter-human conflict. It continues in Genesis 4 with the murder of Abel by Cain and has been confirmed by human violence and inhumanity ever since. The Hebrew Scriptures do not gloss over this but tell it as it is. Human differences become not a means of enrichment but an occasion for fear, conflict, and hatred. In yet a further *ecological* dimension, human beings who were created for a responsible role within the community of creation now find themselves in conflict with nature itself; the world they were called to "subdue" now becomes intractable and out of control (3:17-18). Productive and creative work now becomes back-breaking and arduous labor (3:19). Human beings have vandalized the *shalom*, the peace of creation, and continue to do so throughout their history. They are driven out of Eden. The fear and dread of humans falls upon the animal kingdom (Gen 9:2). At every level of their development human beings are in crisis and the root of their discord is their estrangement from their creator.

The multiple alienations identified in the course of Genesis 3 ring true to human experience throughout their history. One further dimension can be identified and that is at the *eschatological* level, or the level of ultimate and final reality (sometimes called the "last things"). Sin divorces human beings from their future, the goal towards which they are moving. Although it is popularly thought that Genesis 3 narrates a fall from an original perfection in creation, this is not the claim these passages make. Neither humankind nor creation should be thought of as perfect in the beginning since this would suggest that they had already arrived at the goal that lay before them. Instead, what we see described here is a good beginning given by God that is then distorted through irrational human choices. Adam and Eve are at the beginning of their lives setting out to fulfill their calling to have dominion over creation. They forsake their calling almost as soon as they have begun, just as human beings waste no time in deviating from the proper pathway. So they become incapable of achieving the future. God indeed proclaims creation and humans within it as "very good" (1:31), but this means not that the creation is already perfected but that it suits God's purpose, that it is fit for the purpose God has in mind, and this involves the progressive development of humankind as they learn to seek and to know God (Acts 17:26-27).

God's work in creation is well thought of as a "project," an initiative through which God intends to accomplish certain ends through particular means. This is to be done through divine-human co-operation, but the co-operation is refused from the human side. It is to this end that Christ has come. As the redeemer and Savior he has restored and renewed humanity in his own life, death, and resurrection. He has reversed the multiple alienations that human beings have brought, and do bring, upon themselves. God was in Christ reconciling the world to himself (2 Cor 5:19). At the theological level he has lived as one fully reconciled to God. At the psychological level he has lived as a whole, complete human being, knowing and embracing his own identity, whose sufferings are a consequence not of his own lifestyle but of "bearing the sins of many." At the sociological level he has lived in love for neighbor and for enemy alike. In ecological terms he showed himself both to be in touch with nature and to have dominion over it. Finally, he has restored the human race to its intended future, brought it back on track, and demonstrated this in the resurrection by which he restores to us and opens up for us a future of inexpressible joy and hope. All of this he does out of love as God acting in our own humanity.

BEING HUMAN

A number of other matters remain to be discussed in relation to humanity by way of clarification and explanation. It is sometimes claimed that human beings are "basically evil." It would be more accurate to say that human beings are basically good but radically fallen. To call something that is made in the image of God "basically evil" is to risk demeaning God's good creation. Even in their sin, human beings do not completely lose the image of God, as Genesis 9:6 makes clear. They retain that image but are like mirrors that are now turned away from the object they are intended to reflect. Once turned back in the right direction they will reflect the divine likeness, but even turned away they retain the capacity to reflect that image. Human beings retain their fundamental goodness but are radically fallen and fail to be what they are supposed to be. Sometimes it is also said that they are "totally depraved," and this also is not true if it means that there are no shreds of goodness left to them. Human beings are not as evil as they could possibly be since this would make them devils not humans. Yet they are indeed "totally" depraved in the sense that every part of them has been affected and distorted through their fallenness. There is not one part of the human make-up that has not been affected by sin, whether this be their reasoning capacity, their emotions, their sexuality, their ambitions, their spirituality, or their will. It is in this sense a total dislocation. Even when we are at our best we are still touched by sin. Our spiritual and religious desires are tainted by self-interest and misdirected motivations, and at those times when we do good we often accompany this with a sense of pride and self-congratulation. Even our best is therefore sullied. We do well not to delude ourselves about our moral capacity. Jesus understood this about us. He knew what was in all people (John 2:24-25; Matt 7:11) and took account of it. Yet there are degrees of depravity and not all humans are equally corrupt. Even though all are fallen and inclined to the wrong, there are still "noble sinners" who struggle to do what is right.

It has been a traditional Christian belief that human beings possess immortal souls. On this account, the human constitution is comprised of three distinct parts: body, soul, and spirit (1 Thess 5:23) that can in part be separated from each other. On the death of the body therefore the immortal spirit or soul survives beyond death and endures forever, either in heaven or in hell. Traditional though it may be, there are very good reasons for doubting this way of thinking and seeing it as an intrusion into Christian faith of an alien form of thought. The New Testament is clear that God *alone* "has immortality and dwells in unapproachable light" (1 Tim 6:16). In the Genesis account there is in the midst of the Garden a tree of life of which the first humans could freely eat (Gen 2:9). This is a symbol of the eternal life that humans could enter into and enjoy as they developed and grew in response to God. Immortality was not for them a present possession but a future possibility into which they could enter as they trusted in and walked with God. Consistent with this, the New Testament portrays immortality as a future gift that will be given through Christ in the resurrection to those who trust in him, the foretaste of which can be enjoyed now (Rom 8:11; 1 Cor 15:42–58). Immortality is something that our mortal bodies must "put on" in the future (1 Cor 15:54). The biblical picture then is not one that suggests we already have immortal souls but rather that we are mortal and finite creatures who enter into eternal life and immortality as a gift that comes to us through communion with God in faith and trust. God has made us from the dust to become fully human persons who are unities of body and soul, inner and outer. The language of body, soul, and spirit is not to suggest that we are tri-partite beings but, rather, unified wholes that can be looked at from different perspectives—as embodied selves with rich emotional, intellectual, and spiritual lives and in relation to God. This does not deny the fact that it is possible for a person's essential self, the "soul," to be preserved by God apart from the body, simply to deny that the soul has inherent immortality apart from the gift and grace of God. To summarize this section, we might say that as human beings born mortal and finite, we are nonetheless capable of not dying eternally, but only in living communion with the God who alone has immortality. To be "capable of not dying" is not the same as being "not capable of dying." In the resurrection we will be transformed into immortality and only then, sharing in the divine nature through Christ (2 Pet 1:4), will we be not capable of dying, truly immortal.

ORIGINAL SIN

Finally, we address the question of "original sin." This is the conviction that the sin into which human beings have deviated is universal, affecting all human beings of whatever class, gender, or ethnic group they may be. It is also corporate in that it affects the human race as a whole in its shared existence and embraces whatever common activities we engage in and institutions that we create. The religious, political, economic, and social "powers" that emerge from shared human existence are not likely to prove more moral than individual human beings themselves and tend, like them, to be self-interested, open to corruption, and concerned with their own survival. Although not a biblical saying, the dictum that "power tends to corrupt and absolute power tends to corrupt absolutely" rings true. Further, original sin indicates that human fallenness is structural, that is, when we are born into the human race we are already sharing in its fallen, self-centered nature, and this is only compounded once we are formed and shaped into the likeness of those around us, all of whom are fallen creatures. From birth we have a tendency to prefer sin rather than to love God and are therefore imprisoned in the fallen human condition until we encounter one who can unlock the prison and set us free, a savior and redeemer: "You were dead through the trespasses and sins in which you once lived, following the course of this world, following the ruler of the power of the air, the spirit that is now at work among those who are disobedient. All of us once lived among them in the passions of our flesh, following the desires of flesh and senses, and we were by nature children of wrath, like everyone else" (Eph 2:1–2). Apart from Christ himself, the person who "can do no wrong" does not exist.

The doctrine of original sin is a great leveler in that it places princes and paupers on the same level—nobody is exempt. On the other hand, it need not imply that all are equally sinful. It is a matter of observation that some, sinners though they may be, live lives of outstanding decency and kindness. The distance between the depraved criminal and the compassionate humanitarian is great. The sparks of goodness we continue to find in human beings can be attributed not only to the responsible individuals but to the influences that have formed and shaped them, and most of all to the fact that God continues to preserve human society from collapsing into evil by the exercise of "common grace," God's continuing activity in inspiring that which is good and true and humanizing a fallen world. However, any who think they stand should take care, lest they fall.

Neither should original sin be confused, as it often has been, with "original guilt." This is the idea that not only have our first parents and those who preceded us in the human story bequeathed to us the fallen condition into which we were born, but also that because they represented us we were "in them" when they sinned and therefore their guilt for sin is also attributed to us. Now it is certainly true that as well as being culpable for our own actions there is a more general sense in which, being embedded within the human race as a whole, we share in a general culpability for its sins of both commission and omission. Yet on several occasions the biblical traditions make it clear that we are directly responsible and accountable only for those sins that we consciously commit and not for anybody else's. Although it is certainly true that we constantly suffer the fallout from the wrong things others do, most of all those closest to us, it is clearly stated that we are only guilty for those things we do ourselves: "When the son has done what is lawful and right, and has been careful to observe all my statutes, he shall surely live. The person who sins shall die. A child shall not suffer for the iniquity of a parent nor a parent for the iniquity of a child; the righteousness of the righteous shall be his own, and the wickedness of the wicked shall be his own" (Ezek 18:19–20). This seems to be what Paul had in mind when he wrote: "Sin was indeed in the world before the law, but sin is not reckoned where there is no law. Yet death exercised dominion from Adam to Moses, even over those whose sins were not like the transgression of Adam, who is a type of the one to come" (Rom 5:12–14). Adam's sin was a conscious transgression of a known command and for sin to be "reckoned" there has to be a known law, either of conscience or Scripture. Where the distinction between original sin and guilt is particularly important is in understanding the status of children. Although born into a fallen world by no fault of our own, we only become guilty of sin when there is a law of conscience or morality known to us. Children therefore do not incur guilt until they reach an age of accountability for their actions.

The human condition, fallen as it is, is a precarious one. Original sin makes it clear that its remedy is more than a question of human beings "trying harder," though of course they should. Their situation is chronic. What they need is more than improvement: they need salvation and are unable to supply it to themselves. Because it cannot come from within them it must come from beyond them. Yet the analysis we have made requires us always to hold together both the dignity and the depravity of humankind and not to forget the one in the light of the other. Sober though it may be, the portrait of radical human fallenness we have painted is actually the point at which our salvation begins. The first step in transforming the situation is the recognition of what is wrong. Jesus said, "and you will know the truth and the truth will make you free" (John 8:32). Although human beings have fallen away from communion with God, and so from so much else, they have not fallen out of God's loving care nor out of God's purpose of salvation. In the moment in which the project of creation was conceived in the heart of the creator, it was already known to God what human beings would make of the life God had given them and how God would respond. God has the sovereign power and the fullness of grace to triumph over human sin and to restore the world to the divine purpose. This is our hope and confidence.

7

God's Original Creation

THROUGH THE PRECEDING CHAPTERS we have taken it as given that God is the creator of the world. Everything that exists has its origins in God. Scientifically speaking, it is now accepted that the universe we know had a beginning. This is sometimes called the "Big Bang" and posits a massive outburst of energy that propelled the universe into being within a fraction of a second and that caused a spectacular expansion of the universe which continues to today. This is consistent with the idea that in the beginning "God created the heavens and the earth" (Gen 1:1), though that it was indeed God who created is an idea that cannot be proven, only received by faith as a reasonable and coherent interpretation of the things that are. Moreover, the Christian community has been persuaded that God created all things and did so "out of nothing" (Heb 11:3). In other words, God did not create out of pre-existent matter that existed eternally but called all things into being from non-existence. This is the most complete form of creation there could possibly be since all other forms of creativity involve fashioning that which already exists. This establishes that God is the sole and ultimate reality, unique and without parallel, the source of all that exists. It also means that God did not create the universe out of God's own self since that would imply that the world itself is divine. Although there are those who indeed do believe the world to be divine, the Christian belief allows the world to be other than God, over against God, with its own identity, yet without being in itself opposed to God. Rather the universe is God's good creation with its own kinds of freedom and its own integrity.

Creation is an act of love by which God freely wills there to be creatures who might enjoy life and might receive the love and grace of a generous creator. The conviction that God exists as Father, Son, and Spirit mutually indwelling each other in a communion of perfect love allows us to imagine that the love of God is not confined within God's own being but overflows with creative and generative power. God's love goes out from God's own self, first to create, then to preserve and sustain, then to redeem and reconcile, and finally to complete and fulfill. Creation, therefore, is not simply about what happened "in the beginning." Every day is a new creation as the universe draws its existence immediately from God. In all these movements of grace, God acts creatively to fulfill the original, divine purpose of bestowing love. Love is the motivation that lies behind creation.

BELIEF IN THE CREATOR

Although logically creation must belong to the first of God's acts, and although it has been assumed in everything that has so far been considered, we might ask why it is that only now in this exposition of convictions do we come specifically to reflect upon it? In delaying a consideration of creation to this point we are in fact following the patterns that we find within the history of Israel and then in the early church. Israel's faith was rooted in the deliverance from Egypt and the salvation experienced at the Red Sea (or Reed Sea as some translate it). It was in the events of Exodus 14 that Israel was saved by God's intervention from destruction by Pharaoh's army. First of all, Israel became persuaded that God was their God and that God would preserve and protect God's own people. Israel owed exclusive loyalty to the Lord and was to worship God alone and none other (Exod 20:1–4). At first they may well have believed that there were other gods that belonged to the nations but that the Lord was the only God for them. In time this belief developed to the point of true monotheism—the Lord was the only God that existed in reality outside human imaginations. Moreover, the one who could save in such mighty fashion by holding back the waters of the Red Sea possessed such power because this God was the creator of the world in the first place. Israel's convictions therefore developed from the belief that God was the only God *for them* to the idea that God was the only God *at all* and all other claims to divinity were pretensions (Deut 4:39; Isa 45:20–22). It was, therefore, through the experience of salvation that they came to their convictions about creation. A God who could save was a God who could create in the first place.

Although the first followers of Jesus, as Jewish believers, inherited this belief in God as creator and savior, we find a similar progression in their understanding of creation in relation to Jesus. First of all, they were persuaded that he was risen from the dead and that this was the sign that he had power to save and people should call on his name (Acts 2:22–24; 4:12). But within a very short time they were not only attributing salvation to Jesus but also creation: "In these last days he has spoken to us by a Son, whom he appointed heir of all things, through whom he also created the world . . . he sustains all things by his powerful word" (Heb 1:1–3); "He is the image of the invisible God, the firstborn of all creation; for in him all things in heaven and earth were created, things visible and invisible" (Col 1:15–17); "All things came into being through him, and without him not one thing came into being" (John 1:3). This astonishing leap, as already noted, is made more comprehensible once we see that salvation is an act of God. If Christ is savior, he is placed firmly on God's side of the divine-human distinction, and so he must be associated with creation as well as salvation. Furthermore, Christ is the incarnation of God's Word and God's Wisdom. "By the word of the LORD the heavens were made, and all their host by the breath of his mouth" (Ps 33:6), and "The Lord possessed me [Wisdom] at the beginning of his work" (Prov 8:22 NIV margin). Christ is therefore very definitely identified with the work of creation. The God who saves through him is the same God who first of all created, also through him. Christ is the mediator of both salvation and creation.

A CHRIST-CENTERED CREATION

In the last chapter we drew attention to the centrality of humanity in God's purposes for the creation project. This assertion now needs to be qualified. It is not for human beings that creation has been brought into being but for Christ himself. He is at the centre of all things. "All things have been created through him and for him" (Col 1:16). Although human beings occupy a primary role within creation, this is subordinate to that of Christ. Human beings should not imagine that what exists does so primarily for them, but rather that they and the whole creation exist for Christ's sake. Human beings have a tendency to judge the value of all things by assessing how those things relate to the human race and how we may profit through them. But the first goal of creation is for it to exist for the one through whom all things were made, not for human beings as such. Most of what happens in the natural world happens beyond and outside the gaze of human beings. But nothing that happens escapes God's own gaze and attention, indeed it exists for God's own pleasure. God takes pleasure in that which is created. In Christ, therefore, there is to be found a special kind of knowledge. It is the calling of science to investigate freely and fairly how it is that the world functions and operates, to explain on a causal level the workings of the creation or "to think God's thoughts after him." Science is unable to give an account, however, of *why* it is that creation exists in the first place and what its goal might be. This is made known in Christ. The end and purpose of creation is to conform to Christ and to learn to live in communion with God in the same way that Christ does. This is the hidden and spiritual meaning of the creation, which is made known to us by divine revelation in the incarnate Christ. It is the ultimate purpose to which all other subsidiary purposes are subject.

THE CREATION NARRATIVES

Understanding the purpose of creation helps us to grasp more fully the nature of the first creation narrative to be found in Genesis 1:1—2:3. This portrays creation taking place over a six-day period, culminating in the creation of humankind on the sixth day. Each of the days is introduced, God's work for that day described, and each day closes with a refrain, "And there was evening and there was morning." Unlike us, the Jews reckoned the start of each day from one evening until the beginning of the next. Each day has a beginning and an end. However, on the seventh day (the number seven in Jewish thinking represents completeness), we are told that God rested and blessed the seventh day and made it holy (2:3). This day is, therefore, different from all the others, not least so in the fact that there is no end to the day: it is a day that continues. The seventh day expresses God's purpose for the creation and is the true climax to the creation narrative, that creation might enjoy *shalom*, peace and well-being in communion with the creator. Creation was not made for discord but for harmony, for cooperation and communion, not for conflict. The later institution of the Jewish Sabbath on the seventh day was intended to be a perpetual reminder of this purpose, a revisiting of the divine harmony and peace so that life would not become submerged in laborious work and oppression (Exod 20:8–11). It was a way of re-establishing priorities. The idea of "rest" also continued as a symbol of the salvation that God holds open for those who will enter into it by faith in God's own self (Heb 3:18—4:3).

The creation narrative with which the book of Genesis begins describes for us in poetic and worshipful forms the origin of creation in the love and power of God. Its object is to celebrate God's good creation and to give praise to the creator from whom all good things have come. It is not a scientific account of the creation, of the "how" of the world's becoming, although there are some insightful parallels with what we believe we now know through science. As a piece of literature it resembles a liturgical act of worship, possibly enacted in the Jewish temple. It is broken down into stanzas, or days, and has elements of repetition that may have been contributed by a choir closing each of the stanzas. It is a hymn of worship. Although it opens the Bible, this is not a sign that it is the first part of the Bible to be written. In all probability it had its composition in the period of the Jewish exile in Babylon after a large proportion of the people had been uprooted from their own land and taken as slaves into captivity in what seemed to them like a reversal of the exodus from Egypt. This was a highly distressing period of Jewish history when God's people needed the reassurance that God was ordering the chaos by which they were surrounded. The basic scenario of the chapter is of a creative and sovereign God who holds back and subdues the chaos and progressively brings order to an unruly world. So God did in the beginning and so this same God is able to do in the present, whatever our circumstances and however overwhelming they may seem. So it can be seen that this passage has a pastoral as well as a theological intent.

We should not read Genesis 1 as though it were a scientific account of creation. To do so would be a category mistake confusing the poetic language of the passage with that of scientific research. A literal reading of the passage only creates an unnecessary conflict with scientific accounts of the age of the earth, the billions of years that it has been in formation, and the means by which it has arrived at its present point. Genesis 1 deals with the why of creation rather than the how and as such is complementary to science, supplying understandings that can never be achieved by empirical enquiry. Yet there are some parallels discernible here to what is currently generally agreed in science. The first of these is the conviction that the universe has an origin and so has not always existed. It came into being at a particular point, catapulted into existence by a mighty event. Since that point, life on earth has been in development as one form of life after another has come into being, following generally the same progression as Genesis outlines from mineral to vegetable to animal to human life. Furthermore, life has produced further life as species have propagated and multiplied to the point of filling the earth. Thus, God's creative activity can be seen to take place in various ways. First of all, God summons creation into being. God then orders and shapes the basic framework of the world, providing the context within which organic life can be created. God commands creation to "put forth" (v. 11) vegetation and plant life, all of which has the power to self-propagate. The animal creation is created as the earth "brings forth"

(vv. 20, 24). As the various species are created they are placed under a divine constraint to reproduce and multiply (v. 22). All of this emerges from the earth that God has made fruitful and bountiful. Even human beings are made of the dust of the ground (Gen 2:7). It can be seen, therefore, that part of God's creative activity is to bestow upon creatures themselves the power to create through procreation. Under God, and within the framework God has provided, the creation creates itself. The hand of God empowers the cosmos as it evolves, and gifts it with both abundance and freedom. The world of nature is interconnected and integrated in its development. Such an astonishing world is made by a gracious and glorious God, who is rightly to be praised for the glory and wonder of it all. A further stage of creation is then seen in the creation of humankind, which God brings into a form of partnership with God's own self as Adam is invited to name and categorize the living creatures (Gen 2:19–20). Human beings made in the image of God are partners with God in the continuing work of creation and the drama of life.

CREATION AS ORGANISM

Although the Bible sometimes uses the idea of God as an architect and builder (Job 38:4: "Where were you when I laid the foundation of the earth?"), this is not the preferred way of thinking of God in creation. Creation is more of an organism than a building; it is living and active and displays its own forms of intelligence and adaptability. In the light of this, it is perhaps apt to think of God as more like a parent to creation rather than an architect, though with the significant distinction that creation is not born from God but made by God out of nothing. God brings forth creation by speaking the creative word and then by further speaking requires the earth to bring forth plant and animal species. The dominant note in Genesis 1 is "Let there be . . . ." God then lays organic life under the necessity of being fruitful and multiplying. Creation, therefore, may be thought of in part as "letting be." God creates and then actively allows creation to live out its own potential in reproduction and progression. There is space here for evolutionary development. As the species are brought forth from the earth so they now bring forth all kinds of life. To this we can attribute not only the vast diversity of the biosphere but the range of life from the exquisitely beautiful to the astonishingly ugly. There is no need to imagine that God has specifically and individually designed all these—rather, this is the creative diversity that creation has produced as it has responded to the divine command. It is an outworking of the potential that God has given from the beginning. God lets creation be and takes pleasure in what it produces. By utilizing the idea of the creative divine word we might also find a way to conceive of evolution taking place not only within species but from one species to another, as envisaged in evolutionary theory. If the development of the evolutionary tree of life involves such progression, we may imagine God speaking new words into creation that require creation to move from one stage to another as a result of divine constraint. The theory of "punctuated equilibria" envisages something similar to this, with nature remaining constant for long periods of time and then taking sudden and momentous leaps forward, propelling life to a new stage.

It is undoubtedly the case that the scale, intricacy, beauty, and grandeur of creation impresses upon human beings a sense of transcendent wonder and raises questions about the origins and existence of such an abundant, living reality. For those who have eyes to see, the glory of God is displayed in the things created. "The heavens are telling the glory of God" (Ps 19:1). Whether we look up to the stars or down into the subatomic depths we cannot help but be impressed and overawed by what we find. The same is true of the human body, especially the human brain and consciousness, which as yet are so little understood: "I praise you, for I am fearfully and wonderfully made" (Ps 139:14). It is only with a degree of effort that humans evade seeing God's handiwork in these things. Paul is right to say, "Ever since the creation of the world his eternal power and divine nature, invisible though they are, have been understood and seen through the things he has made" (Rom 1:20). Although they do not consider nature to be divine, Christians certainly consider it mysterious and wonderful, even "magical" and "enchanted" in the poetic sense that it captures our wonder and amazement. Yet neither can we or should we overlook the "dark side" of the natural world. Nature and evolution are characterized by peaceful, mutually beneficial cooperation between species and yet also by conflict, apparent cruelty, and predation. Animals are equipped to sting, entrap, capture, and kill, and have evolved to protect themselves against other species from which they are under constant threat, or sometimes from their own species. In evolutionary terms all of this may serve a purpose, maintaining a proper balance between species so that one kind does not devastate the habitat and destroy it, both for others and themselves, or ensuring that only the fit survive and so strengthen life along the way. Nonetheless, it is hard not to ask questions about how the apparent waste, conflict, and cruelties of the animal kingdom relate to the unequivocal affirmation of the sheer goodness of creation emphasized in Genesis 1.

FIT FOR PURPOSE

When God pronounces the creation with humans within it "very good" (Gen 1:31), this does not imply the perfection of creation, rather that it is "fit for purpose." That purpose is that it provides a fit context within which human beings may face the challenges of life, and develop in depth and humanity as they explore and actualize their God-given potential, and grow into that kind of relationship with God through faith and trust that will issue in eternal life and final immortality. From this point of view the natural world and the historical process were never intended to be a threat-free zone but one that would present human beings with difficulties to overcome, failures over which to triumph, losses through which to become sensitized, and achievements to which to attain. As creatures made from the dust and yet in the image of God—that is, earthy and finite and caught between heaven and earth—it might be imagined that anxiety would accompany them. Yet such anxiety could either precisely be the spur that would cause them to trust in their creator or the occasion for turning in on themselves and finding their security in themselves. Characteristically humans choose the latter course, when they should make the former. The point is, however, that creation, even with its dark side, is an appropriate "valley of soul-making," not an unthreatening or bland context that would give rise to shallow people but a demanding one that would require strong and resilient persons to emerge.

Such an analysis might well suggest that creation as it is, with its dark side, is what God intended there to be. Or it may be possible to imagine that human beings, emerging into a world of conflict and predation, were placed there in order to tame it, to "subdue it" (Gen 1:28) by exercising dominion over it and guiding it to a better place. This is the vocation that they have refused to fulfill but instead have joined in with the unruly nature of the creation. It may also be the meaning of the enigmatic verse Romans 8:20: "For the creation was subjected to futility, not of its own will but by the will of the one who subjected it." In the fulfillment of God's purposes for the world there are hopes and expectations in the Bible that the present conflicted creation will give way to a peaceful one in which "the wolf shall live with the lamb, the leopard shall lie down with the kid. . . . They will not hurt or destroy on all my holy mountain; for the earth will be full of the knowledge of the LORD as the waters cover the sea" (Isa 11:6–9). Until the creation attains to this final peacefulness it is appropriate to think of the world itself, not only human beings, as "fallen," not yet attaining to the highest good that was intended for it but falling short of the glory that is to be. Yet despite this, it is still God's good world, structurally good, even if frequently deviating from the true path. The vocation that human beings were to fulfill and yet have forsaken is now being fulfilled in Jesus Christ, the last Adam. He is the one who will now, in the light of humankind's defection, lead creation to its completion, restoration, and healing: "Now in subjecting all things to [humans], God left nothing outside their control. As it is we do not yet see everything in subjection to them, but we do see Jesus, who for a little while was made lower than the angels, now crowned with glory and honor because of the suffering of death, so that by the grace of God he might taste death for everyone" (Heb 2:8–9).

More will be said about the presence of suffering in God's world in a later chapter. For the moment, we are able to affirm that creation comes from God and is therefore a good and gracious gift to be enjoyed. Its origin is in God but its moment-by-moment preservation is also an act of God. We are told that Christ, through whom the world was created, "sustains all things by his powerful word" (Heb 1:3). The preservation of the world from collapsing back into nothing is a continuing gift of the creator. In this sense the creation and preservation of the world is a work of salvation as well as of creation. God saves the world from disappearing into chaos by paying constant attention to it, by upholding it so that it may continue to be. It is not, then, as though God has made the world and then abandoned it. God has granted to the world its own existence and integrity, its freedom to be and to become, to realize its own potential. In this sense, as we have noted, God has engaged in an act of self-limitation, making space for that which is not God. The world has, therefore, a measure of independence from the creator but is at the same time utterly and completely dependent upon God for its existence. God and the world are responsive to each other as living realities. The world is not a mere machine. In this responsive openness we once more locate the reality of prayer with human beings seeking for and finding God, and God speaking into and influencing the world.

CREATION AND DISCIPLESHIP

For the Christian community and Christian disciples, to affirm that the worlds have been made through Christ and for Christ is of the highest significance. The Christian is concerned to honor Christ above all and this means honoring and respecting that which belongs to him. Respect for and care of creation is therefore an aspect of Christian discipleship. Christ's presence may be found within the created sphere, within the explorations of science and mathematics, of art and sculpture, of music and literature, of architecture and engineering. We do not have to escape the created world in order to find that which is truly spiritual and truly Christ-like. To enjoy creation is to share with the creator in taking pleasure in the things that have been made. Although the present form of the world may be destined to pass away (1 John 2:17), this is not to say that the world God has made has no future. Its future, as we shall see, is to be restored in "a new heavens and a new earth, where righteousness is at home" (2 Pet 3:13).

8

God's New Creation

IT SHOULD NOT BE imagined that the defection of the human race took God by surprise. From the moment of creation's conception it was already known to God what would happen within it and how God in grace and faithfulness would respond. It has, therefore, always been the purpose of God that once the old creation had gone astray God would act to renew, restore, and redeem it, and would do so first of all at the point where it had failed, namely in the salvation of human beings whom God had created in the divine image. Christ renews the human race and through them will in time renew the whole creation. Christian convictions centre therefore around a story of salvation focused upon Jesus Christ as the savior. Christ is raised up and has come from God to be the means by which all things are reconciled to God, are liberated from their human-imposed alienation, and are restored to active cooperation with God in bringing creation to its true goal. "So if anyone is in Christ, there is a new creation: everything old has passed away; see, everything has become new!" (2 Cor 5:17).

Christ the savior is prophet, priest, and king in God's work of new creation. He has done that which is necessary to be the world's redeemer. It may be said that he has "lived the human race round" so that it can now face in the right direction. In effect, in Christ the world has been converted so that in him it now turns towards God rather than away. This is God's own work and gift. What now remains is for human beings to enter into what Christ has done on their behalf and to experience the salvation that comes from him. What has been done *for* them needs to be realized *within* them, the objective needs to become subjective and to issue in transformed lives.

Having been alienated they need now to be brought near so that they are "in Christ" receiving his benefits. It is those who are "in Christ" who are free to become "new creations." This chapter deals with how fallen human beings find new life in Christ and how this is crucial for the whole of the creation.

THE STORY OF THE NEW CREATION

Although they are at a distance from God, human beings have not been abandoned. It is not simply that God continues to show divine kindness and forbearance. God continues to impress God's own self upon them. There is the wordless witness of nature to the reality of God's power (Rom 1:20; Ps 19:1–4), and there are few people who have not been caused to ask themselves about the origins of the world by contemplating it. There is the voice of conscience by which we are prompted to believe that there is a moral law to which we owe obedience (Rom 2:14–16). There is the sense that we are not alone in the universe but that our actions are being watched and weighed. These are more than convenient survival mechanisms that have evolved to prevent humans from destroying each other. They are witnesses. "In past generations he allowed all the nations to follow their own ways; yet he has not left himself a witness in doing good—giving you rains from heaven and fruitful seasons, and filling you with food and your hearts with joy" (Acts 14:17). There is a sense of God therefore in all human hearts, an instinct to believe, even where this is smothered or flatly denied. Moreover, Christ is the light that shines on all people. "All things came into being through him, and without him not one thing came into being. What has come into being in him was life and the life was the light of all people" (John 1:3). This chapter goes on to read, "He was in the world and the world came into being through him; yet the world did not know him. He came to what was his own, and his own people did not accept him" (1:10–11). These words could refer to the incarnation of Christ and the way he was rejected by his own, Jewish people. Their position in the passage, however, suggests that they refer not first to the incarnation but to the cosmic presence of Christ throughout the world and the way in which people (who have been created through him) continue to resist him when he, the eternal Word, impresses himself upon them. All people, therefore, are aware of the light of Christ at some level, even though they may then reject and discard it (Rom 1:20–23). It is this light that preserves the human race from falling into total ruin and it is sometimes called, as already noted, "common grace," the grace and kindness that God shows to all human beings and to which we attribute the many good and kind things that continue even in a fallen world.

As we have seen, it is characteristic of fallen people to resist God's call on their lives. The entire story of the Bible, even with the people of Israel, is a story of stubborn resistance and disobedience to God. Human beings are willful and corrupt so that even when God draws near to them they prefer the darkness to the light: "And this is the judgment, that the light has come into the world, and people loved darkness rather than light because their deeds were evil" (John 3:19). We might wish that the picture were more positive, but it is not. There is a stark realism to the Christian understanding of humankind. But over against it is another reality, the reality of God's grace and mercy and the persistence with which God refuses to let go of the world that is rightfully God's own. Christians do not have great confidence in human nature, as some appear to do, but they do have confidence in the goodness of God and in God's faithfulness to the eternal purpose. Human beings are past the point of being able to help themselves and so need more than a little help to realize the good life: they need radical transformation from the inside out. In their current state they are prisoners of their condition and are no longer free. They incur guilt through their actions and stand in need of both forgiveness and healing.

THE BONDAGE OF THE WILL

The extent to which human beings in their fallen, imprisoned condition have "free will" is worth considering. It should be clear enough that within a certain range human beings do have freedom of action and choice. They are constrained by nature and so must live within limits. They are also strongly conditioned by their social context and formation, by traditions and conventions, fashions and the expectations and behaviors of their social group. In other words, they are probably less free than they think they are and more enslaved to the ruling and controlling "elemental spirits of the universe" (Col 2:20) than they would like to think. Yet they still possess "agency," the power to direct their lives in certain respects, to choose between one alternative and another, moral or otherwise, and they remain responsible for their choices such that, in the extreme, they can be penalized or punished for wrong or criminal acts on the basis that they could have chosen to act differently and so are culpable in the eyes of others. It would be wrong, therefore, to deny people the capacity to make responsible and moral choices. But while affirming this, there are two ways in which they could be said not to have wills that are totally free. The first is that although we often know what is right to do, we do not always have the power to do it. At this point sin is like an addiction—we are helpless to help ourselves; we continually prove incapable of resisting temptation or of overcoming it, but weakly give in. Paul described this condition in Romans 7:21–24: "So I find it to be a law that when I want to do what is good, evil lies close at hand.... I see in my members another law at war with my mind, making me captive to the law of sin that dwells in my members. Wretched man that I am!" It is this proneness to sin that the New Testament often calls "the flesh." This word means more than "the body." It is rather our human nature governed by the self-centered compulsion to do wrong. The flesh understood in this way, and not just as our bodily existence, is something to fight against and to overcome.

One way to think about this is to imagine that behind the will that each of us possesses there is another will—the will behind the will. All of us are familiar with the fact that before we can set our wills in certain directions, to complete difficult or uncongenial tasks for instance, we have to "want to," that is, we have to summon up the determination to apply our wills in those directions. Without this our wills are effectively paralyzed, but by "wanting to want to" we can mobilize and motivate our wills to achieve. It is in the "wanting to want to" that the problem lies. Technically we have the "will-power" to do whatever we want, but the "wanting" is lacking. This is where our wills are not free—what we want is crippled by selfishness and self-centeredness. So this leads to the second way in which our wills are not free.

This second way concerns our relationship to God. We are "dead through trespasses and sins" (Eph 2:1). This means that we are spiritually insensitive and unable to stir ourselves up to seek God and restore from our side the relationship with God that we lack. We are so at a distance from God and so alienated that we cannot find the way back. We, like Adam and Eve in Eden, have developed an aversion to God and hide from God's presence. Left to ourselves we are hopelessly lost and incapable. Thankfully, however, we are not left to ourselves. When we are disinterested in looking for God, God comes looking for us. Just as it was the case that "while we still were sinners Christ died for us" (Rom 5:8), so it is that even before we begin to think about God, God has taken the initiative in seeking us out. Here we find one of the great solid facts of the whole of the biblical story: just as creation began with God, so does salvation. God's grace, God's unmerited and undeserved favor and kindness, precedes any actions on our part. Indeed, anything that we do in relation to God has the character of response—we respond to what God first does in relation to us. Grace is prior to our faith and is the cause and origin of whatever faith we possess.

This pattern can be traced back to the very beginnings of the story of salvation. It was God who took the initiative in choosing and calling

Abraham to be the father of many nations (Gen 12:1–3). Moreover, it was not because Abraham, or the people of Israel descended from him, possessed any merit of their own. Quite the contrary: "It was not because you were more numerous than any other people that the LORD set his heart on you and chose you—for you were the fewest of all peoples. It was because the LORD loved you and kept the oath that he swore to your ancestors" (Deut 7:7–8). As far as the Bible is concerned, "Salvation comes from the LORD" (Jonah 2:9 NIV). It is not a human achievement but a divine gift. Its origin and fulfillment is in the will, purpose, and love of God, not in any human works or merits. If human beings seek after God, as they must, it is because God has already prompted them inwardly through the Spirit to do so. If our thoughts turn to the divine, it is because God has already turned towards us and not left himself without a witness but is quietly impressing God's own self upon us. God's ways are mysterious and hidden. As the wind "blows where it chooses, and you hear the sound of it, but you do not know where it comes from or where it goes," so it is with God's Spirit (John 3:8). Yet God's ways are purposeful and sure.

It should be clear then that no one can find themselves to be "in Christ," recipients of the gift of salvation, without God's prior activity in gathering a people to God's own self who will be the people of God, the community of the redeemed. No individual can be found to be among the people of God without the prior activity of God in awakening them, convicting them and enlivening them to their own need and to the resolution of that need in Christ. This is called "prevenient grace," the grace that goes before any response that we are enabled to make. Paul's version of this has already been touched upon: "But God, who is rich in mercy, out of the great love with which he loved us even when we were dead through our trespasses, made us alive together with Christ—by grace you have been saved—and raised us up with him" (Eph 2:4–5). Since the human will is not free in relation to God and the will behind the will, the "wanting to want to," is defective, the prevenient grace of God is directed towards renewing and regenerating the inner desire to seek after God that is necessary before we can find. It is those who are hungry for God who will be filled, those who are thirsty who will be satisfied. But the hunger and the thirst are gifts of God in the first place. It is not that some people are by nature holier or more spiritual than others, rather, it is the grace of God that starts us on the road to salvation.

THE ROAD TO CONVERSION

As with the birth of a child there must first of all be an initial conception and a period of gestation before the live birth becomes possible, so it is with those who come to the point of spiritual birth. Jesus talked about the process of sowing the word of God (Matt 13:18–23). The seed of the gospel is first sown into a person's life and begins to take root. It grows to the point where it can yield fruit. But first of all people need to be made aware of the reality of God and then to desire to know God. We may think of this as a period of awakening whereby those who are spiritually insensitive towards God, spiritually "dead," begin to become alive or to waken up to the call of God upon their lives. Jesus said of the Holy Spirit, "And when he comes, he will prove the world wrong about sin and righteousness and judgment" (John 16:8). The Spirit convicts people about their own sin, their need to be made right with God and for their lives to be judged by God. This is a process in which we are stirred up to see that our lives are not as they should be; we are facing in the wrong direction, we are alienated from God and that Christ can be for us "the way, the truth, and the life" (John 14:6). It is, in effect, a conversion, a turning away from one way of living to find another and better way in Christ: "You turned to God from idols, to serve a living and true God, and to wait for his Son from heaven, whom he raised from the dead—Jesus, who rescues us from the wrath that is coming" (1 Thess 1:9–10). Just, then, as Christ was the turning point for the human race as a whole, opening up a new creation and re-orientating us towards God the Father, so each of us must face a turning point of our own, whether it be sudden or gradual, whereby we repent of our sins and our self-centered lives, turn to God through Jesus Christ, and begin a new life in him.

It is clear then that we cannot reconcile ourselves to God, but simply accept God's forgiveness and God's acceptance of ourselves as a gracious gift. It is also clear that we are not "saved by works," neither the works of ritual ceremony and observance nor even the moral good works that we do. Even our best is flawed because we can never escape the fact that even when we do good things we are already congratulating ourselves for doing them. Nothing that we do is without self-interest. We are saved by faith alone—that is, by trusting in the savior and in what the savior has done for us by offering his own life as an atonement for human sin. Faith is more than believing certain things to be true. It is necessary that we do this, but faith properly understood is about personal trust in Jesus Christ as our present and living mediator and go-between, our way to God (1 Tim 2:5). At this point we must give up our pride and self-reliance and be humble enough to accept that we need help, a help that comes from beyond ourselves and is not found within ourselves.

This new relationship with God can be thought of in a variety of ways. It can be thought of as the reconciliation of parties that were previously estranged. We have now been reconciled to God through Jesus Christ: "All of this is from God, who reconciled us to himself through Christ, and has given us the ministry of reconciliation; that is, in Christ God was reconciling the world to himself" (2 Cor 5:18–19). What remains is for us to accept that we have been accepted even though we might still consider ourselves unacceptable. God accepts us as we repent, turn to God, and trust in Christ. "There is therefore now no condemnation for those who are in Christ Jesus" (Rom 8:1). This is essentially a relational image rooted in the idea of the family, and can be seen to have close links with the crucial parable told by Jesus about the lost son who returned home to be joyfully accepted by his father (Luke 15:11–32). Jesus gave us no clearer vision of God than this one. In a restored relationship with the Father through Christ we experience union with Christ (Rom 6:5; Phil 2:1). Through this relationship everything that Christ is can now be communicated to us. The new relationship can also be thought of in legal terms: In a court of law we have been declared to be in the right. Even though we have been in the wrong, the judge has now ruled in our favor and the charges against us have been lifted. Through faith we have been "justified" and declared righteous: "For there is no distinction, since all have sinned and fall short of the glory of God; they are now justified by his grace as a gift, through the redemption that is in Christ Jesus, whom God put forward as a sacrifice of atonement, effective through faith" (Rom 3:22–25). One value of this legal image of salvation is its objectivity: Christ has made atonement for us in such a way as to wipe our record clean when we accept what he has done. This then stands firm as a legal judgment in the courts of heaven that cannot be overturned. A further image that we might stress has already been mentioned. Conversion is like being "born again." Through the work of spiritual awakening and conviction of sin we have been made alive and brought to the place where spiritually we come to birth. As we were born one time physically, so now we are born spiritually and come alive to God and the life of the kingdom of God: "Jesus answered, 'Very truly, I tell you, no-one can enter the kingdom of God without being born of water and the Spirit. What is born of the flesh is flesh, and what is born of the Spirit is spirit'" (John 3:6). The image of Christ as the life-giver is entirely appropriate and forms a key theme in the Gospel of John. "I came that they may have life, and have it abundantly" (John 10:10).

Christian conversion is a profound and life-changing experience, but to say this is not to make any assumptions about how it may happen. Christ is the one way to the Father, but there are many ways to Christ, from the sudden and dramatic to the gradual and apparently straightforward. What should be common to all conversions and all Christians, however, is the sacrament of baptism. Jesus commanded his disciples to baptize (Matt 28:19). At Pentecost Peter exhorted those who were turning to Christ: "Repent, and be baptized every one of you in the name of Jesus Christ so that your sins will be forgiven; and you will receive the gift of the Holy Spirit" (Acts 2:38). Baptism is the rite prescribed by Christ by which people may seal their inward commitment to him, renew their experience of conversion, anchor their faith in an act of confession, and witness and signify that they are now no longer their own but Christ's. Baptism itself as a very physical and dramatic action may be thought of as an act of cleansing from sin (Titus 3:5); of the burial of the old life and of rising to a new life (Rom 6:1–4); of immersion into the realm of the Holy Spirit (Acts 1:4–5), and of new birth as a person passes through the waters, as though in childbirth, to a new life (John 3:5). In practical and spiritual terms it marks a person out as now belonging fully to Christ and the Christian community. It is, in other words, the prescribed act by which people signify they are choosing to become Christians, and as such will be explored more fully in the final chapter.

FAITH, WORKS, AND ADOPTION

If conversion to Christ is such a life-changing reality then it is clear it must be evidenced in the way people live their lives. It is true that we are not reconciled to God by works that we do, since that would give us a ground for boasting about ourselves (Eph 2:8–9), but equally true that faith without works is dead (Jas 2:14–17). Good works are the evidence that lives have been transformed through regeneration, repentance, and faith: "For we are what he has made us, created in Christ Jesus for good works" (Eph 2:10). It is for this reason that the works we do, not the claims we make for ourselves, are the basis on which we are judged (Matt 16:27). Faith is more than intellectual assent to a number of propositions. It represents a whole-hearted turning to God and as such cannot but have profound effects on the way we think and live. If it does not do this then plainly nothing transformative has happened. Although our ritual or even moral works do not achieve right-standing before God, once we have been reconciled to God by grace alone God's purpose is to establish us in a way of life in which works of goodness, kindness, and compassion become instinctive to us. "I will put my law within them, and I will write it on their hearts; and I will be their God, and they shall be my people" (Jer 31:33). We are now being shaped and fashioned in the likeness of Christ himself (Rom 8:29). Most of all, because we are now "in Christ," we gain the privilege of being children of God.

In one sense, all human beings may be thought of as children or offspring of God in that by their creation they owe their origin to God (Acts 17:28). But there is a much deeper reality whereby in Christ we enter into the relationship that Christ has with the Father. "But to all who received him, who believed in his name, he gave power to become children of God, who were born, not of blood or of the will of the flesh or of the will of man, but of God" (John 1:12–13). We have received the "Spirit of adoption." "When we cry, 'Abba! Father!' it is that very Spirit bearing witness with our spirit that we are children of God" (Rom 8:15). To be a child of God is a higher status than that of being justified, or made right with God, in that it is an advance upon this condition. We could have been forgiven and restored to fellowship with God without necessarily becoming God's children. But as it is, through Christ the eternal Son we have been drawn into a relationship with the Father that opens up to us the intimacy of knowing God as Jesus knows the Father. In fact, it is significant that the much-quoted verse John 14:6 reads, "I am the way, and the truth, and the life. No one comes to the Father except through me." This verse is often misquoted to read, "No one comes to *God* except through me," but the fact that it specifies the Father is significant. "The Father" is the distinctively Christian way of thinking of God and it implies a closeness, an intimacy, and a degree of loving affection that is striking. "See what love the Father has given us, that we should be called the children of God; and that is what we are" (1 John 3:1). Adoption is that practice by which a child who was born of one family is accepted into another family with the same status and on the same basis as children born to that family. Although we were strangers to God, God has accepted us as children and allowed us the privilege and joy of sharing with the Son and the Spirit in the fellowship of God's own communion. This is what is meant when it says we have become "participants in the divine nature" (2 Pet 1:4). It is not that we have been made into gods but that we have come to share in the relationships of Father, Son, and Spirit and are sustained in eternal life through that communion.

Out of our relationship through Christ to the Father comes the instinct for worship and prayer that are expressions of thanksgiving for Christians. Communion with God is the medium in which the believer exists, and it finds expression in particular moments of worship, personal or collective, and in concentrated or spontaneous prayer. The depth and quality of the communion with God we now enjoy gives rise to an inner sense of assurance that we are indeed God's children. We are entitled to feel ourselves secure in our relationship with God on the basis of the promises we have received, such as in Jesus' words, "anyone who comes to me I will never drive away" (John 6:37). But in addition to this there is "that very Spirit bearing witness with our spirit that we are children of God" (Rom 8:16). This refers to an inner witness, an inward-rising persuasion that we are indeed recipients of God's love and favor and are related to the Father as children. So although any Christian will undergo moments of doubt and self-questioning, there is also here an inner resource that gives confidence and assurance about our relationship with God and which, among other things, creates the desire to bear witness to the reality of God in personal experience.

Conversion is the beginning of a way of life and a process of progressive spiritual change that should continue for the rest of a person's life. Justification, God's work of declaring us right with God's own self by grace through faith, is understood to be immediate. By contrast, sanctification, the progressive process of becoming righteous and holy persons, of growing in the virtues of faith, hope, and love (1 Cor 13:13; Gal 5:22–26) is ongoing and continuous. We should develop and grow in the practice of a virtuous life. We are to offer ourselves to God for the renewal of our minds and the transforming of our lives. In effect, having been formed and shaped by the forces that surround us we have now to be re-formed and re-shaped so that we become like God (Rom 12:1–2). This is not an easy process and it involves inner struggle and the clear intention on our part to love God with all that we are and have (Matt 22:34–40). In all these things God's Spirit helps us. Although we have turned to God in conversion, we are not wholly free of our old lives, nor will we ever be in this present life. Realism indicates that temptation and sin continue to beset the believer and that we do well not to think more highly of ourselves than we ought to think but to be sober and realistic (Rom 12:3). Despite this we do well also to know that God is purposeful and that what God begins God will one day complete: "I am confident of this, that the one who began a good work among you will bring it to completion by the day of Jesus Christ" (Phil 1:6).

A VISION FOR "ALL THINGS"

In union with Jesus Christ our savior and mediator human beings can become new creations, sharing in a new community and looking forward to a new heaven and a new earth in which righteousness dwells. Although human beings are key elements in bringing about God's new creation and may be regarded as the first fruits of all God's creatures (Jas 1:18), God's work of salvation does not end with them. They are simply the first fruits of a greater harvest. In a remarkable passage (Col 1:15–20), the apostle Paul envisages the cross of Christ as the means by which not only human beings but "all things" will be reconciled to God. When referring, as he frequently does, to "all things" it means that nothing is left out. This is a truly universal, cosmic vision, and in a future chapter it will be further explored. For the moment it is sufficient to note that at the cross, where Christ proclaimed in the moment of his dying that, "It is finished" (John 19:30), his death had significance not only for people but also for the whole creation: "For in him all the fullness of God was pleased to dwell, and through him God was pleased to reconcile to himself all things, whether on earth or in heaven, by making peace through the blood of his cross" (Col 1:19–20).

We have already asserted more than once that the one who offered his own self as an atoning sacrifice for sins was first of all the Word through whom all things were made and on whom creation continued to depend (John 1:3; Heb 1:1–3). We might imagine that his death would make its impact upon every atom in the universe. In that he came as the last Adam to be everything humankind has failed to be, and in that at the cross he did what was sufficient to cover human sin and to reconcile human beings to God, he has decisively created the conditions through which both fallen creatures and the fallen world itself might now be restored to their place of communion with God and might progress to that end for which they were always destined: shalom, Sabbath-rest, peace with God. In this sense the "blood of the cross," which means Christ's life poured out in sacrifice, is the point at which all things are reconciled to God. It is also possible to reflect at this point upon the fact that in becoming a human being, a finite creature, without ever ceasing to be the eternal, divine Word, Christ not only assumed a human identity but embraced every level of existence that precedes and is included within that. That is to say, he entered into the world of chemical, organic, animal, and human existence, investing himself in the creation as that creation presents and recapitulates itself in every human life. In this way, Christ was qualified to represent not only the human dimension of the creation but every other dimension and level of the created sphere as well, gathering it all up into his incarnation. He brings it all to newness of life by participating within it and in the resurrection takes it on as the "pioneer of salvation" (Heb 2:10) to its next stage as the one who blazes the trail and opens up the future.

9

God's Spirit in Creation and in Christ

ACCORDING TO CHRISTIANS THERE is one God, Father, Son, and Holy Spirit. More needs to be said at this point about the Holy Spirit, who is at work in the creation and in the new creation. A crucial conviction of the Christian community is that God is close to us. Although God is rightly understood as exalted beyond this creation as the transcendent source of all things, and although in Christ it is firmly believed that God is with us as one who shares our history from within, it also belongs to the church's convictions to say that God is in the depths, at the heart and core of all things, on the inside of the creation and of the created. "In him we live and move and have our being" (Acts 17:28). We have already noted the freedom by which God is able to project God's own self into the world. We can now affirm that it is through God's own Spirit that God does this. "Where can I go from your Spirit? Or where can I flee from your presence? If I ascend to heaven, you are there; if I make my bed in Sheol you are there" (Ps 139:7–8).

In the unfolding story of biblical revelation, it is only in the later stages, especially after the book of Acts, that the Spirit of God comes into the clearest focus. Likewise, as the growing Christian community honed and developed its convictions in its creeds, it was only after it had achieved relative clarity about what it believed about Jesus the Messiah that it could turn its full attention to the Holy Spirit. Once again, however, we encounter the difference between the order of being and the order of knowing. The fact that the Spirit of God comes into fuller focus in the later stages of revelation does not mean or imply that the Spirit has not been present with God from eternity, nor that the Spirit has not been active from the beginning in the work of creation and the work of salvation. Indeed, as we shall see, God's Spirit is intimately involved in all these things as the Spirit of the Father and the Son, God's agent in bringing God's purposes for the world to fulfillment. From the beginning this Spirit has been at work with the Father and the Son, both in creation and in redemption.

GOD'S THIRD WAY OF BEING GOD

The Spirit may be thought of as God at God's closest to us or as God's third way of being what God is. In both Hebrew (Old Testament) and Greek (the Septuagint and the New Testament) the words for "Spirit" (*ruach* and *pneuma* respectively) carry three meanings: spirit, wind, and breath. The words imply something invisible, universally present, essential for existence, and free, and so it is with God's Spirit. By the Spirit, God works in the world in ways that are at the same time clear and mysterious: clear in that there would be no creation without the regular provision that the Spirit gives, yet mysterious in that we do not fully comprehend the workings of God. "The wind blows where it chooses, and you hear the sound of it, but you do not know where it comes from or where it goes. So it is with everyone who is born of the Spirit" (John 3:8). It is entirely correct to think of the Spirit as immensely powerful, just as the wind can operate at hurricane force. But it would be wrong to imagine that the Spirit is merely a force or power and therefore impersonal. The Christian community is persuaded that God is personal, that this is further emphasized in the incarnation of God in the person of Christ and that the Spirit of God also bears personal characteristics. To make the point, the neuter noun *pneuma* in the New Testament is on occasion even given personal pronouns in defiance of Greek grammar (John 16:13). This same verse indicates that the Spirit guides into the truth. Related verses in John speak of the Spirit as one who teaches and reminds (14:26), testifies (15:26), convicts (16:8), and brings glory to Christ (16:14). The Spirit is spoken of as possessing intelligence and knowledge (John 14:26), a will (1 Cor 12:11), and emotions (Eph 4:30). The Spirit can be lied to (Acts 5:3–4), grieved (Eph 4:30), and resisted (Acts 7:51). All this is indication that as the Father and the Son, so the Spirit is personal in nature. It is no surprise therefore that Jesus, according to John's Gospel, speaks of the Spirit as "another Advocate" (John 14:16), and here the word "another" has the meaning not of "other and different" but "another *of the same kind*." As Jesus is "another of the same kind" as the Father so the Spirit is "another of the same kind" as Jesus, that is to say, fully divine and fully personal.

We return here to the mystery of the Trinity, namely that God has three ways of being God: Father, Son, and Spirit. Within this statement the whole history of divine revelation is told, and indeed the whole story of salvation. The Spirit is personal and also fully divine. This is emphasized by indicating that the Spirit does what God does, whether this be creation (Gen 1:2; Ps 104:30), the resurrection of Christ (Rom 8:11), or the inspiration of Scripture (2 Tim 3:16). The Spirit, we are told, is the "eternal Spirit" (Heb 9:14), and such eternity is a divine characteristic. "For the Spirit searches everything, even the depths of God. For what human being knows what is truly human except the human spirit that is within? So also no one comprehends what is truly God's except the Spirit of God" (1 Cor 2:10–11). The logic here is clear: the Spirit can search the mind of God definitively because the Spirit is truly and fully God—God on the inside.

When we speak of the Spirit, therefore, we are speaking of one who is fully divine, fully personal, and fully at one within the life of God's being with the Father and the Son. God works in the world by means of the Spirit who goes out from God. To deal with the Spirit is to deal with God's own self. More than this, because we are able to imagine the Spirit as being on the inside of God, we might also think of the Spirit working on the inside of the Christian community and of the Christian believer. The Christian blessing also known as "the grace" takes us one step further: "The grace of the Lord Jesus Christ, the love of God, and the communion of the Holy Spirit be with all of you" (2 Cor 13:13). As Christ is characterized by grace, and the Father by love, so the Spirit is characterized here by "communion," or fellowship. Wherever the Spirit is at work the Spirit creates fellowship, making connections and bringing unity. This is so within the very life of God as the Spirit unites Father and Son in the bond of love. It is so in creation as the Spirit holds the fabric of the universe together. It is so in the Christian community, where the Spirit is the "bond of peace" that unites those who believe (Eph 4:3). It is so within believers whom the Spirit unites with the Father through the Son. Working on the inside, the Spirit draws and holds things together as the holy bonding agent of God.

THE SPIRIT OF CHRIST IN CREATION

Because the Spirit comes into focus only in the later stages of the biblical revelation, there is a tendency to associate the Spirit with the work of salvation and the life of the church. This would in itself, of course, be entirely correct. But it would be a mistake to confine the Spirit to these realms. For one thing, this would reduce the scope of how we think of the Spirit, and for another, it would reinforce a division between the church (in which God's Spirit is thought to be active) and the world (from which the Spirit is thought to be absent). It is better to understand that the Spirit is at work in the creation as a whole and then also active in the new creation that is being brought to pass in the midst of the old. The Spirit of God is the Spirit of life on whom all creation depends and whose handiwork is seen in the beauty and majesty of all created things. The Scriptures associate the Spirit in various places with water, oil, wine, and wind and these are very basic elements in the fabric of life. The Spirit was present in the original creative work of God. Even while the creation was "formless and empty," the Spirit of God "was hovering over the waters" (Gen 1:2 NIV), presumably working to bring order and form out of the chaos. We have noted how the biblical depiction of creation gives priority to the word of God as the agency through which God creates. Repeatedly God speaks and the creation springs into being at God's command. Already here we can with some imagination detect the presence of the Triune God. The Father speaks, the Son is the word that is spoken, and the Spirit is the breath by which the word is uttered. Creation is a cooperative act of the one God, Father, Son, and Spirit. The Spirit goes out from God's own self to let creation be, to give it shape and order and sustain it as it responds to God's command to flourish and grow. So the Spirit is present and active in the very origins of the created sphere and continues to be active as the creation unfolds its potential before the Lord. The Spirit is always inseparably active in whatever the Father and the Son may do since God cannot be divided. "By the word of the Lord the heavens were made, and all their host by the breath of his mouth" (Ps 33:6). "The spirit of God has made me, and the breath of the Almighty gives me life" (Job 33:4).

Since God continues to sustain the creation, the Spirit is also at work for this purpose: "When you hide your face, they are dismayed; when you take away their breath they die and return to the dust. When you send forth your spirit, they are created; and you renew the face of the ground" (Ps 104:30). Furthermore, we are to attribute to the Spirit the skills and gifts granted to human beings that enable them to enrich and beautify life. Bezalel and Oholiab were the creative geniuses who furnished the tabernacle in which Israel worshiped God for several centuries. They were gifted by the Spirit of God for this purpose: "The LORD spoke to Moses: See I have called by name Bezalel son of Uri son of Hur, of the tribe of Judah; and I have filled him with divine spirit [or "with the Spirit of God," margin], with ability, intelligence, and knowledge in every kind of craft, to devise artistic designs, to work in gold, silver, and bronze, in cutting stones for setting, and in carving wood, in every kind of craft. Moreover, I have appointed with him Oholiab son of Ahisamach, of the tribe of Dan; and I have given skill to all the skilful, so that they may make all that I have commanded you" (Exod 31:2–6). By derivation from these verses we may conclude that all artistic abilities are given by God, though the way they are put to use is a matter of human responsibility. "Every generous act of giving, with every perfect gift, is from above, coming down from the Father of lights" (Jas 1:17). Believing in the Spirit of God enables us to see that although God's saving purposes may focus upon the people of Israel and on that enlarged Israel that we call the Christian community, God's activity is not confined to these communities. God is the Lord of the whole earth and is active in hidden ways in the histories of all peoples. This, at least, is the claim of the book of Amos: "'Are you not like the Ethiopians to me, O people of Israel?' says the Lord. 'Did I not bring Israel up from the land of Egypt, and the Philistines from Caphtor and the Arameans from Kir?'" (Amos 9:7). The universal Spirit of God is the means by which God is active in creation and throughout its varied expanses and manifestations. God's Spirit cannot be confined or limited by human imagination, and wherever the Spirit is active, creating communion and fellowship is a hallmark of what the Spirit does.

Having made these universal and inclusive claims, however, we do need at this point to add a qualification. The Spirit of God is the Spirit of *Christ*. Not everything that looks spiritual or claims to be so can be said to be of Christ, and therefore not everything that is apparently spiritual can be owned as the Spirit of God. Amongst the most significant of Jesus' statements recorded by John is John 16:13–14: "When the Spirit of truth comes, he will guide you into all the truth; for he will not speak on his own, but will speak whatever he hears, and he will declare to you the things that are to come. He will glorify me, because he will take what is mine and declare it to you." This is a crucial guiding statement for the Christian community in its practice of discerning between what is true and what is false. The Spirit is not to be found in any idea, practice, or deed that plainly contradicts Jesus or is in conflict with his life and teaching. The Spirit, however, may be found at work in everything that is true, compassionate, gracious, and beautiful (Gal 5:22; Phil 4:8–9). Whatever makes for a Christlike world can be said to be of the Spirit of God.

THE SPIRIT OF CHRIST IN NEW CREATION

If the Spirit is the Spirit of life and is active in the creation then all the more can it be claimed that the Spirit is active in bringing to pass the new creation. This must mean that the Spirit is intimately involved in the life and ministry of Jesus, who is the one in whom that new creation is coming to be. Once more we may deploy the image of the spoken word. Christ is the Word spoken to us by the Father and the Spirit is the breath by which that Word comes to expression. Christ has come to renew the old humanity and the old creation, each in its own ways falling short of God's will and intention, and does so from within, by first of all participating in the life of the creation that he might raise it from the depths and into the heights. It is God's Spirit within Jesus who enabled him to be who he was and to do what he did. The Christian community is fully persuaded that the Spirit comes to us through Jesus, that Christ is the one who "baptizes with the Holy Spirit." But Christ can only do this because first of all he was the one on whom the Spirit descended and remained (John 1:32-34). Christians are used to giving thanks to the risen Lord for granting them the gift of the Holy Spirit. They should equally give thanks to the Spirit of God for giving them the Christ, the anointed one. Jesus is the product of the Holy Spirit working through history and in the affairs of human beings to raise up God's Messiah in the person of Jesus of Nazareth.

This theme is most clearly developed in the Gospel of Luke. As in the book of Acts by the same author, Luke shows a particular interest in the Holy Spirit. He makes it clear that before the birth of Jesus the Spirit was already active, preparing the way for the coming of the Messiah. Of John the Baptist, the forerunner to Jesus, it was said, "Even before his birth he will be filled with the Holy Spirit" (1:15). When the angel-messenger appeared to Mary he promised, "the Holy Spirit will come upon you, and the power of the Most High will overshadow you" (1:35). When Mary met her cousin, the mother of John, Elizabeth was "filled with the Holy Spirit" and pronounced a blessing on her (1:41-42). In a moment of ecstasy, we read that Mary's spirit "rejoices in God my Savior" (1:46), while when John the Baptist was born, "his father Zechariah was filled with the Holy Spirit" and prophesied that his son would be a prophet of the Most High (1:67, 76).

Once Jesus was born his parents were blessed by a righteous man called Simeon, of whom it is recorded that "the Holy Spirit rested on him. It had been revealed to him by the Holy Spirit that he would not see death before he had seen the Lord's Messiah" (2:25-26). These pictures suggest that Jesus was born into a network of devout Jewish believers who were alive in the Holy Spirit and were being made ready to receive the one through whom the world would be transformed. This prepares us for the fact that in Jesus himself God's eternal Word was being entrusted to the womb of a young peasant woman by the work of the Holy Spirit, whose power, as we have noted, overshadowed her, and caused her to bear a son: "Therefore the child to be born will be holy; he will be called Son of God" (1:35). Jesus was born of the Holy Spirit and of Mary. In this we see God at work entering into the hereditary flow of the human race whilst at the same time doing what was necessary to renew that race from within in a way that human beings could not themselves achieve. The fact that Jesus was born of a virgin indicates that just as the Spirit hovered over the waters in the original creation so now, as the Spirit hovered over Mary, an act of new creation was taking place in the midst of the old. Jesus was not the product of the human race, not even in its most devout and godly expression, and certainly not "of the will of the flesh or the will of man" (John 1:13), but of God working through the Spirit. The virginal conception is a sign of something surprising and new beyond imagination, the embracing by the person of the eternal Son of a specific human identity in order that he might be present among human beings for all human beings as the embodiment of the love and grace of God. By the work of the Holy Spirit it was possible for Jesus to be utterly and truly human, "born of a woman, born under the law" (Gal 4:4), whilst remaining utterly and truly God's own Son.

JESUS AND THE SPIRIT

Being born of the Spirit it is no surprise to go on to read in the New Testament that Jesus' life and ministry were understood by reference to the same Spirit. "The child grew and became strong, filled with wisdom; and the favor of God was upon him" (Luke 2:40, compare Isa 11:1–5). It was at his baptism that he entered into the fullness of his mission. This baptism is recorded or referred to in all four Gospels as the time when, "The heaven was opened, and the Holy Spirit descended on him in bodily form like a dove" (Luke 3:21–22). This should not be taken to imply that the Spirit was not present in Jesus prior to this time. The Spirit who had always been *within* Jesus now came *upon* him for the fulfillment of his work. What happened here was the inauguration of the age of messianic fulfillment. Jesus, having proven his obedience to the Father in the largely hidden years of his childhood and early adulthood, was now ready to fulfill his calling and was empowered by the Spirit for the work that awaited him. His baptism in water by John indicated his identification with repentant Israel and his solidarity with fallen humankind, while the coming of the Spirit upon him was the sign of the new age of messianic salvation of which he was the agent. As Jesus set out on his mission this new day now dawned. The later coming of the Spirit at Pentecost was understood to be the fulfillment of the prophecy of the book of Joel: "I will pour out my Spirit on all flesh" (Joel 2:28; Acts 2:16–21); but it was first of all through the ministry and work of Jesus that that day became possible. And the Spirit was integral to its happening.

The ministry of Jesus—his healings, teaching, and acts of deliverance—took place in the power of the Spirit. After his baptism, and "filled with the Spirit," Jesus was "led by the Spirit" into the wilderness to be put to the test. Having proved he was more than equal to it, the same Spirit led him out of the wilderness (Luke 4:1, 14). In his inaugural sermon at Nazareth, in what is sometimes called "the Nazareth Manifesto," Jesus declared, "The Spirit of the Lord is upon me, because he has anointed me to bring good news to the poor" (Luke 4:18). Jesus now showed himself to be profoundly conscious of the Spirit. He heard the Spirit speaking in the Hebrew Scriptures (Matt 22:41-44) and proclaimed concerning his acts of deliverance, "But if it is by the Spirit of God that I cast out demons, then the kingdom of God has come to you" (Matt 12:28; Luke 11:20). He spoke to the disciples of the Father's willingness to give the Holy Spirit to those who ask (Luke 11:13), assured them that the Holy Spirit would help them when they were on trial (Luke 12:12), and commanded them to baptize in the name of the Father, Son, and Holy Spirit (Matt 28:19). The prominence of the Holy Spirit in the whole ministry of Jesus is highly significant. It enables us to make the claim that the mighty works of Jesus were not performed by virtue of his power as the Son of God incarnate but by the Spirit. Even though he was God's Son, he came in humility as one who was fully dependent on the Spirit. In humbling himself in the incarnation and embracing a frail human identity (Phil 2:5-8), Jesus was laying aside his divine prerogatives and making himself fully dependent on God's Spirit to accomplish his mighty acts of healing and deliverance. And God's Spirit was given to him without measure. This is the manifestation of divine power through voluntary human weakness.

It is not only in the mighty works of Jesus that we can discern the presence of the Spirit but also in the motivation and will-power that led him to the cross. The writer of the book of Hebrews proclaims, "how much more will the blood of Christ, who through the eternal Spirit offered himself without blemish to God, purify our conscience from dead works to worship the living God!" (Heb 9:13-14). Here the "eternal Spirit," God's Spirit, is understood as the power at work within Jesus enabling him to offer to God a holy life without blemish, culminating in giving himself in sacrifice upon the cross. The Spirit is not only to be associated with acts of power, therefore, but with costly self-giving and with that work through which Christ made atonement for the sins of the world. More mysterious even than this is the question of what happened to Jesus in between his dying on the cross and his being raised from the dead. The closest the New Testament comes to disclosing this is in 1 Peter 3:18-20, which states: "For Christ also suffered for sins once for all, the righteous for the unrighteous, in order to bring you to God. He was put to death in the flesh, but made alive in the spirit, in which also he went and made a proclamation to the spirits in prison, who in former times did not obey, when God waited patiently in the days of Noah, during the building of the ark, in which a few, that is, eight people, were saved through water." Although this passage raises many questions, the reference to "in the spirit" is suggestive. It is the Spirit of God who was the agent of being "made alive" in this way: there is no other source. It can be imagined, therefore, that the Spirit accompanied Jesus on his journey into death in order that he might retrieve him from there. The Spirit did not allow Jesus to be "abandoned to Hades" or to experience corruption (Acts 2:31).

This sets the scene for what is then stated unambiguously: by the Holy Spirit Jesus was raised from the dead and "declared to be the Son of God with power according to the Spirit of holiness by resurrection from the dead" (Rom 1:4). With even greater clarity Romans 8:11 declares, "If the Spirit of him who raised Jesus from the dead dwells in you, he who raised Christ from the dead will give life to your mortal bodies also through his Spirit that dwells in you." The Spirit who gave birth to Jesus in Mary's womb and then accompanied him through life and so into death and beyond, is the same one who then caused his body to be raised out of death into that new level of glorified life in God that we call the resurrection. Having endured what it meant for our sakes to know himself forsaken by the Father (Mark 15:34), Jesus was restored to full and intimate communion with the Father by the Spirit, who is the Spirit of communion and fellowship.

THE SPIRIT IS TO BE HONORED

The Spirit then is the Spirit of creation and new creation, the one who creates and recreates. The Spirit is God active in the world bringing the gracious, surprising, and compassionate will of God to pass. The Spirit should neither be restricted nor neglected. God's Spirit should not be constrained in our minds by being confined to the life of the church or the individual believer alone; rather the Spirit is universally active, giving life to everything that has breath, inspiring that which is good, true, and beautiful, since anything that is good in the creation and all that we celebrate in the new creation should be understood as the gift of God. Neither should the Spirit be neglected as though the Spirit is always "in third place," after the Father and the Son. Wherever Father and Son are to be found, the Spirit is already there as the one who creates fellowship and enables connection. The life of the Spirit is deep and rich and is to be further explored as we turn to the life of the church and of Christians.

10

God's Spirit in the Church and in Christians

If the Spirit of God and of Christ is the Spirit of the new creation then the church of Christ and those who belong to it are themselves the product of the Spirit's influence and work. Although there are many images of the church in the New Testament (ninety-six on one calculation), three primary images predominate.

THREE PRIMARY IMAGES

The first is that of *the people of God* (1 Pet 2:9). This immediately connects the community of Christ with the backstory of Israel as the people God had chosen to be the agents of the divine purpose on earth (Exod 19:3–6). Israel experienced God's saving power at the Red Sea when they were delivered from destruction by Pharaoh's armies. In response to God's saving work they were called to enter into a covenant with the Lord to be God's own people, living according to God's purpose and ways. They were to be distinguished from the nations by practices such as the Sabbath, circumcision, temple worship, and food laws. All of these marked them out as having a distinct identity as witnesses to the Lord. In Christ the scope of who belonged to the people of God was increased so that all who had faith in Christ might be considered children of Abraham (Rom 4:16–17), having experienced a spiritual "circumcision of the heart" (Rom 2:28–29). The church then is the enlarged people of God gathered from all the nations. As such, although

Jewish Christians might continue to practice the rituals and customs they have inherited from their tradition, gentile Christians are not under the same obligation: their faith in Christ confessed in baptism and manifested in the life of discipleship is enough to mark them out as members of the people of God. As the people of God, the followers of Jesus are joined and bound together by the Spirit of God, who is (once more) the Spirit of fellowship and connectedness shared by all Christian believers (Eph 4:1–6).

The second major image is that of *the body of Christ*. In this image Christ is understood to be the head of a living body of believing people in which every believer is connected both to the head and to other members of the body. It is by the Spirit that we are brought into participation in the body and into relationship with the head (1 Cor 12:12–13). The Spirit may be thought of then as the soul that gives life to the body, the animating Spirit that gives life (Gen 2:7). As with the human body, each part of the body can be seen to have a role and a function so that the body works with maximum effectiveness when all the parts are coordinated and cooperative (Eph 4:15–16). The church, following this image, is not first of all an institution but an organic, developing, and mobile community of persons in fellowship. Whatever organizational or institutional features it may have are there to support the reality of living fellowship and personal engagement.

If it is the case that the people of God can be understood in relation to the Father and the body of Christ in relation to the Son, the third primary image focuses on the Spirit's own self and is that of *the temple of the Holy Spirit*. According to this image, the church is built upon the foundation of the apostles and the prophets, with Christ himself as the "cornerstone," and each believer is like a living stone inserted into the walls (Eph 2:19–22; 1 Pet 2:4–5). Together we provide a place where God's Spirit may dwell and make a home. It is to this community, then, that people may come to find and to worship the living God as once they did to the temple. The church, scattered as it is among the nations, is the place were God's Spirit may be found to be particularly, though by no means exclusively, at work in the affairs of human beings.

THE SPIRIT AND THE COMMUNITY

It can be seen in each of these images how the Spirit of God is active in creating, forming, and sustaining the Christian community. It is entirely consistent with this that the church as we know it today came into being by means of a powerful outpouring of the Spirit on the day of Pentecost as recorded in Acts 2. Although the roots of the church reach back, as we have seen, into God's call of Abraham to be the father of a multitude through whom the families of earth would be blessed (Gen 12:1-3), and although Jesus himself gathered an embryonic community around himself in which the foundations of the church were laid, it is at Pentecost that the church burst upon the scene with explosive force. None of this is to imply that the Spirit was previously absent, since it is only through the Spirit that the people of Israel could be formed in the faith and that Christ could fulfill his ministry. What is implied, however, is that the Spirit signifies the coming of the age of messianic fulfillment, and a new dawn opens up in the dealings of God with human beings. The Spirit is the power of the new age, the presence now of the future that is to come (Heb 6:4-5). It is significant that it is after Christ had offered himself by the Spirit as an atonement for sin, and after he had been raised from the dead and had ascended to the Father, that the full coming of the Spirit could be experienced. "Being therefore exalted at the right hand of God, and having received from the Father the promise of the Holy Spirit, he has poured out this that you both see and hear" (Acts 2:33). The work of Christ is the necessary foundation for the work of the Spirit in reconciling human beings to God and gathering them together across the barriers and boundaries we so readily erect into a new, united humanity (Eph 2:15-18). It is on the basis of the self-sacrifice of the Messiah that the messianic age can be extended beyond the embryonic community of the first disciples into all the world. Those first disciples became the first and definitive witnesses to Christ and his kingdom, the apostles and prophets upon whose testimony the church is built (Eph 2:20). Because we can all find new life, forgiveness, and a new start at the cross, the potential for building a new human community began to be realized. By the Spirit the knowledge of Christ, and through him of the Father, can be made universal since the Spirit is not subject to limitations of space, time, and geography. Through the Spirit Christ can be present to save wherever he chooses.

On the basis of Christ's work, the Spirit gathers the church from among all peoples. The gathering began in Jerusalem and those upon whom the Spirit came at first were Jews and converts to Judaism who happened to be gathered in the city for the festival called Pentecost (Acts 2:5-13). Pentecost celebrated the barley harvest and was also known as the "day of the first-fruits" (Exod 23:16-17). Those who received Christ through the Spirit on that day were indeed the first-fruits of a great harvest. The harvest continued as the same Spirit broke first into the Samaritan community (Acts 8:4-8, 14-17) and then into the gentile world (Acts 10). Since that time the community of the Spirit has spread across the face of the earth. In these successive Pentecosts (Jewish, Samaritan, and gentile in nature), we are entitled to see the fulfillment of John the Baptist's prophecy, "I baptize you with water for repentance, but one who is more powerful than I is coming after me; I am not worthy to carry his sandals. He will baptize you with the Holy Spirit and with fire" (Matt 3:11). The risen Christ confirmed this when he said, "This . . . is what you have heard from me; for John baptized with water, but you will be baptized with the Holy Spirit not many days from now" (Acts 1:4–5). The baptism of the Holy Spirit is the outpouring of the Spirit by God that first gathered the church and then impelled it into the mission that was to take it into the nations and across the face of the earth. It is the event predicted by the prophet Joel and cited by Peter on the day of Pentecost by way of interpretation of the events that people were witnessing: "In the last days it will be, God declares, that I will pour out my Spirit upon all flesh, and your sons and your daughters shall prophesy, and your young men shall see visions, and your old men shall dream dreams" (Acts 2:17, compare Joel 2:28–32). Whatever else it was, the accounts suggest that Pentecost was dramatic, forceful, and unmistakable, and that it resulted in intense experiences of spiritual enthusiasm. It was the impetus for the emergence and growth of the church, which continues to make its impact upon the nations.

It is appropriate that those who were converted to Christ on the day of Pentecost were urged to be baptized in the name of Jesus Christ (Acts 2:38, 41). This symbolized the washing away of their sins, but it also spoke volumes about the fact that these converts were being plunged into the new realm of the Spirit, immersed in the power and presence of the Spirit who could transform them and bring them into possession of the good things that are in Christ. Christian communities are more than ordinary gatherings of people with a common interest. They are spiritual communities. By the Spirit Christ is present within them. They are possessed of a dimension of spiritual vitality that lifts them beyond the merely human and makes them places of spiritual energy and communion. They have the potential to transform those who participate in them, to connect them through the Word and the Spirit to the living God. The Spirit is the hallmark of the church and of the believer within the church, which explains how Paul can write, "Anyone who does not have the Spirit of Christ does not belong to him" (Rom 8:9). It is the Spirit who draws us into and makes us effective participants in the life of the church: "For in the one Spirit we were all baptized into one body—Jews or Greeks, slaves or free—and we were all made to drink of one Spirit" (1 Cor 12:13). It should be clear then that the Spirit is not the exclusive interest of only a certain kind of Christian, or Christian denomination. Without the Spirit it is not possible to be the church at all. When the apostle Paul encountered a group of apparent disciples and asked them whether they received the Spirit when they became believers, they answered, "No, we have not even heard that there is a Holy Spirit." Paul's response was to take them back to the very beginning, to baptize them in the name of the Lord Jesus and ensure that the Spirit was imparted to them. Their faith, sincere as far as it went, did not go far enough, and before they could go any further they needed the Spirit of God to set them on the right road (Acts 19:1–7).

THE SPIRIT OF WORSHIP

It is significant that when we read of the impartation of the Holy Spirit in the book of Acts, the record indicates that those who received the Spirit would regularly "speak in tongues and prophesy" (Acts 2:4; 10:45–46; 19:6). We need not conclude that the manifestation of these gifts is mandatory for all, but we ought indeed to infer that when the Spirit comes, overflowing worship often follows. The Spirit inspires and enables praise of God. Worship is a consequence of the Spirit-led life. On the day of Pentecost the witnesses of the event were astonished because, "we hear them speaking about God's deeds of power" (Acts 2:11). It is a mark of the community of the Spirit that believers worship, both in the name of Christ and in the power of the Holy Spirit. Paul could write, "For it is we who are the circumcision, who worship in the Spirit of God and boast in Christ Jesus and have no confidence in the flesh" (Phil 3:3). This verse may suggest a contrast with some forms of ritual Jewish worship that were outwardly correct but inwardly lacking. The Hebrew Scriptures do themselves point to this danger: "When you stretch out your hands, I will hide my eyes from you; even though you make many prayers, I will not listen; your hands are full of blood. Wash yourselves; make yourselves clean; remove the evil of your doings from before my eyes; learn to do good; seek justice, rescue the oppressed, defend the orphan, plead for the widow" (Isa 1:15–17; see also Ps 51:15–17). Religious acts without heartfelt obedience and concern for others are not pleasing to God. The contrast may also be with forms of gentile worship: "When you are praying, do not heap up empty phrases as the gentiles do; for they think that they will be heard because of their many words" (Matt 6:7). But worship in the Spirit comes from the heart and is inward before it is outward.

According to Jesus, true worship comes from the Spirit: "But the hour is coming, and is now here, when the true worshippers will worship the Father in spirit and truth, for the Father seeks such as these to worship him. God is spirit and those who worship him must worship in spirit and truth" (John 4:23–24). Jesus himself gave us an example of such worship in a rare glimpse into his own inner life and relation to the Father. On an occasion when his disciples returned triumphant from a preaching and healing mission on which he had sent them, we read, "At that same hour Jesus rejoiced in the Holy Spirit and said, 'I thank you, Father, Lord of heaven and earth, because you have hidden these things from the wise and the intelligent and have revealed them to infants'" (Luke 10:21). To be noticed here is that in this moment of intense emotion, created within him by the Holy Spirit who relates us to the Father, Jesus was filled with joy and thanksgiving. Joy in God and thanksgiving for God's good and gracious works are characteristic of the Spirit and of our relationship to God. They should mark our worship, which, although it must have room for solemnity, would be severely lacking if it did not make space for joyful praise. Jesus' worship showed a remarkable blend of the intimacy that he knew with the one he called Father, and the profound sense that the Father was also the Lord of heaven and earth. This brings together both the immanence of God, God's freedom to draw near to us, and God's transcendence, the sense that God engulfs us and is far beyond anything we can think or imagine. As these experiences are centrally rooted in the relationship of Jesus to the Father in the Spirit, we might say that they are normative for Christian communities and the quality of worship to which they aspire.

EARLY CHRISTIAN WORSHIP

It is certainly the case that the first church in Jerusalem experienced all these aspects of deeply felt Christian worship, and that for them worship was a matter of the heart. At the same time, it is clear that these first believers observed a rhythm of worship in the Jewish temple and that they saw no contradiction between following the outward patterns of Jewish worship combined with deeply personal engagement with God and with each other (Acts 2:42, 46). In combination with observance of the Jewish Sabbath, the first Christians quickly developed the custom of meeting for worship on the first day of the week (Acts 20:7; 1 Cor 16:2). This was the day on which Christ had risen from the dead and it came to be known as "the Lord's day" (Rev 1:10). It was also, of course, according to the Genesis narrative, the day on which God began to create (Gen 1). The basic components of the first church's worship were the teaching they received from the apostles (now contained in the New Testament), fellowship with God and with each other, shared meals (probably including the Lord's supper), and prayers of both spontaneous and ordered kinds (Acts 2:42). The earliest Christian community was a deeply worshiping one and this was a sign of the coming of the Spirit to bring this community to birth after the ascension of Christ to the

Father. Because of the Spirit they were not left as orphans (John 14:18) but enjoyed the continuing experience of the presence of the risen Lord. Truly Christian worship only happens when believers enter into fellowship with the Father through Christ by the Spirit, and such an experience is both a sign and demonstration of the power of the worshiping community to unite us beyond the barriers that might otherwise divide us: "So he came and proclaimed peace to you who were far off and peace to those who were near; for through him [Christ] we both [Jews and gentiles] have access in one Spirit to the Father" (Eph 2:17–18).

Worship as we encounter it in the New Testament community is very much a Spirit-filled and participative activity. It is clear that within the community of believers there are times when one who is commissioned to teach and instruct might lead the conversation (Acts 20:7). But other glimpses of these early communities suggest that gatherings for worship were neither like theatres in which the great majority were observers of a dramatic activity carried through by only a few (such as the celebration of communion in some traditions); nor were they like lecture-halls in which only one spoke and all the others listened (such as preaching in some other traditions). Rather, they were community gatherings with freedom for many to bring their own contributions to worship. This is most clearly portrayed in 1 Corinthians 12 and 14. Here the church gathering is described as though it is a body, the body of Christ, in which the Spirit of Christ imparts to each member gifts that they are able to share with all the others. 1 Corinthians 12:7 makes the point that, "To each is given the manifestation of the Spirit for the common good." The Spirit works in each person so that each may contribute to the well-being of the whole. Nobody who has the Spirit need be excluded from this, though it is surely the case that not everybody contributed on each occasion. The picture then is of a dynamic community led by the Spirit, with each person free and able to minister in what is sometimes called "the priesthood of all believers." This is more than an affirmation of each individual member and certainly is not intended to promote "individualism" or exhibitionism. It is rather a declaration that the church as a whole is "a royal priesthood" (1 Pet 2:9) and that we may all contribute to that whole in worship and service of God. Paul's instructions in 1 Corinthians 14 have it as their purpose to ensure that the worship of the community is well-ordered and considerate, thereby enabling each individual contribution to be properly valued and considered. Enthusiasm should not lead to the neglect of good order (1 Cor 14:26–33), and good order properly understood is the servant of freedom and participation.

SPIRITUAL GIFTS

It is in this context that the New Testament addresses the question of spiritual gifts imparted by the Holy Spirit. It is clear on the day of Pentecost that when the Spirit came upon the church, the community of believers was lifted into a new realm of spiritual perception. Those on whom the Spirit came spoke in tongues and prophesied (Acts 2:4). They were carried beyond how they would normally behave and became capable of heightened spiritual emotions and activities. Similarly, as Paul described the young Christian community in Corinth, he listed a number of gifts that were being expressed among them: the utterance of wisdom, the utterance of knowledge, the gift of faith, gifts of healing, the working of miracles, prophecy, discernment of spirits, speaking in tongues and the interpretation of tongues. All these gifts were imparted by the Spirit and were for the common good, for building up the body of Christ (1 Cor 12:4–11). There is no need to imagine that this is an exhaustive list; rather they are illustrative of the kinds of activity in which the Spirit may freely engage. It also becomes clear that the value and authenticity of these gifts is in direct proportion to how much they benefit the Christian community, building it up in faith, hope, and love (1 Cor 13:13; 14:12).

At our present distance from the New Testament era it is not always straightforward to identity what these gifts are and how they function. They do point collectively, however, to the intuitive dimensions of Christian experience. Alongside the reasoned, intellectual content of the faith there is an intuitive dimension in which the Spirit of God is felt as much as thought. In contrasting the gift of tongues and prophecy, for instance, Paul writes, "For those who speak in a tongue do not speak to other people but to God; for nobody understands them, since they are speaking mysteries in the Spirit. On the other hand, those who prophesy speak to other people for their building up and encouragement and consolation" (1 Cor 14:2–4). Such gifts of the Spirit are received by believers in the intuitive parts of their lives. They may be rooted in our natural abilities but become heightened by the Holy Spirit so that we go beyond that of which we are normally capable. In this way the Spirit gives more of God's grace to people. For instance, a person may have natural abilities as a public speaker, but this only becomes preaching when the content is truly right and the way it is delivered is empowered by the Spirit. So it is with the other spiritual gifts. The gift of tongues is a form of unlearned speech through which a believer expresses praise to God. In this sense it is like spontaneously created music through which people might voice their response to God's goodness. It expresses what is in the heart without needing to be mentally formulated. Paul clearly valued tongues, but believed prophecy was a higher gift because it benefited other people and not the speaker alone (14:18–19). In the instructions he gave, he was aiming at a proper blend of the mind and the "spirit," the intellectual and the intuitive: "What should I do then? I will pray with the spirit, but I will pray with the mind also; I will sing praise with the spirit, but I will sing praise with the mind also" (14:15).

Not all the gifts that Paul mentions are necessarily to be used in the Christian community's gathering for worship. The body of Christ is not always at worship and most of the time is serving God in other ways. Nonetheless, the Spirit gives gifts to all its members, some of which are at the intuitive end of the spectrum and some of them not. There are, as examples, gifts of service, teaching, giving, and compassion (Rom 12:3–8). What makes a gift "spiritual" is that it is dedicated to God and filled with God's Spirit, so that in some way it might serve God's kingdom and purpose. However, if a gift is truly to be regarded as a gift, then however we serve God, whether in prominent or not so prominent ways, it is best to remember that none of us has anything that we did not first receive from God (1 Cor 4:7). We are stewards of all that we have been given and will one day need to give an account of what we have done with it (Matt 25:14–30).

FRUITS OF THE SPIRIT

To complement the gifts of the Spirit, the New Testament also speaks of the "fruit of the Spirit." If Christians are made into new creatures by the Spirit by being "born of the Spirit," then the same principle applies to the ways in which we live for God. The Holy Spirit produces holy lives by changing us from within and giving to us "new hearts and new spirits" (Ezek 36:26; Heb 8:8–12). This means that obedience to God is no longer a matter of outward duty and external law, rather: "I will put my law within them, and I will write it on their hearts; and I will be their God, and they shall be my people. No longer shall they teach one another, or say to each other 'Know the Lord,' for they shall all know me, from the least of them to the greatest, says the Lord" (Jer 31:33–34). It is by the Spirit working within us that this happens. So, the fruit of good and virtuous lives is something that comes from within us; something we want to do rather than being a burdensome requirement. "The fruit of the Spirit is love, joy, peace, patience, kindness, generosity, faithfulness, gentleness, and self-control. There is no law against such things" (Gal 5:22–23). Love for God inspired by the Spirit is bound to issue in love for our neighbors and even our enemies.

The Spirit-empowered community that has been gathered by the Spirit in the first place and is sustained by the Spirit throughout its journey is also guided by the Spirit in the fulfillment of its mission. From its origins in Jerusalem, the church has had to face the challenges of numerous cultural changes and transitions and has been in need of the Spirit's guidance at many points. This is not to say that it has always made the right decisions—since, though God's Spirit may speak, we do not always hear—but it is duty bound to seek for the Spirit's help. Jesus did say, "When the Spirit of truth comes, he will guide you into all the truth; for he will not speak on his own, but will speak whatever he hears, and he will declare to you the things that are to come" (John 16:13). Reliance on the Holy Spirit does not mean we are saved the hard work of thinking and struggling our way through problems that may face us, but that as we do so we should be seeking the mind of the Spirit as well as our own. When the early church held a conference in Jerusalem to face a particularly thorny issue, and found after much discussion they could come to an agreed conclusion, they completed their deliberations by saying, "For it has seemed good to the Holy Spirit and to us" (Acts 15:28). This is the right balance between a human search for understanding and divine guidance.

REALIZING GOD'S KINGDOM

The Christian community is the product of the Spirit's work in gathering and empowering God's people. It is the community of the Spirit and could not exist without the Spirit's grace. When we read of the Spirit-led and Spirit-filled community in the early chapters of the book of Acts, this is intended to be far more than a historical record. These chapters are laying down what is to be considered normal for the church, principles and practices that are to identify the church throughout the world, though adjusted to different contexts and conditions. We are presented with a picture of a missionary church that is expanding into the ancient world as it wins the allegiance of new members from the Jewish and gentile communities of its day. The foundation of new churches that would then carry on the work of the gospel in their own contexts was the heart of the early church's and apostles' strategy for expansion. Although it is wise to maintain our focus on the importance of community and togetherness in the Christian enterprise, we also do well to remember that each person who discovers life in Christ has his or her own story to tell and each of these stories is itself also the work of the Holy Spirit. If the church might be likened to a temple, then each believing person is like a stone in the temple, a living stone being built into a "spiritual house" (1 Pet 2:4-5). The Holy Spirit works in the community, but also in all members of that community as they are incorporated into the body. Furthermore, if we are to understand Jesus the Messiah as the "first-born within a large family" into whose image we are being conformed (Rom 8:29), then the work the Spirit does in each of us must reflect and parallel the work that was first done in Christ.

Jesus is the pioneer of our salvation, the last Adam in whom the work of human redemption is accomplished in and by his own humanity. If the Spirit prepared the way for the coming of Jesus in order that the world might receive him, the Spirit also prepares the way for each of us to come to Christ, awakening us from the death of spiritual apathy and insensitivity in order that we might begin to hear and heed the voice of God. If the Spirit caused Jesus to be conceived in Mary's womb and then to be born as the holy one of God (Matt 1:20-21; Luke 1:35), so the Spirit works in our inner life to regenerate us, to do that in us which by nature we ourselves cannot do, to repent of our sin, turn to Christ in trust and faith, and be reconciled to God (Titus 3:4-5). If the Spirit enabled Jesus to live a holy life fully pleasing to God by sanctifying him for the service of God, so the Spirit claims our own lives, inclines us towards what is good and holy, and enables us in faith to please God (Heb 11:6). If the Spirit dwelt within Jesus so that he became the bodily temple of God, so the Spirit who dwells within us makes us together into the temple of God (2 Cor 6:16). If the Spirit of God equipped Jesus for the ministry that was before him and gave him the power to work the works of God, the same Spirit also rests upon us and baptizes us into the realm of spiritual power and potential (Acts 1:8). If the Spirit of God enabled Jesus to give himself in self-sacrifice upon the cross, so the Spirit inspires us to give ourselves for the sake of others and to bear the fruit of peace, love, and joy (Gal 5:22-25). If the Spirit was the source of Jesus' assurance that he was the Son of the Father, so the Spirit brings inward assurance also to us that we are now the children of God by adoption (Rom 8:15-16; Eph 1:5). If it was by the Spirit that Jesus was raised from the dead, so it will be by the Spirit that our own bodies will one day be raised (Rom 8:11). In short, the Spirit worked in Jesus all that made him the prototype of a new humanity, and now the Spirit's work is to incorporate others into the same new humanity in Christ. By communion with Christ in the Spirit we are being transformed into his likeness: "Now the Lord is the Spirit, and where the Spirit of the Lord is, there is freedom. And all of us, with unveiled faces, seeing the glory of the Lord as though reflected in a mirror, are being transformed into the same image from one degree of glory to another; for this comes from the Lord, the Spirit" (2 Cor 3:17-18).

The Spirit of God is the agent of God, powerful and fully personal, at work in creation and Christ, in the church and in Christians. The Spirit is God at God's closest to us, the one who is closer to us than our own breath. The Spirit is at work in the deep places, creating fellowship and making connections. Without the force-field of God's Spirit, everything would spin apart and chaos would ensue. Without the Spirit we would not be held in communion with God and with each other. A further perspective is added when we also say that the Spirit is the Spirit of the future at work in the present. To enter into the knowledge of God in Christ is to have been "enlightened, and have tasted the heavenly gift, and have shared in the Holy Spirit, and have tasted the goodness of the word of God and the powers of the age to come" (Heb 6:4-5). The "powers of the age to come" refers to the future coming of God's kingdom in all its fullness, which will be time of "universal restoration" (Acts 3:21). It is the time of the final Sabbath, of peace and shalom, of all things being one in Christ (Eph 1:10). It is a time that has yet to come but in Christ it has already come upon us in part, and it is through the Spirit that it is known.

The kingdom of God was inaugurated in Christ, but has yet to be consummated, to be brought to completion. The Spirit is "the pledge of our inheritance towards redemption as God's own people" (Eph 1:14). In so far as we have the Spirit, therefore, the Christian community is already experiencing the power and presence of God's future, but not yet in its completed form. The whole work of the Holy Spirit in the church and in Christians may be understood as the Spirit bringing to pass within us now the realities which will be gloriously universal when the fullness of God's plan is brought to pass.

11

God's Gracious Election

ACCORDING TO JOHN'S GOSPEL, Jesus said to his disciples, "You did not choose me, but I chose you. And I appointed you to go and bear fruit, fruit that will last" (John 15:16). In saying this, Jesus was restating a conviction that is fundamental to the vision of God and of God's activity in the biblical revelation, namely, that before any of us ever made any kind of movement towards God, God had already moved towards us. God chose us before we chose God. More than this, any kind of response that we make towards God is a result and consequence of God's first having taken the initiative in drawing near to us. The Bible bears witness to a God who first initiates the work of creation and then the work of salvation, and does so not because God is asked or persuaded to do so but out of sheer, unmerited love that arises solely from within God's own self. We call this the "grace" of God and its distinguishing mark is not simply that it is more than we deserve but that it is the precise opposite of what we deserve.

UNIVERSAL AND PARTICULAR

The God who created us and all things did so for a purpose. This purpose is most plainly spoken of in Ephesians 1:8–10, which asserts, "With all wisdom and insight he has made known to us the mystery of his will, according to his good pleasure that he set forth in Christ, as a plan for the fullness of time, to gather up all things in him, things in heaven and things on earth." God's ultimate purpose is to restore all those things that are currently broken and fractured into a new unity in Christ so that there is one whole, healed, and harmonious universe in him. It is towards this final goal that God is currently working in the church and in history, even though much of the time God's providential rule is not obvious to us. The means by which God is working this purpose out is that of election, the choice of a people who will uniquely represent God's revelation of God's own self and so be witnesses of it to the nations of the world. It should be stressed that God's intention is *universal,* to bless all the nations, but the means towards this goal is *particular,* through the choice of specific groups and persons who will be witnesses to the whole world of the grace of God, firstly the people of Israel and then the varied and scattered communities of the Christian church. The people of Israel and the church together are at the centre of God's saving purposes for the world. From before the foundation of the world God has chosen them and called them for this particular purpose, and so it can be said that God has "foreknown" them and "predestined" them to play this part in the divine plan (Rom 8:28–30).

The priority of divine grace, the fact that God takes the initiative in the work of salvation, is evident in the whole sweep of the biblical narrative. If the book of Genesis is concerned with "origins," as its name implies, not only does it identify the origins of creation, fall, and human sin but the origins of God's work of salvation. God called Abraham to leave his own country and to set out on a journey to a new land. God spoke to him and promised, "I will make of you a great nation, and I will bless you, and make your name great, so that you will be a blessing. I will bless those you bless you, and the one who curses you I will curse; and in you all the families of the earth shall be blessed" (Gen 12:2–3). The importance of these words cannot be overemphasized since with them the whole story of the people of Israel and the Christian church began. God's call was specific—it came to Abraham and was continued through his posterity, Isaac and Jacob. God's promise was clear—that Abraham would give rise to a great nation that would be blessed by God. God's intention was plain—that through this initiative all the families of the earth would be blessed. So although Abraham was called into a great privilege, this was intended not for him alone but for the whole world. Abraham's vocation was to live in a special relationship with the Lord in which he would obey God and God would protect, preserve, and provide for the people of the call. This was to be a distinctive people marked out by God and with a particular vocation. Much of the Hebrew Scriptures concerns the story of this people, their trials and tribulations, their battles and wars, their captivity and liberation in Egypt, their life as they settled in the promised land marked out for them. In addition, we read both of their willing response to the Lord and frank accounts of their stubborn disobedience as a "stiff-necked" and rebellious people (Exod 33:3–5; Ezek 2:3–5; 3:7–11).

THE COVENANT PEOPLE

God's "covenant" with Abraham that God would bless his posterity, and with the people that "I will be their God," was renewed on a number of occasions (Gen 15:1–6; 17:1–17), as was the prescription that the covenant would be marked in the flesh by the sign of male circumcision (17:13–14). The covenant entered into a new and more specific phase after the people of Israel had been delivered under Moses out of captivity in Egypt and as they were being led into the promised land in Canaan. Here Moses encountered God on Mount Sinai and God said,

> Thus shall you say to the house of Jacob, and tell the Israelites: You have seen what I did to the Egyptians, and how I bore you on eagles' wings and brought you to myself. Now therefore, if you obey my voice and keep my covenant, you shall be my treasured possession out of all the peoples. Indeed, the whole earth is mine, but you shall be for me a priestly kingdom and a holy nation. These are the words that you shall speak to the Israelites.
> (Exod 19:3–6)

Israel now was not only aware that they were a people called by God but that God had the power to save them, as he did at the Red Sea. In grateful response for this act of salvation they were to enter into a covenant of obedience to God that would be marked by adherence to God's law, by male circumcision as a sign that they belonged body and soul to God, by worship in the tabernacle they were commanded to make, and by Sabbath rest, allowing them opportunity for renewal and also time to honor God by remembering God's mighty acts on their behalf. In these ways, they were to live distinctively as God's own people, and so to bear witness to the nations. Their willingness and ability to live up to this high calling was to fluctuate greatly, given the natural human tendency to forget those things that are most important. Because of this, God would in time raise up prophets who would call them and their rulers back to their duty and primary vocation to be true to the covenant made at Sinai. But the years to come were to put them to extreme tests, in the course of which their understanding of God's ways would be greatly deepened.

Israel's calling to be an elect people was renewed immediately prior to entering the promised land. The whole of the book of Deuteronomy is a reminder of the goodness God had shown them, of the distinctive way of life to which they were called, of the blessings that follow obedience to God and the curses that flow from turning away (chapter 28), and of the covenant that God was making afresh with them at that very time. Supremely, it calls Israel repeatedly to love God and identifies what Jesus was later to characterize as the greatest commandment of all: "Hear O Israel: The LORD is our God, the LORD alone. You shall love the LORD your God with all your heart, and with all your soul and with all your might" (Deut 6:4–5; Matt 22:34–40). And it clearly sets out its understanding of Israel's election:

> For you are a people holy to the LORD your God; the LORD your God has chosen you out of all the peoples on earth to be his people, his treasured possession. It was not because you were more numerous than any other people that the LORD set his heart on you and chose you—for you were the fewest of all people. It was because the LORD loved you and kept the oath that he swore to your ancestors, that the LORD has brought you out with a mighty hand and redeemed you from the house of slavery, from the hand of Pharaoh king of Egypt. Know therefore that the LORD your God is God, the faithful God who maintains covenant loyalty with those who love him and keep his commandments to a thousand generations, and who repays in their own person those who reject him.
> (Deut 7:6–10)

Although the covenant relationship made demands upon Israel, it should primarily be understood as a relationship of mutual love in which the laws and expectations laid upon Israel would not be burdensome, but light. One great prophet compared Israel's hard-heartedness towards the LORD, drawing from his own experience, to that of a wayward spouse who found it impossible to be faithful to her husband (Hos 1:2–3). Despite this, God persisted with the covenant: "How can I give you up, Ephraim? How can I hand you over, O Israel? . . . My heart recoils within me; my compassion grows warm and tender. I will not execute my fierce anger; I will not again destroy Ephraim; for I am God and no mortal, the Holy One in your midst, and I will not come in wrath" (11:8–9). Despite this, the divine patience being pushed to the limit, God was first to hand Israel (the northern kingdom) over to the Assyrians and then Judah (the southern kingdom) over to the Babylonians to be judged for their many compromises with idol-worship and their neglect of the covenant. God's characteristic way of judging and disciplining the people was to hand them over to the logic of their own actions so that they could reap what they sowed. To be sent into exile, as Israel had at one time been sent into Egypt, was a profoundly painful event in her history. Yet even this was to be seen as a sign of God's love since "the LORD reproves the one he loves" (Prov 3:11–12; Deut 28:47–68; Heb 12:5–11).

THE WITNESS OF THE JEWISH PEOPLE

In exile, Israel, now developing recognizably into the Jewish people, was to find repentance and renewal. It was here that the Scriptures were to begin to take form and to be studied closely. It was here that, in the absence of the temple, the earliest synagogues were to emerge. It was here that prophets such as Ezekiel and (Second) Isaiah (Isa 40–55) were to give new hope to the people and to speak of a renewed covenant and a restoration to the promised land. The judgment of the exile came to be seen not as an ultimate catastrophe but as a work of God providing the opportunity for Israel to recover her vocation; and that vocation was to be a light to the gentiles: "I am the LORD, I have called you in righteousness, I have taken you by the hand and kept you; I have given you as a covenant to the people, a light to the nations, to open the eyes that are blind" (Isa 42:6–7: these words can be understood to apply both to the Messiah and to the people of the Messiah, Israel). "I will give you as a light to the nations, that my salvation may reach to the end of the earth" (Isa 49:6). From now, the vision of Israel as a missionary people emerges with great clarity: "Many peoples and strong nations shall come to seek the LORD of hosts in Jerusalem, and to entreat the favor of the LORD. Thus says the LORD of hosts: In those days ten men from nations of every language shall take hold of a Jew, grasping his garment and saying, 'Let us go with you, for we have heard that God is with you'" (Zech 8:22–23; Isa 56:6–8).

The significance of the Jewish people in the story of salvation is hard to over-estimate. The apostle Paul summarized the debt that is owed to them in the following way: "They are Israelites, and to them belong the adoption, the glory, the covenants, the giving of the law, the worship, and the promises; to them belong the patriarchs, and from them, according to the flesh, comes the Messiah, who is over all, God blessed for ever. Amen" (Rom 9:4–5). It is in the coming of the Messiah that God's purpose in calling Israel comes into focus. Jesus could not have been who he was were it not for the people from whom he came. Almost everything that we see in Jesus, and all the ways in which we have come to understand him, bear the marks of his Jewish inheritance. The Hebrew background to Jesus has given us the categories, ideas, and vocabulary with which to interpret him as the Son of God and the Son of Man. He is God's servant, called and chosen to impart salvation, not only to the Jewish people, but to all other peoples. Because of him the work of election has progressed through and yet beyond Israel to encompass the nations too. The church is the enlarged people of God. For this reason, the New Testament speaks of the church with language that closely parallels that used of Israel many years before: "But you are a chosen race, a royal priesthood, a holy nation, God's own people, in order that you may proclaim the mighty acts of him who called you out of darkness into his marvelous light. Once you were not a people, but now you are God's people; once you had not received mercy, but now you have received mercy" (1 Pet 2:9–10).

In the election of the church as the expanded Israel (Gal 6:16) we find the same marks as in Israel herself. The church is chosen not by virtue of any merits of its own but solely because of the love of God. Once we were no people but now God has made us God's own people. There are, therefore, no grounds for boasting, since whatever the church has, it owes to God's grace, not to its own achievements. Those who boast should boast in the Lord (2 Cor 10:17; Eph 2:8–9). Although election is a privilege, it is primarily a vocation to a mission and a task. We are to "proclaim the mighty deeds of him who called us." We are to "bear fruit that will last." By living as a distinctive people in the service of God and by bearing witness in word and deed to God as made known in Christ, the church is a light to the world (Matt 5:14), reflecting the true light that is Christ himself (John 8:12). The church is a series of particular communities, but the purpose of God does not stop with those communities. It has in view the bringing of light to all the world.

PERSONAL ELECTION

Although the church is central to the divine purpose, the church is a community of persons, so we must also speak of the election of individuals to be drawn to Christ and into the commonwealth of the Christian community through regeneration and conversion. Once more, the principle holds good that election precedes conversion. Jesus said both, "And I, when I am lifted up from the earth, will draw all people to myself" (John 12:32) and, "No one can come to me unless drawn by the Father who sent me; and I will raise that person up on the last day" (John 6:44). Without the grace of God going before and enabling any decision we ourselves make, it is impossible to believe. God frees us from ourselves in order that we might respond to grace. We have nothing that we did not first receive as a gift, therefore self-congratulation is ruled out (1 Cor 4:7). The only appropriate response the Christian can make towards God is to live a life of gratitude, humility, and service. The fact that our salvation depends upon God from first to last is also a source of encouragement and comfort to us. This was Paul's intention when he wrote: "We know that all things work together for good for those who love God, who are called according to his purpose. For those whom he foreknew he also predestined to be conformed to the image of his Son, in order that he might be the firstborn within a large family. And those whom he predestined he also called, and those whom he called he also justified; and those whom he justified he also glorified" (Rom 8:28–30). God is able to begin and end the divine purpose for us, even against the most difficult of circumstances, and is absolutely steadfast in pursuing the goal that awaits us.

At the same time, the fact that some, an apparent minority, on hearing the gospel come to believe it and others do not raises a series of questions. The most common answer to this mystery is to say that although Christ draws all people to himself, many, perhaps the majority, resist his invitation. As in Jesus' Parable of the Great Dinner, "they all alike began to make excuses" (Luke 14:15–24). In effect, they "reject it and judge [themselves] to be unworthy of eternal life" (Acts 13:46). There can be no doubt that such attitudes of resistance are encountered every day—many choose not to believe the gospel, claiming it not to be true. Others may think it to be true but find it inconvenient. People therefore exclude themselves from the grace of God, either by their own deliberate decision or their slothful lack of response. However, an alternative position is to say that God does not, in fact, choose all to find salvation, but has already determined that he will save some and add them to his church, and simply leave others in their sins or even deliberately consign them to be lost. Moreover, this is a decision, the claim runs, that God made even before time began, in an "eternity past," not on the basis of anything done by those chosen or not chosen, but solely on the basis of God's free decision. The human race is thus divided into the elect and the "reprobate." Biblical verses that are cited to support this alternative approach, which asserts God's right to do what God wants, include, "I have loved Jacob, but I have hated Esau" (Rom 9:13; see Mal 1:2–3), and,

> But who indeed are you, a human being, to argue with God? Will what is molded say to the one who molds it, "Why have you made me like this?" Has the potter no right over the clay, to make out of the same lump one object for special use and another for ordinary use? What if God, desiring to show his wrath and to make known his power, has endured with much patience the objects of wrath that are made for destruction; and what if he has done so in order to make known the riches of his glory for the objects of mercy, which he has prepared beforehand for glory?
> (Rom 9:20–23)

From this second point of view there usually follows a further conclusion, namely that Christ has not died for all people, but only for the elect that God intends to save. The promise given to Mary, after all, was that "he will save *his people* from their sins" (Matt 1:21), and this is interpreted to mean that Christ has not died for all but only for those he counts as "his people."

Both these ways of interpreting the fact of people being in two groups, those who believe and are for Christ and those who do not believe and are against him, face challenges. Those who place the stress on the choice not to believe run the danger of suggesting that God is ultimately powerless to save since human beings can thwart the divine purpose. They ultimately are in control and leave God in the status of an observer who offers salvation but then is forced to wait and see who takes up the offer. This position might also suggest that some people are residually good, good enough to choose to believe, whereas others are more deeply corrupted, when actually it is these who are most in need of salvation. The relative fewness of those who do believe, compared with the totality of the world's population, does not leave us with great hopes for the salvation of the human race. Could not God do more to draw people in, to persuade them of their sin and of the joyful salvation that is in Christ? If God truly loves, could God not persist to the point that human resistance is broken down and the number of those who believe is infinitely greater?

On the other hand, the notion that God has already divided the human race into the "elect" and the "reprobate" and has never intended to bring salvation to the reprobate but rather only to confirm them in their position, is deeply problematic and leaves us asking questions about the very nature of God's goodness. There are many reasons to question it. For a start, there are the clear affirmations that "God so loved *the world* that he gave his only Son" (John 3:16). Then there are the frequent affirmations that the death of Christ was for the whole world: "Here is the Lamb of God who takes away the sin of *the world*!" (John 1:29). "He is the atoning sacrifice for our sins, and not for ours only but also for the sins *of the whole world*"(1 John 2:2). To claim that *the world* here means "all without distinction" (that is: all types and ethnicities of people) as opposed to "all without exception" (nobody excluded), is not enough to blunt the case for a universal atonement, since it avoids the obvious meaning of the word "all." Moreover, the will of God to save all and not just some is clearly stated: "This is right and is acceptable in the sight of God our Savior, who desires everyone to be saved and to come to the knowledge of the truth" (1 Tim 2:3-4). "For to this end we toil and struggle, because we have our hope set on the living God, who is the savior of all people, especially of those who believe" (1 Tim 4:10). "For the love of Christ urges us on, because we are convinced that one has died for all; therefore all have died" (2 Cor 5:14). "For God has imprisoned all in disobedience so that he may be merciful to all" (Rom 11:32). Most tellingly, the idea that we are amongst either the elect or the reprobate because of a divine decision before the world was even created, and that with no regard to anything we may have done or not done, begins to sound more like luck, or lack of it, than grace.

There is more at stake in these discussions than might at first appear. Clearly, how we think of God's saving purpose makes a difference to our vision of God and the reasons for which we give praise to God. If we think of God's saving love embracing all humanity, we also have a firm foundation on which to build a church that is concerned for all and open to all. If the saving purpose of God does not extend to all people then we are more likely to see the church as a closed gathering of the elect in the midst of communities that are ultimately destined to perish. Is it possible for us then, to state our convictions about divine election in a way that is both fully honoring to a gracious God and challenging for the kind of church we wish to be? The answer to this is firmly, Yes, and we now seek to set out those convictions in a way that shows how God's work of election is both good news for the world and a central teaching of a generous church.

THE GOOD NEWS OF DIVINE ELECTION

Election begins with God. God has first of all elected God's own self to be our God. From eternity God has chosen that "you shall be my people, and *I will be your God*" (Jer 30:22; Ezek 11:20; 36:28). The first decision that has been made therefore in "eternity past" is one in which God determines to be *for us*. This is the language of self-determination and covenant and expresses the idea that God from eternity wills to enter into a binding and permanent relationship with a people called for this purpose, and then to extend this to the whole world (Rev 21:1–4). In this way, it may be said that God turns God's own self towards humankind and wills to do them good, to bless them through friendship and covenant relationship with God's own self. The creation is brought into being as the context in which this drama of personal engagement and relationship might be worked out and into which the blessings of the covenant might flow for the good of all. Yet in the moment in which God conceived the purpose of forging covenant within the project of creation, it was already known to God how human beings would misuse their freedom, estrange themselves from God, and vandalize the creation. Equally it was known to God how to respond to this and bring about the salvation of the world.

So, secondly, this desire for covenant and for the restoration of a broken world was purposed from before the foundation of the world and has come to be revealed in the person of Jesus Christ. Christ is above all God's chosen one (Matt 3:17; Mark 1:11; Luke 3:22). "Here is my servant, whom I uphold, *my chosen* in whom my soul delights" (Isa 42:1). In him God's Son became incarnate to be the supreme covenant partner with the Father, the one who works out fully what it means to be in a loving relationship to the Father and to do God's will utterly and completely. In him God achieves the salvation of the world. Christ is both the electing God and the elected human, the God who chooses and the human being who is chosen. In this way he is the mediator between God and humankind, the one who both offers to God a fully obedient life on behalf of us all and so atones for our failure to do so, and also "takes away the sin of the world" so that the divine life might flow into human hearts and the world (John 1:29). In Jesus Christ as the last Adam the whole of humanity is chosen. To be "in Christ" is to be chosen by God, "just as he chose us in Christ before the foundation of the world to be holy and blameless before him in love" (Eph 1:4–5). At one level, therefore, it can be said that since all human beings are potentially "in Christ," all human beings are potentially amongst the elect. To place faith in Christ and embrace him as savior is to pass from being "not a people" to being "God's people," from those who "had not received mercy" to those who "have received mercy" (1 Pet 2:10). Our relationship to Christ is what determines all.

At this point we might think of God's work of election as an expanding circle. The circle of those who are among the elect people of God is always increasing. It does so as by the Holy Spirit more people become convicted of their sin and are moved to put their faith in Christ. Although God's purpose centered in Christ and in the church is predestined, intended beforehand from all eternity, the work of election is a present, ongoing activity of God. Rather than think of it as a fixed decision made in eternity past to save particular people and not others, we should see it as a work of the eternal God in our present as God in grace and by the Spirit goes before us, preparing the way for people to believe, regenerating them by the Spirit, and calling them into the church. As Jesus said, "All things have been handed over to me by my Father; and no one knows who the Son is except the Father, or who the Father is except the Son and *anyone to whom the Son chooses to reveal him*" (Luke 10:22). In a parallel claim to unique status, Jesus says, "I am the way, the truth, and the life. No one comes to the Father except through me" (John 14:6). Who has entered into truth and life is for Jesus to say since *he* is the way. Sovereignty belongs to God and is being worked out through Christ. Furthermore, because Christ has died for all, and because in him the Word through whom all things were made has become incarnate and has brought about a new creation, there is no one who is in principle excluded from the salvation he brings. Christ, by the Spirit, is still actively choosing to reveal the Father to people and calling them to himself.

We can set no limits to the scope of salvation. Nor can we set limits to the persistence of God in pursuing the lost. As with Israel, as with the church, so today, the God who sent his Son to "seek out and to save the lost" (Luke 19:10), and who now sends the Spirit of the Son into the world to grow and expand the church, persists in seeking the lost. If anyone comes to find the truth in Christ, it is because God has persisted with them to the point of their eyes being opened to that truth. Generally it has been thought that God's search for lost humanity takes place in this life and ceases when a person dies. On the basis of a verse such as Hebrews 9:27—"it is appointed for mortals to die once, and after that the judgment"—it has been considered that death is the threshold beyond which it is impossible to come to believe. Yet "judgment" here need not necessarily imply condemnation: judgment is God's work of delivering justice. We should not discount the possibility that God's persistence in seeking the lost continues beyond the grave, especially given that many of God's human creatures do not receive any kind of justice in this life.

What are we to say about the aborted, the stillborn, the children who die in early infancy, the mentally ill, the innocent victims of holocaust, famine, disaster and war, and those who in their lives have never had opportunity even to hear the gospel, let alone understand it? "Indeed, God did not send the Son into the world to condemn the world, but in order that the world might be saved through him" (John 3:17). Although death might be a barrier to human beings, it is not so to the God who has demonstrated power over death by the resurrection. There are good reasons to believe that God's search for a lost humanity continues even beyond death, that the children of Abraham will in time number more than the stars in the heavens that we cannot count (Gen 15:5-6), or the grains of sand by the seashore (Heb 11:12), and that at the last we shall join with "a great multitude that no one could count, from every nation, from all tribes and peoples and languages, standing before the throne and before the Lamb" (Rev 7:9). Although there are many things we do not know, there are good reasons to be abundantly hopeful about the final outcomes of God's saving purpose. After an encounter with a rich young man Jesus once proclaimed, "It is easier for a camel to go through the eye of a needle than for someone who is rich to enter the kingdom of God," to which his followers exclaimed in amazement (and not surprisingly), "Then who can be saved?" Jesus' reply is instructive: "What is impossible for mortals is possible for God" (Luke 18:24-27). When it comes to divine election we can set no limits since all things are possible for the God who is able to "accomplish abundantly far more than all we ask or imagine" (Eph 3:20). In divine freedom and mercy, God has always been and ever will be the God of surprises.

ETERNAL SECURITY

A conviction related to the Christian community's understanding of election is that of the security of a believer's relationship with God. It stands to reason that if God has a purpose that is being worked out through election then what God begins, God will complete: "I am confident of this, that the one who began a good work among you will bring it to completion by the day of Jesus Christ" (Phil 1:6). In addition, ideas such as being "born again" suggest that once we are born of God we remain God's children. On the other hand, there are stern warnings in the New Testament about falling away from faith and of being excluded from the enlarged Israel that is the church (Heb 6:1–8; Rom 11:20–22). There is also the example of Judas who, although he was chosen to be in the company of Christ and although Jesus entrusted him with the responsibility of handling the money, went out from the Last Supper determined to betray him (Luke 22:14–23; John 13:21–30). Even though he was to all intents and purposes a disciple of Jesus, Jesus was later to call him, "the one destined to be lost" (John 17:12).

Although we look for a straightforward answer to our curiosity over this question, the New Testament is reluctant to give us one. It seems there is enough there to give assurance that as we trust in Christ we are secure in him and have grounds for confidence. At the same time, there is enough to warn us that should we turn away we have no such grounds. We have enough to comfort us but not enough to breed complacency, and in this is a wholesome tension. "So if you think you are standing, watch out that you do not fall" (1 Cor 10:12). There are no grounds for presumption, but only for humility. It is not enough to have the right words. Jesus warned, "Not everyone who says to me, 'Lord, Lord,' will enter the kingdom of heaven, but only one who does the will of my Father in heaven" (Matt 7:21). Doing the will of God by persevering in the service of Christ is the true evidence that we have been inwardly transformed by God's grace. Keeping close to God who "is the source of your life in Christ Jesus, who became for us wisdom from God, and righteousness and sanctification and redemption" (1 Cor 1:30) is the proper ground for our hope and confidence. As with salvation, so with perseverance and endurance: they are gifts of God, the God who is faithful: "If we are faithless, he remains faithful—for he cannot deny himself" (2 Tim 2:13). For believers, true confidence is in the Lord and not themselves.

12

The Powers of Darkness and their Defeat

ENCOUNTER WITH EVIL IS a fact of life, and the Christian community is persuaded that there are dark and destructive forces at work in the world over and beyond the evil acts of human beings. The central evidence for this is not first of all human history or personal experience, although these are compelling enough. Rather, it is the testimony of the New Testament to Jesus. Jesus was tempted by the devil in the wilderness (Luke 4:1–13). He exercised a highly effective ministry as an exorcist, one who expels evil influences (Mark 1:21–28; 5:1–20). He understood his own death as an overcoming of "the ruler of this world" (John 12:31; 16:11). And his mission is summed up as being "to destroy the works of the devil" (1 John 3:8). At the heart of Christian revelation there is an awareness of the power of evil. The redeeming work of Christ is understood therefore against the backdrop of the reality of evil, and this dimension cannot be omitted from any account of the life of Jesus without radically changing the nature of that life and of the Christian faith.

Yet particular care needs to be taken in how we think through this aspect of the content of faith. Evil needs to be reckoned with and taken seriously, yet not so seriously as to obscure our vision of God or to direct our attention in ways that will do us little good. For evil to occupy our attention too much would itself be a victory for the powers of evil, potentially robbing us of a proper sense of God's gracious supremacy in all things. We shall therefore cast them only a short, sharp glance. In fact, it should be the case that we do not "believe in" the devil in anything like the way we believe in

God. To believe in God is not only to accept God's reality but also to invest our trust and our hope in God, to open up our lives to grace and goodness unreservedly. By contrast, even as we believe in God, we *renounce* the devil and all his works. We do not believe *in* but *against* the devil. Our act of faith in God is simultaneously an act of *disbelief* in the devil, not as a refusal to accept its reality, but as a rejection of all that it stands for. There have been times and places when Christians have "believed in" the devil too much and have themselves become obsessed, and this is not an error we wish to repeat. To guard against this we need to guard how we think and speak of evil so that from the very beginning we put the power of darkness in its place as having been overcome by Christ.

This chapter is different from others that have preceded it in that it offers two possible ways of approaching this subject. One has the strength of being traditional and might be thought of as the "majority report" in the church's history. The second, a minority report, follows a less familiar path and develops the idea that evil is a wholly negative phenomenon and so is fundamentally the emptiness that ensues when God is excluded from human life and community. Both approaches insist that evil is "real," but real in differing ways. It may be possible to reconcile the two approaches, but approaching the subject from two perspectives ought to add depth to our understanding. This chapter reviews these two perspectives and then returns at the end to the nature of the Christian community's convictions about the powers of darkness.

EVIL AND THE FALL OF ANGELS

The first version of evil's reality locates evil supremely in supra-human realities of a "spiritual" kind, specifically in a being identified as "Satan" (the names means "accuser": Rev 12:10) or "the devil" (which means "slanderer") or by a variety of other names and titles. As all things ultimately derive from a good God who is the "Father of lights" (Jas 1:17), it is deduced that Satan must have been created as a good angel, named Lucifer (Isa 14:12 KJV: the name means "Day Star" or "son of dawn"), who by an act of rebellion fell away from his vocation, persuaded other angels to rebel (Jude 6), and so became the fountainhead of evil in all its forms. According to this view it is Satan who is in view in the Garden of Eden, taking form as a serpent in order to tempt Adam and Eve away from their primeval devotion to God (Gen 3:1–7; compare Rev 20:2). It is the devil who acts in concert with "principalities and powers," "cosmic powers of this present darkness," and the "spiritual forces of evil in the heavenly places" (Eph 6:12) to make "war against the saints" (Rev 13:7), and also, of course, God.

Evil, then, following this version, which makes ample reference to biblical texts, is the reality of an intensely evil spiritual being, surrounded by cohorts of lesser such beings that operate in a spiritual dimension to distort, negate, and oppose the purposes of God. As God's creation is good, and these beings must owe their origin to God, these beings could not have been created in their present state, but assumed their condition by the misuse of angelic free will. This posits a fall or "catastrophe" in the created sphere at some point prior to the creation of human beings. Humans have then in their turn fallen prey to evil by yielding to temptation and have become implicated in the rebellion and responsible for their part within it. Human life is thereafter defined by the struggle between good and evil, God and the devil. Indeed, for many Christians belief in a personal devil amounts to an article of faith, despite the absence of any such statement in the church's historic creeds. Yet to balance this, it is firmly believed that in Jesus Christ God has decisively reclaimed the creation and overcome evil through his death and resurrection. The fruits of that victory are currently only partly felt and their full effect awaits the consummation when God will be "all in all" (1 Cor 15:28). The coming of this glad day is assured, even if it is delayed.

This account of evil will be familiar to anyone who is acquainted with Christian history or those cultures that have been influenced by Christian faith. It is also assumed to be thoroughly biblical in content. Yet in reality it faces challenges, both biblically and theologically. It derives some of its justification from Ezekiel 28, especially vv. 12–17, and Isaiah 14:12–21, passages that speak of the fall of two exceptional but flawed individuals who aspired to equality with God, and, as noted, it is from the latter passage that the name Lucifer is drawn (v. 12). However, both these passages refer not to an angelic catastrophe but to identifiable historical persons (the king of Tyre and the king of Babylon respectively) and the process of interpretation that can make them refer to a supra-historical spiritual power is by no means clear, if indeed it is possible. For most of those who use these passages as proof-texts, the association is simply assumed, with no attempt to justify how. So they are proof-texts that do not prove their case. Furthermore, where Satan is identified in the Hebrew Scriptures (which is very rarely) it is not with the same nature and role he was later to assume. In Job 1–2, where he makes his most extended appearance, "the satan" (a title, not a proper name) is God's servant, God's "holy sifter," agent provocateur, or "enforcer." The book of Job is a remarkable literary masterpiece and it is undoubtedly better to see (the) Satan here as a literary figure within the book's overall narrative, rather than as an actual being. Only later does the figure of Satan take a turn towards the irreducibly sinister in Hebrew religion.

Even the New Testament texts concerning Satan's, the devil's, or the fallen angels' origins are less than clear. Jude 6 ("The angels who did not keep their own position, but left their proper dwelling") and 2 Peter 2:4 ("For if God did not spare the angels when they sinned, but cast them into hell and committed them to chains of deepest darkness") are more likely to relate to the enigmatic passage in Genesis 6:1–5, which refers to the "sons of God" taking human wives. This passage attracted much attention in Jewish mythology and the New Testament references may be to that mythology, rather than biblical sources. At any rate, the passages refer to such angels being held prisoner, rather than being active in the world as principalities and powers. Jesus' reference to watching "Satan fall from heaven like a flash of lightning" (Luke 10:18) and the "war in heaven" of Revelation 12:7 clearly apply to the mission of Jesus and of his followers, rather than to the pre-historical origins of evil in an angelic fall. So although securely placed within the history of Christian imagery and thought, it is by no means clear that there is as solid a biblical basis for this first version of the reality of evil as is normally assumed.

There remain, of course, good theological reasons for finding the origin of evil in some kind of creaturely aberration through the misuse of freedom within a good world. This allows us to affirm the fundamental goodness of God's creation, enables us to deny that God is the originator of evil, and allows us to see the conflict between good and evil not as an eternal one but one that had a beginning and will have an end. Moreover, there is something very compelling about the idea of an intensely evil agent at work in the world. The worst forms of sin are not those of a physical but a spiritual nature: pure pride, pure arrogance, pure malevolence. The worst forms of sin can therefore arguably only be produced by a pure spirit whose sin would be irreversible, unforgivable, and incurable. Satan fits the bill. On the other hand, the idea of a *personal* devil creates problems. For a start, even such a devil would be limited in scope, whereas experience suggests that wherever humans are to be found temptation and sin lie close to hand. And in what sense could the devil be called "personal" if personhood is a reflection, echo, and image of divine personhood? There is no sense in which the devil could be thought to be remotely in God's image as a person since evil is the negation and contradiction of all that is divine. A further question concerns the idea that Satan is a fallen creature, originally made by God. If this is so, and if God has compassion over all that God has made (Ps 145:9) and seeks the reconciliation of all things visible and invisible (Col 1:20), are we not led to imagine that even Satan might be redeemed? Some

Christian thinkers have affirmed this final restoration, but the Bible itself gives no such hope—quite to the contrary (Rev 20:10). This in turn suggests that what we mean by "Satan" is not a creature originally created by God but some other kind of reality.

EVIL AS EMPTINESS AND DEPRIVATION

The various questions raised lead to a second way of thinking and speaking of the undoubted reality of evil in the world, one that accepts the reality of evil as a force within human spiritual and social existence but views the biblical language that describes it as "mythic." That is, the power of darkness is real, but the language in which it is described is a personification of a power that is essentially impersonal or even anti-personal, aimed at the destruction of personhood.

Personification is used at several points in the Bible. The apostle Paul portrayed both sin and the law as though they were personal powers (Rom 7:5, 11) and Revelation describes both Death and Hades as though they were personal agents in themselves (20:13–14). So the biblical language that describes evil may be narrative and mythic in form, even though the reality to which it refers is far from mythical. Otherwise put, the devil is a product of sinful human society rather than the other way round, the symbol of an entire society alienated from God. Evil is literally godlessness, the destructive spirituality created when God, the beneficent source and sustainer of life, is excluded from human communal existence by multiple human choices to be godless. It is ultimate emptiness.

Although this is a minority report it has long been proposed within the history of Christian thought as a way of pushing beyond the traditional, mythic, and pictorial language of the New Testament to ask more precise questions about the nature of evil. It concerns itself with the question: what are you left with when God, and therefore all goodness, is excluded? We are left with the absence of the good, and this means evil. It is like only darkness being left when the light is removed. Such evil only exists by being parasitical on life. It exists by negation and has no positive value or potential of its own. Rather than being an ordered kingdom of evil, it is pure chaos with no rhyme or reason of its own other than to negate and to destroy that which is ordered and good. In this way, it is the precise opposite of the good, ordered, and purposeful work of creation that God has accomplished. Evil distorts what is good and is as death compared with fullness of life. The parallel with death is significant and is an association often made in the Bible. To turn to evil is to die (Gen 2:17; Ezek 18:4, 20; Rom 6:23). Death is a powerful reality that casts its shadow over all of life. We feel its encroachment and fear its power to turn all things to bitterness. Death is a power, it is real, but it is not something in itself. It is not a being or an entity; rather it is the absence of life. It can be personified as though it were itself something, the "last enemy" (1 Cor 15:26, 55), but actually it has no being in itself. This could be instructive in helping us understand the nature of evil.

This alternative view also faces challenges. If evil is emptiness and chaos, why does the New Testament speak of it as though it had intentions and agency? "And we do this so that we may not be outwitted by Satan; for we are not ignorant of his designs" (2 Cor 2:11). Yet chaotic forces sometimes result in patterns that have the appearance of design or intention. Evil as this alternative view describes it has the power to take form in the affairs of human being and impinge upon them. According to Paul, Satan is a master of disguise, even to the point of appearing on the side of the good: "Even Satan disguises himself as an angel of light" (2 Cor 11:14). The NIV translates this as: "And no wonder, for Satan himself masquerades as an angel of light." The word "masquerade" is a useful one here. Jesus said of the devil, "He was a murderer from the beginning and does not stand in the truth. When he lies, he speaks according to his own nature, for he is a liar and the father of lies" (John 8:44). Evil, therefore, is inherently deceptive. It contains nothing of the truth. It can take form in a variety of ways, even masquerading as divine, but these are all outward appearance concealing an inner reality that is determined to distort and destroy. Those who imagine that they have mapped the territory of the evil empire are in danger of being deceived. Although evil may masquerade as a "personal" devil and present itself to human beings in this way, we do well to be cautious. Most of all we are called to renounce evil and embrace the good.

These two approaches to evil may be able to inform each other. The "fall of angels" approach faces questions as to how a purely spiritual being, created by God as part of the good creation, could even conceive the possibility of rebelling against God. Where does such a thought come from? It might well be concluded that this is an unanswerable question beyond which we cannot penetrate and that the nature of evil is so irrational that it is folly to expect a rational explanation. Or it might be imagined that when God created the world as it is, he also, by doing so, created the possibility of its opposite, an exclusion of what is good to give rise to a contradictory and rival reality. This is not to say that God created evil, but that the possibility of evil became inevitable once the world was created. It then took creatures with "free will," angelic or human, to actualize that possibility. The alternative view, which argues that evil is the absence of the good, still must take seriously the ways in which this same evil takes form and force in human experience as darkness, death, the devil, and demons (however these realities are understood).

What can be agreed as a conviction of the Christian community is that there is a power of darkness and that it is a kind of supra-human power standing over against human beings. It therefore has an objective reality and is truly to be encountered, being more than a reality of the mind. It has no goodness inherent within it, but is wholly hostile to God and so to what is good, true, and beautiful. Whatever its nature, here the language of "agency" becomes inevitable. It tempts human beings towards disobedience, distorts their lives, and sometimes impinges upon them to the extent that they are held in bondage and are inwardly imprisoned to sins, addictions, deceptions and delusions. This is where we may think of the ministry of Jesus as an exorcist as he liberated people from evil influences that infested and oppressed them and against which they were powerless. The power of darkness, as we shall see, also distorts the structures of human society, bending them in the wrong directions and towards the wrong ends, so the holy struggle in which Christians are involved is not solely personal and individual but communal, corporate, and institutional: "For our struggle is not against enemies of blood and flesh, but against the rulers, against the authorities, against the cosmic powers of this present darkness, against the spiritual forces of evil in the heavenly places" (Eph 6:12).

The New Testament says little in the way of where these powers of darkness come from but is clear that they exist and they confront us. In John 1 it speaks of the light shining in the darkness and declares "the darkness did not overcome it" (v. 3); yet as to where the darkness came from in the first place the passage says nothing. In Colossians 1 we are told that in Christ "all things in heaven and earth were created, things visible and invisible, whether thrones or dominions or rulers or powers—all things have been created through him and for him" (v. 16). We are then told that through Christ, "God was pleased to reconcile to himself all things, whether on earth or in heaven" (v. 20). But as to how things came to be estranged from Christ and why they needed to be reconciled we are left uninformed, at least in this passage. After Christ himself was anointed with God's Spirit at his baptism we are told that he was led by the Spirit into the wilderness where he was tempted by the devil (Luke 4:1–2). But as to the devil's origin we are here left in ignorance. It seems that we are to come to terms with the realities of the powers of darkness without necessarily understanding how such powers have originated. And it is possible to do so.

EVIL AND COMPLEXITY

Traditionally, in Christian conviction, the three enemies of the soul are the world, the flesh, and the devil. Together these three unholy dimensions of a fallen world comprise a matrix of opposition and resistance to the coming of God's kingdom. They intermesh and interact and feed upon each other and in themselves explain how it is that the human situation cannot be resolved by human beings alone. It is too overwhelmingly complex. They also explain why it is that the Christian life is not easily lived since the disciple of Christ is pressured from all three directions.

The words "flesh" and "world" need to be understood carefully. On the great majority of occasions that the New Testament uses the word "flesh" it does so simply to refer to physical bodies as created by God. There is therefore no negative suggestion. If the eternal Word became flesh (John 1:14) then we can be assured that bodily existence as such is wholesome and good. But the word is also used to refer to our fallen condition in which we are enslaved to passions that control us: "For we know that the law is spiritual; but I am of the flesh, sold into slavery under sin. . . . For I know that nothing good dwells within me, that is, in my flesh" (Rom 7:14, 18). Our unruly physical passions pull us down and sometimes feel as though they are at war with the call to holiness (Rom 8:2–4). "Flesh" therefore comes to represent our personal vulnerability to temptation and sin, the parts of our life that are as yet unregenerate. In a similar way, the New Testament uses the word "world" ambiguously. On the one hand, it refers to the creation as made by God and as loved by God: "God so loved the world . . ." (John 3:16). On the other hand, it can refer to human society as it is organized in alienation from God and without love for God. In this sense Christians are warned against the world in case it enmeshes us within its own godless systems and draws us away from devotion to the true God in favor of humanly created idols: "Do not love the world or the things in the world. The love of the Father is not in those who love the world; for all that is in the world—the desire of the flesh, the desire of the eyes, the pride in riches—comes not from the Father but from the world" (1 John 2:15–16). Healthy Christian living includes the ability both to celebrate embodied, physical existence and the delights of nature and human achievement without giving way either to uncontrolled passion or to conformity to unrighteous values and practices. Yet every Christian will recognize the struggle that it is to stay true to the way of Christ when there are powerful gravitational pulls in the opposite direction (Rom 7:18–20). All of this is compounded if we also reckon with those supra-human forces that are identified through the term "the devil" and that mean "our struggle is not against enemies of flesh and blood" (Eph 6:12). Sometimes such powers feel overwhelming and anything but defeated.

The "principalities and powers" that are referred to in the New Testament require some explanation. In creating human beings God gave them the command to "fill the earth and subdue it; and have dominion" (Gen 1:28). As well as the obvious reproductive implications of these words and their implications for the stewardship of nature, they include what is sometimes called "the cultural mandate," the responsibility to develop artistically and culturally, to build communities, institutions, and civilizations. It stands to reason that human beings who have fallen from the divine communion and become inwardly corrupted will give rise to institutions and structures that are themselves fallen and corrupted. The "powers" are therefore both created (in that the potential for their creation was given to human beings by God—see Col 1:16) and fallen. It can also be conceived how those institutions and powers, as they increase in size and significance, will then come to dominate and control the very human beings who gave rise to them in the first place. It is wisely said that institutions can become more than the sum of their individual parts and assume a life of their own. People create things of which they then lose control. The powers become lord-less and lawless. Human beings thus become prisoners of the powers: the religions, governments, ideologies, institutions, business houses, corporations, multinationals, political parties, and other assorted entities that they themselves have established. 1 Corinthians 2:6–8 speaks of the "rulers of this age" that "crucified the Lord of glory," so we are entitled to see in the death of Christ how the powers of political, religious, and popular rule, represented respectively by the chief priests, Herod and Pontius Pilate, and the mob, played their part in conspiring against Jesus and doing away with him. In this we can also see the potential for evil that is contained in any of the powers that human beings create and their inclination away from, rather than towards, the living God. This does not render them irreducibly evil, but it does make them inherently unstable. They are necessary for human existence, since we could not flourish without them, but, as history clearly testifies, they always carry the risk that they might do more harm than good. Especially is this the case if there are indeed powers of darkness and spiritual emptiness that exercise their influence upon them and incline them to do wrong.

JESUS IS VICTOR!

It can be seen, therefore, how the world, the flesh, and the devil constitute a system that stands in need of being overcome and then redeemed. Christ is both the victor and the redeemer. He was the victor in that he lived free from the world, the flesh, and the devil. He was dominated and controlled by none of them. Moreover he did what was necessary in his life, death, and resurrection to enable others to enter into his freedom and share it with him. That he overcame the flesh and lived a life of communion with and devotion to the Father has already been claimed. Alone among human beings, Christ is to be seen as the one who, although he shared our nature in every respect, was without sin (Heb 4:15). Unlike Adam and Eve in the Garden, who stand for all human beings, when Jesus was tempted he did not capitulate but overcame (Luke 4:1–13). Jesus loved God with all his heart, soul, mind, and strength (Matt 22:34–40) and in so far as we live in communion and solidarity with him we too are able to love God sincerely and to triumph over the flesh. Jesus also said, "In the world you face persecution. But take courage! I have conquered the world!" (John 16:33). It is strange to consider death on the cross as a kind of victory, but this is what it was. Rather than collapse under the pressure of the world and conform to its demands, Jesus had resisted it and had completed his course of obedience to the Father (Phil 2:5–11). Neither the powers of the corrupted religious establishment, nor the intimidating might of Rome, nor the clamor of the mob were enough to dissuade him from taking the road to the cross. The victory he won was that of remaining fully himself and doing the Father's will, rather than giving in to the world's pressure. This victory was then revealed and proclaimed when God raised him from the dead and vindicated him.

It was the Father's will that Jesus should give himself on the cross as an atoning sacrifice for the sins of humanity. The cross was the place where atonement was made for the sins of the world and so it has become for us a place of liberation, liberation from sin and guilt and from the oppressive powers of darkness that hold us in their thrall only because our sins alienate us from God and render us vulnerable to their influence. Once our sins are borne away, we are set free; Satan can no longer accuse us nor the devil slander us: "He himself bore our sins in his body on the cross, so that, free from sins, we might live for righteousness; by his wounds you have been healed" (1 Pet 2:24). Because of this it can be said that the powers of darkness have been overcome and defeated at the cross and this defeat is then made manifest in the resurrection. "And when you were dead in trespasses and the uncircumcision of your flesh, God made you alive together with him, when he forgave us all our trespasses, erasing the record that stood against us with its legal demands. He set this aside, nailing it to the cross. He disarmed the rulers and authorities and made a public example of them, triumphing over them in it" (Col 2:13–15). "But thanks be to God, who in Christ always leads us in triumphal procession, and through us spreads in every place the fragrance that comes from knowing him" (2 Cor 2:14). Christ "has gone into heaven and is at the right hand of God, with angels, authorities, and powers made subject to him" (1 Pet 3:22).

When Christians wish to assert victory over the powers of darkness it is in and through Christ alone that they can do this. He is both the victim and the victor, the one who gave himself up to be abused and rejected in order that he might then absorb and remove the world's hostility against himself and against the Father in whose name he came. Having achieved this through his sufferings and then his death, he demonstrated that death could not hold him (Acts 2:24), and rose from the dead. Our hope is in Christ. Although evil has been *decisively* overcome, it remains true, and is evident all around us, that it has not yet been *finally* overcome. The parallel is sometimes drawn here between D-Day and VE-Day. In World War 2 D-Day was the event when the Allied forces landed in Normandy and won a foothold in Nazi occupied territory. It took almost a further year before Victory in Europe Day came and the war was finally won, a year of fierce and costly fighting. Yet the decisive victory on which everything else depended had already been won. The end was in sight and could be anticipated, even if it had not yet arrived. And so it is with Christ's victory on the cross. In principle, the powers of darkness have been overcome; their end is near, but the struggle is not yet ended and remains fierce.

The Christian community lives in the victory of Christ and by his Spirit shares in what he has accomplished. In communion with Christ and as we are held by the Spirit of God we are enabled to live holy lives, to begin to overcome the "flesh" that pulls us down. Although we live in the world and play our legitimate parts in its affairs, we also draw upon resources within the Christian community that enable us to resist the gravitational pull towards idols of human manufacture. The Christian community exists as a company of those who acknowledge the claim of the true God upon their lives and who therefore orientate themselves personally and communally towards God's will: "You turned to God from idols, to serve a living and true God, and to wait for his Son from heaven, whom he raised from the dead" (1 Thess 1:9–10). The Christian church is a community of resistance that deliberately fosters a style of life distinct from that advocated by the world, whilst at the same time it encourages its members to take their place within that world as faithful servants of God and good citizens (Rom 12:1–2; 13:1–7). Within its community life a distinctive spirituality is practiced, one that centers upon Jesus Christ, follows in his way and brings worship to the God who is Father, Son, and Spirit. This is a gravitational pull in the right direction, towards the one who is "the Father of lights, with whom there is no variation or shadow due to change" (Jas 1:17).

13

Future Hope
The Restoration of All Things

THERE ARE, ACCORDING TO 1 Corinthians 13:13, three great virtues: faith, hope, and love. Much has been said in preceding chapters about faith, which we have understood as reasonable and informed trust in God and in God's Son, Jesus Christ. The life of faith issues in love for God and love for others, and this is the key quality of the Christian life, reflecting the love of God for the world. Hope is a quality that in particular looks to the future and anticipates good things yet to come. Hope is profoundly important since it is the source of motivation for living. If there is nothing to hope for, there is nothing to live for, and life is reduced to drudgery or even despair. Hope is therefore full of health-giving and joyful possibilities and gives meaning to both faith and love. It is a Christian conviction that because there is a God who is faithful to creation, there is everything to hope for in this world: "For surely I know the plans I have for you, says the Lord, plans for your welfare and not for harm, to give you a future with hope" (Jer 29:11).

HOPE FOR THE COSMOS

Hope may be thought of in two dimensions, the hope we have for individuals and the hope we have for the whole cosmos. This chapter deals with hope for the cosmos and the next chapter with hope for persons. Christian hope is as broad as creation, since it stands to reason that if God has created the world then God has a purpose for it that will not be deflected even despite human rebellion. Although Christian hope includes the hope of heaven (to be explored in the next chapter), it is a much reduced understanding of the Christian Scriptures that imagines salvation to be solely about souls "going to heaven." This is a phrase that as such rarely if ever occurs in the Bible, not because the hope is not there, but because it is included in a much broader understanding of what salvation involves. The sense that history is going somewhere, heading towards a final goal, and not just going round in circles, is fundamental to the whole biblical narrative. We may imagine this sense of a final goal emerged from the nomadic lifestyle that has shaped the early stages of the biblical story. Abraham and the first recipients of the knowledge of the LORD were nomads whose life consisted in pursuing the horizon. This same experience was bequeathed to the early Israelites as they migrated from Egypt into the land of Canaan. There was a horizon to be pursued, and when this was reached there was another horizon that awaited them. So there developed the sense that history itself was moving towards a final horizon where God was awaiting them. God was in the future as surely as God was in the present. This was the idea of the kingdom of God, a future reality of life in the divine presence when all things would be restored and everything would take its rightful place. Isaiah could speak of it in these terms:

> In days to come the mountain of the LORD's house shall be established as the highest of the mountains and shall be raised above the hills; all the nations shall stream to it. Many people shall come and say, "Come, let us go up to the mountain of the LORD, to the house of the God of Jacob; that he may teach us his ways and that we may walk in his paths." For out of Zion shall go forth instruction, and the word of the LORD from Jerusalem. He shall judge between the nations, and shall arbitrate for many peoples; they shall beat their swords into ploughshares, and their spears into pruning hooks; nation shall not lift up sword against nation, neither shall they learn war any more.
> (Isa 2:2–4)

Other visions are cast in order to anticipate the coming days of peace. In another place, Isaiah declares that "The wolf shall live with the lamb, the leopard shall lie down with the kid, the calf and the lion and the fatling together, and a little child shall lead them.... They will not hurt or destroy on all my holy mountain; for the earth will be full of the knowledge of the LORD as the waters cover the sea" (11:6–9). For Zechariah, "On that day living waters shall flow out of Jerusalem, half of them to the eastern sea and half of them to the western sea; it shall continue in summer as in winter. And the

Lord will become king over all the earth; on that day the Lord will be one and his name one" (14:8–9). The vision of a peaceful and blessed future is carried over into the New Testament, so that according to Jesus, "I tell you, many will come from east and west and will eat with Abraham and Isaac and Jacob in the kingdom of heaven" (Matt 8:11), and in the book of Revelation, "See, the home of God is among mortals. He will dwell with them; they will be his peoples, and God himself will be with them; he will wipe away every tear from their eyes. Death will be no more; mourning and crying and pain will be no more, for the first things have passed away" (21:3–4).

Such powerful visions draw the imagination towards a future that will be unlike the present in that the sorrows and sins of the present age will be taken away and peace and blessedness will prevail. This is not the future that we can calculate by projecting forward today's statistics into tomorrow's world, but the future we can imagine on the basis of the promises of God. Such a day is seen not as a human achievement but as a divine gift, an age that God will bring to pass out of undeserved divine goodness and faithfulness. It is a much richer picture than the idea of "going to heaven" since it is communal (we share in this with others) and it involves the wider creation, which, far from being abandoned as worthless, shares in the newness of life that is envisaged. The future gives hope for the present. The Christian hope for the future is therefore not one that is restricted to personal survival beyond death but one which embraces all things.

THE USE OF IMAGERY

Important things need to be said at this point about the use of imagination. It has sadly been the case that some Christians, when speaking of the "last things" or the "end of the world," have done so in terms that are both disturbing and frightening. The future is imagined as a doomsday scenario in which things fall apart, are burned up and disintegrate, and untold disasters abound. Those who are among the saved are rescued from the catastrophe that engulfs the creation as "a brand plucked from the fire" (Zech 3:2). A certain kind of preaching has majored on describing the disasters that are about to fall upon the earth before making the appeal for people to "save yourselves from this corrupt generation" (Acts 2:40); and it is true that such preaching is well able to appeal to the Scriptures for support. It can be said then that there are two strands of thought running through the Bible when it comes to thinking of the future of the planet. One strand appears to predict the destruction of all things while the other offers a more optimistic expectation of the renewal of heaven and earth.

Before attempting to reconcile these two strands it is worth investigating each further. The first strand is represented in the New Testament in a number of ways. When predicting the coming of the Messiah, John the Baptist warned the people, "His winnowing fork is in his hand, to clear his threshing-floor and to gather the wheat into his granary, but the chaff he will burn with unquenchable fire" (Luke 3:17). When the apostle Peter preached on the Day of Pentecost, he quoted from the prophet Joel in saying, "And I will show portents in the heavens above and signs on the earth below, blood, and fire, and smoky mist. The sun shall be turned to darkness and the moon to blood, before the coming of the Lord's great and glorious day. Then everyone who calls on the name of the Lord shall be saved" (Acts 2:19-21, citing Joel 2:30-32). Second Peter is particularly striking: "But the day of the Lord will come like a thief, and then the heavens will pass away with a loud noise, and the elements will be dissolved with fire, and the earth and everything that is done on it will be dissolved. Since all these things are to be dissolved in this way, what sort of people ought you to be in leading lives of holiness and godliness, waiting for and hastening the coming of the day of God, because of which the heavens will be set ablaze and dissolved, and the elements will melt with fire?" (3:10-12). These verses reflect a kind of literature that is known as "apocalyptic" and that is fully represented in the Hebrew Scriptures by the book of Daniel and in the New Testament by the book of Revelation. It is in the nature of apocalyptic to use dramatic and heightened language to depict events in ways that could be said to be akin to the contemporary genres of science fiction or even, amazingly, horror. It is not surprising that many find these books difficult to interpret. Nor is it a surprise that they have suggested imagery to others of the most dramatic and disturbing kind when it comes to imagining the "end of the world." The fact is that the language is meant to be disturbing, forewarning people of earth-shattering events that are likely to befall them. Over the years modern voices have attempted to awaken people to impending threats by creating their own forms of secular apocalyptic in predicting nuclear war, global famine, race war, a new ice age, pestilence, and global warming, and who is to say that the threats have not been or are not real? However, this first strand of biblical testimony suggests that the world as we know it is going to perish, being dissolved by fire, with only those who "call on the name of the Lord" being saved out of it.

The second strand of testimony suggests rather that creation will itself participate in God's work of salvation and renewal. This is "the time of universal restoration that God announced long ago through his holy prophets" (Acts 3:21), and refers back to the scriptural passages cited at the beginning of this chapter. Creation comes from God, belongs to God, exists for

God, and will share at the last in God's work of re-creation. So, Colossians 1:15–20 can claim "in [Christ] all things in heaven and earth were created, things visible and invisible... all things have been created through him and for him" (v. 16) and also, "and through him God was pleased to reconcile to himself all things, whether on earth or in heaven, by making peace through the blood of his cross" (v. 20). What has been created will be reconciled. "All things" appears to leave nothing out and to be universal in its embrace. Romans 8:19–25 is even more explicit: "For the creation waits with eager longing for the revealing of the children of God; for the creation was subjected to futility, not of its own will, but by the will of the one who subjected it, in hope that the creation itself will be set free from its bondage to decay and will obtain the freedom of the glory of the children of God." The remainder of this passage likens the creation to a woman in the pains of childbirth, ready to give birth to a new creation. Even the passage from 2 Peter that speaks of the dissolution of the creation goes on immediately to claim, "But in accordance with his promise, we wait for new heavens and a new earth, where righteousness is at home" (v. 13). The question here is whether this is a brand new creation that replaces the old or whether it is a renewed creation that takes everything that belongs to the old and makes it into a new creation that captures all that is good in the old and loses nothing. The same vision is reiterated in Revelation 21:1; "Then I saw a new heaven and a new earth; for the first heaven and the first earth had passed away, and the sea was no more." For the Jews of the first century the sea was regarded as a symbol of all that was chaotic and unruly, a remnant of the chaos out of which creation was formed. The new heaven and the new earth contain no evil or chaotic element, for everything is illuminated by the presence of God. What passes away is the sorrow and sadness that belongs to the first creation so that the new creation can be a place of peace and blessedness. It is not therefore a case of God making *all new things*, but of God making *all things new*. The creation itself becomes the dwelling-place of God and therefore is transformed. What passes away is the form of the old creation and the evil that was in it. In the vision of the holy city portrayed in Revelation, the city is in the shape of a cube (21:16), as was the holy of holies in the ancient temple (1 Kgs 6:20). God's presence is immediate throughout the whole of the new creation. Yet the fact that "the kings of the earth will bring their glory into it" (21:24) and that, "People will bring into it the glory and honor of the nations" (21:26) suggests that all that is good, true, and beautiful in the old creation finds its place in the new.

We are able to reconcile the two strands of testimony by affirming that the first indicates how the old creation will pass through judgment, being cleansed and purged of evil and of every distortion of God's good creation.

This is what the language of fire and destruction refers to. But on the other side of judgment there lies restoration, the renewal of all things in the new creation of God. The present creation is not to be treated as though it were insignificant and disposable, but rather respected and honored as a world that has been made through Christ and for Christ (Col 1:16) and that has a future in him, "a plan for the fullness of time, to gather up all things in him, things in heaven and things on earth" (Eph 1:10). It is within this positive and affirming context that we are to imagine the world's end.

REALIZING THE "END"

The language of "end" is ambiguous and of considerable significance. It can signify both a full-stop and cessation, as we might use the word at the end of a book or television program. By it we might mean "it is finished and there is no more." In this sense, it is doubtful whether anybody would look forward to "the end of the world." Or, it might signify a purpose and a goal, as we might mean when we say, "The chief end and duty of humanity is to love God and enjoy him forever." In this sense, the word does not imply a finish but rather a goal and a purpose that gives meaning to our lives. Seen in this way the implication is that of fulfillment, fullness, completing the intended goal of our existence and this is, surely, greatly to be hoped for and anticipated. It must be the case that the world in its present form will one day come to its end (in the first sense); but if this is only to be superseded by the fulfillment of its goal (in the second sense) then this is no loss, but only gain, especially if the new creation takes up into itself all that is good in the first. "Waiting for and hastening the coming of the day of the Lord" (2 Pet 3:12) makes full sense when understood in this way. We want this end to come.

A similar ambiguity is contained in the word "ultimate," which also has to do both with that which comes last and that which truly lasts. This word also suggests that which is of ultimate or final importance, that which is truly significant. Therefore, when the Bible speaks of the last things or the end of the world, its concern is not only, nor even primarily, chronological, focused on issues of *when* things are likely to happen. Rather, it is concerned with those things that are really important, the things that ultimately matter. It is clear that the first disciples were somewhat taken up with questions of when, but Jesus consistently steered them away from this preoccupation: "So when they had come together, they asked him, 'Lord, is this the time when you will restore the kingdom to Israel?' He replied, 'It is not for you to know the times or periods that the Father has set by his own authority. But you will receive power when the Holy Spirit has come upon you; and you will be my witnesses in Jerusalem, in all Judea and Samaria, and to the ends of the earth'" (Acts 1:6–8). Speculative curiosity is not what we are about. Living our best, and redeeming the time in the light of those ultimate truths that we believe, is.

If Christ is the key to all the mysteries of life and creation then he must also be the key to how we think of the end. Put bluntly, *he is the End*. When we are confronted with Jesus, we are confronted with what is ultimate. In the New Testament God's own self is described as the beginning and the end: "And the one who was seated on the throne said . . . 'It is done! I am the Alpha and the Omega, the beginning and the end'" (Rev 21:5–6). Strikingly, and in the very next chapter, the same language is also applied to Christ, the Son of God: "See, I am coming soon; my reward is with me, to repay according to everyone's work. I am the Alpha and the Omega, the first and the last, the beginning and the end" (Rev 22:12–13). Christ, as God incarnate, is the one through whom the worlds were created and he is the one through whom they will come to their destined end. It was through him and for him that all things have come into being and will in the future be reconciled to God. If then we are to understand what is meant by the "end of the world," it is through Christ alone that this should be attempted. Whatever the Scriptures have to say about the end will only finally be understood if we interpret them through Christ; indeed, given the strange ways the Bible has been interpreted, it would be dangerous to understand them in any other way than through Christ himself.

If creation has a goal and a purpose, then it is Christ who has first of all realized that purpose for us and on our behalf. Creation and humanity within it exist for God, to bring glory to God and to enjoy the benefits of God's health-giving life. The goal of creation is that all creatures, according to their kind and capacity, should learn to love God and build together a peaceful and harmonious communion of creation that lives to God's praise. It is clear that at the present time this is far from being the case. The wolf does not lie down with the lamb. The place of human beings within the divine purpose is pivotal and decisive for the whole, and in so far as they turn away from their divine vocation, they suppress the creation and subject it to the futility of not achieving its goal (Rom 8:20). Yet there is one human being in whom the goal of creation has been achieved, and this is Jesus Christ, the Son of God. Christ has entered into our world to take up the challenge that the rest of us have shirked or refused. In him the end has come in the sense that the goal of creation and of a truly human life has been accomplished. Psalm 8 asks the question, "What are human beings that you are mindful of them, mortals that you care for them. You have made them a little lower than God; and crowned them with glory and honor. You have given them dominion over the work of your hands; you have put all things under their feet" (vv. 4-6). In citing this passage, the book of Hebrews goes on to say, "As it is we do not yet see everything in subjection to them, but we do see Jesus, who for a little while was made lower than the angels, now crowned with glory and honor because of the suffering of death, so that by the grace of God he might taste death for everyone" (Heb 2:8-9). In other words, the promise that human beings have failed to fulfill has been realized in Christ, who has participated in suffering and death to redeem us from it. He has shown full obedience to God's will, even though it entailed suffering as a consequence. He has lived the life of love for God with all his heart, soul, mind, and strength. His is the life of ultimate value and significance, for in him is revealed the purpose of God for all creation. In Jesus we are confronted with the end and purpose of the world made manifest, with the ultimate. It is no surprise therefore that the New Testament describes all the time after Jesus as "the last days." "In these last days he has spoken to us by a Son, whom he appointed heir of all things" (Heb 1:2); "He was destined before the salvation of the world, but was revealed at the end of the ages for your sake" (1 Pet 1:20); "Children, it is the last hour!" (1 John 2:18). Chronologically, two thousand years have passed since these words were penned, but *theologically* any time after Christ is the last days.

Christ has realized the end and goal *for* us. And now Christ, risen and ascended, is realizing the end and goal *in* us. "Consequently he is able for all time to save those who approach God through him since he always lives to make intercession for them" (Heb 7:25); "It is Christ Jesus, who died, yes, who was raised, who is at the right hand of God, who indeed intercedes for us" (Rom 8:34). After his ascension Christ did not relinquish his human nature in order to return to his pre-incarnate condition as the eternal Word. Having joined himself to a human identity, he did so for all time and eternity. As such, he "always lives" in the presence of the Father as a human being, a standing reminder of what human beings may now become in him and through him. He does not make intercession with the Father as though the Father still needs to be persuaded that human beings are worth redeeming—it is from the Father that Christ has come in the first place and God's purpose is immovable. Rather, Christ's very presence with the Father as a human being wholly orientated towards the Father is itself the assurance that he is the first-fruits of a new creation and will be followed by many brothers and sisters. The goal that Christ achieved is now being achieved in those who look to him in faith: "For those whom he foreknew he also predestined to be conformed to the image of his Son, in order that he might be the firstborn within a large family" (Rom 8:29). The image of God that we see in its restored form in Jesus is now being reproduced by the Spirit of Jesus in the community of his followers, which is itself ever expanding into a large family with many brothers and sisters. Within the community of faith, therefore, the end is being realized as those who believe are gathered into relationship with God and begin to be conformed to the image of Christ. In this sense, it is rightly said that we belong to those "on whom the ends of the ages have come" (1 Cor 10:11) and that we have tasted "the powers of the age to come" (Heb 6:5). The ultimate goal of communion with God and acceptance of God's reign is being realized in the Christian community. The kingdom of God to which we look forward as the climax of the ages is both present and still to come, and is being anticipated and realized within the community of faith: "But if it is by the Spirit of God that I cast out demons then the kingdom of God has come to you" (Matt 12:28); "Once Jesus was asked by the Pharisees when the kingdom of God was coming, and he answered, 'The kingdom of God is not coming with things that can be observed; nor will they say, "Look, here it is!" or "There it is!" For in fact the kingdom of God is among (or within) you'" (Luke 17:20–21). The kingdom or reign of God signifies the final fulfillment on earth of the divine presence and purpose, and although the full expression of this awaits the climax of the ages, the reality of it can be known now by those who hold the faith within the community of the faith. The church, therefore, is the community of the end-times, the first-fruits of the coming kingdom, the manifestation in the here and now of a future that is to come, God's *avant-garde.*

Christ has realized the end *for* us. Christ is now realizing the end *in* us. And Christ is realizing the end *with* us. Christians are now fellow-workers with Christ in bringing God's kingdom to pass: "For we are God's servant working together; you are God's field, God's building" (1 Cor 3:9). It remains true that the coming of the kingdom is entirely God's gift, but God has chosen to use human beings in its service. Specifically, Christ has commissioned the disciples of Christ to "make disciples of all nations, baptizing them in the name of the Father and of the Son and of the Holy Spirit, and teaching them to obey everything that I have commanded you" (Matt 28:19–20). In this way the Christian community works for and with God to extend God's reign and to work towards the final goal of human history. It is God alone who makes things grow, but the planting and the watering is work that is entrusted to us (1 Cor 3:6–7). It seems that by our responsiveness we are able not only to wait for the coming day of consummation, but even to hasten it (2 Pet 3:12). In this age there is a priority: "And the gospel must first be proclaimed to all nations" (Mark 13:10).

THE CHURCH AS WITNESS

Bearing witness to Christ and making the good news of Christ accessible to all peoples is the priority of the church in its service of Christ. From the beginning, the church has had a sense of urgency in fulfilling this task. It has believed that the coming of Christ is soon: "See, I am coming soon; my reward us with me, to repay according to everyone's work" (Rev 22:12). Jesus said, "But truly I tell you, there are some standing here who will not taste death before they see the kingdom of God" (Luke 9:27), and his words have caused puzzlement, given that the generation to which he spoke has long since "tasted death" and the kingdom has apparently yet to come. These words are easier to understand if we grasp that there are a number of ways in which Christ and the kingdom can be said to have "come." Christ returned to his disciples in the resurrection and he came to them again in the Spirit on the day of Pentecost. The word translated in the New Testament as "coming" in fact means "presence" (*parousia*) and in both the resurrection and the coming of the Spirit at Pentecost Christ can be said to have been present with his followers. In this sense, most of those who heard him speak would have been around to witness the coming of the Spirit. And yet there is a further presence to be awaited, the final coming of Christ to bring history to its ultimate goal. When Jesus ascended to heaven the watching disciples were told, "Men of Galilee, why do you stand looking up towards heaven? This Jesus, who has been taken up from you into heaven, will come in the same way as you saw him go into heaven" (Acts 1:11). This theme is followed in the book of Hebrews: "So Christ, having been offered once to bear the sins of many, will appear a second time, not to deal with sin, but to save those who are eagerly waiting for him" (9:28). Christ, therefore, is the Messiah who appears twice: his first coming was as the suffering servant spoken of in Isaiah 53 who made "his life an offering for sin" (53:10). This coming was in weakness and frailty, in humility and obscurity. Christ came incognito as one "despised and rejected by others; a man of suffering and acquainted with infirmity" (53:3). By contrast, his second coming will be unmistakable, glorious, and universally significant: "For as the lightning flashes and lights up the sky from one side to the other, so will the Son of Man be in his day" (Luke 17:24); "So at the name of Jesus every knee should bend, in heaven and earth and under the earth, and every tongue should confess that Jesus Christ is Lord, to the glory of God the Father" (Phil 2:10–11).

Christ's second coming will be as "King of kings and Lord of lords" (Rev 19:16). A huge contrast exists between Christ's first and second comings, the first in humiliation, the second in exaltation and vindication. Yet we find it hard to imagine Christ's coming in glory in anything other than pictures. Because the kingdom that is yet to come surpasses our powers of description we draw upon imaginative ideas in order to conceive of it. Once more we encounter here the literary form known as "apocalyptic." To make a comparison, the way the New Testament describes Christ's coming has more the character of an impressionist painting than a television documentary. As Jesus warned against trying to predict the time of the end (Acts 1:7), a warning that has been widely ignored by his followers, we do well not to try to join these pictures together as though they were some kind of jigsaw puzzle, but to savor them and their significance as powerful imagery. As an example, 1 Thessalonians 4:16–18 reads:

> For the Lord himself, with a cry of command, with the archangel's call and with the sound of God's trumpet, will descend from heaven, and the dead in Christ will rise first. Then we who are alive, who are left, will be caught up in the clouds together with them to meet the Lord in the air; and so we shall be with the Lord forever. Therefore, encourage one another with these words.

This imagery is drawn from the practices of imperial Rome. When a Roman general returned from making foreign conquests, he would bring his victorious armies along with his captives in a triumphal procession along the Appian Way into Rome. The leading members of the city would go out of the city to meet him and to acclaim him as he made his entry. They would do this as a sign of the honor that was due to him. In similar ways, when Christ returns, those who belong to him will greet him as the victorious and worthy Son of God who comes with power and glory (symbolized by the clouds, which in Scripture are consistently a symbol of the power and presence of God). We should remember that according to Daniel 7, the coming of the Son of Man is not only a coming to earth but also a coming to God to receive "glory and dominion and kingship, that all peoples, nations and languages should serve him" (7:13–14). Similar imagery is employed in 2 Corinthians 2:14: "But thanks be to God, who in Christ always leads us in triumphal procession." The visionary language makes the point.

To summarize: the second coming of Christ will be universally recognized and unmistakable. Christ will not come incognito but to be known for who he truly is. His coming will be visible, personal and bodily. We shall see him as he is. We have yet to discover how and when it will happen, but we do understand its significance as the goal of history and the point when earth's distortions and corruptions will be resolved.

THE "MILLENNIUM" AND ISRAEL

This section ends with brief discussions around two topics that have caused intense debate: the "millennium" and the people of Israel. In Revelation 20 there is a reference to the millennium, a period of a thousand years in which Christ will reign on earth. As the book of Revelation is highly symbolic, there is disagreement as to whether the millennium should be interpreted as an actual period of time, or whether it is a non-literal way of speaking either of Christ's present reign over history, of a period of universal spiritual prosperity to be brought about by the preaching of the gospel, or an actual period of messianic rule after the coming of Christ. At the very least it is a symbol of the final supremacy of Christ over all the powers of darkness and of the vindication of those who have given their lives for him (v. 4). The millennium is a symbol of hope for the future of creation and of human history, that all will finally be well. Our greatest hope is that the one who will come in glory and with great power in order to rule without rival remains exactly the same one who once came in humility, washed the feet of his disciples, and gave his life for many. To see it as symbolic does not deny that there will be a future time when history will be reclaimed for God.

The New Testament is clear that although the people of Israel "stumbled," in that the majority of the people did not embrace the Jesus movement (although all the earliest members of the church were Jewish as were nearly all the New Testament's authors), God's ways and purposes for the people of Israel are not yet at an end. On the one hand, it is quite clear that there is a new covenant that grows out of the old and which supersedes it in its universal reach. This is the thrust of the book of Hebrews and is summed up in the words, "In speaking of a 'new covenant,' (God) has made the first one obsolete. And what is obsolete and growing old will soon disappear" (Heb 8:13). On the other hand, it would be entirely wrong to interpret these words to mean that God has no longer a place and a purpose for the Jewish people. The survival of the Jewish people against all the odds over two thousand years is itself remarkable to the point of miraculous, and some would say it is evidence for the persistence, or even the existence, of God. The apostle Paul made it clear: "I ask then, has God rejected his people? By no means!" (Rom 11:1). He goes on that, although Israel has stumbled, even this stumbling has been used by God as the opportunity to bring the benefit of the gospel to the gentiles (11:12). God's gifts and callings are irrevocable (11:29) and, for this reason, because of God's faithfulness to God's own purpose, in time "all Israel will be saved" (11:26) by being included as a whole within the new covenant. Yet even this needs to be understood correctly. Although there is a rich covenantal history behind them to which

God remains faithful, it is not that the Jewish people have a standing before God that is not now shared with all the other nations. Israel will be included in God's future generosity and blessings because all the nations are now so included and Israel is not to be excluded. "And the leaves of the trees are for the healing of the nations" (Rev 22:2). The good news of Jesus Christ is truly universal and inclusive of all nations and peoples.

14

Future Hope
Heaven and Hell, Death and Judgment

THE DESTINY OF PERSONS needs to be understood within the broader hope for creation, spoken of in the last chapter, and traditionally touches on the four topics of heaven and hell, death and judgment.

HEAVEN

It is commonly conceived that on death we either go to heaven or to hell. This understanding is thought to be reinforced by Jesus' parable of the rich man and Lazarus (Luke 16:19–31). Here Lazarus and the rich man have their fates reversed in the life that is to come, Lazarus being by Abraham's side in paradise and the rich man in torment. This is contrary to what might have been expected, in that the rich man's wealth in life would have been taken as a sign of divine favor and Lazarus' poverty the opposite. Beyond death their true status is revealed, and it is not in the rich man's favor. Their destinies are apparently now fixed. Abraham says: "Between you and us a great chasm has been fixed, so that those who might want to pass from here to you cannot do so, and no one can cross from there to us" (v. 26). Before drawing conclusions, however, some caution needs to be exercised. Not for the first time, in fashioning his parables Jesus is here using a relatively well-known story that would have been told in various ways in his day. As he tells it, he gives it a distinct twist, and the "twist" is what we should consider the meaning of the story. In fact, the parable could be re-titled the "Parable of the Five Brothers," since the rich man had five brothers still alive. Each week in synagogue they listened to "Moses and the prophets" (v. 29) and if they were to do what they there learnt, including fulfilling their responsibilities to the poor, widows, and orphans, whom the rich man so selfishly ignored, they would have no fear about coming into judgment. Or so Abraham says (v. 29). The main point of the story is that when we hear the word of God we should respond to it in repentance and faith and not delay our response, for the issues at stake are serious. The incidental details of the story are not meant to give us information about the life to come; rather, they belong to the texture of the story and, apart from the main points Jesus is making, we should hesitate to derive too many conclusions from them.

Our understanding has been clouded in that older translations of the New Testament, and some newer ones, render the Greek word "Hades" as "hell." Yet the Greek of the New Testament distinguishes between Hades, which is the realm of the dead, and Gehenna, which is the place of final punishment and destruction. The dead wait for the final judgment in Hades, and after the final judgment are either made participants in the new heaven and the new earth or consigned to condemnation in Gehenna, or hell proper. Once more, we have to acknowledge the figurative nature of the language that describes realities of which we have no direct knowledge; but that the language is figurative does not mean that the realities to which it refers are anything less than completely real. In fact, the ways in which the language and imagery referring to the life to come have developed is of particular interest.

In the history and religion of Israel there was no developed doctrine of an "afterlife." The claim sometimes made that religion offers "pie in the sky when you die" in order to offset the sufferings of the present age could not be less true of Hebrew religion. The hope of a long life, a posterity, and a peaceful and prosperous end was for many years the sum total of the Hebrew hope. On death, the human spirit could expect to descend to a shadowy existence in Sheol, or the "Pit," a "hollow place" that represented the state of death in visible terms and was not a place of blessedness: "You have put me in the depths of the Pit, in the regions dark and deep" (Ps 88:6). A more positive view of a life to come emerged only gradually, and when it did so it was out of the realization that since justice could not be delivered in this life, there must be an extension to this life in which justice could by God's power prevail. This emerged clearly in the book of Daniel, when contemplating the martyrdom of many faithful Jews under the persecution of Antiochus Epiphanes in the second century BC. At the last they would be vindicated by being raised from the dead: "Many of those who sleep in the dust of the earth shall awake, some to everlasting life, and some to shame and everlasting contempt. Those who are wise shall shine like the brightness of the sky, and those who lead many to righteousness like the stars for ever and ever" (12:2–3). Even so, not all Jewish groups believed (or believe) in the general resurrection, such as the Sadducees (Matt 22:23–28), because it was not explicitly taught in the Torah, the first five and most sacred books of the Hebrew Bible.

By contrast, the Christian hope is firmly in the resurrection of the body at the end of the age, and in this Christians follow the line that was developing in the later stages of biblical history. The belief was rooted in the conviction that human existence is bodily existence. God has breathed life into bodies (Gen 2:7). It is as bodies that human beings develop and discover their identity. Although there are some references to "body, soul, and spirit" (e.g., 1 Thess 5:23), these are not intended to be separated compartments, but different perspectives on the one, whole human identity in its physical, emotional, and spiritual existence. We have an inner life and an outer life and are "ensouled" bodies or embodied souls. Jewish thinkers divided time into the present age and the age to come, and this perspective passed into Christianity. In this age we die, but we die to be resurrected in the age to come, and resurrection implies (for the redeemed) the full restoration of our personal identity in transformed and glorified bodies. The resurrection of Jesus is here the pattern of our own resurrection. Jesus' body was raised from death in ways that showed both continuity and discontinuity: his body bore the marks of his suffering and the wounds in his hands, feet, and side remained visible (John 20:26–29). Yet he was not limited by time and space. He was recognizable and yet could appear and disappear (Luke 24:30–31). He could pass through locked doors (John 20:19) and could eat and drink with his disciples (Acts 10:39–41). Jesus was raised immortal, death having been defeated, and so shall we be: "If the Spirit of him who raised Jesus from the dead dwells in you, he who raised Christ from the dead will give life to your mortal bodies also through his Spirit that dwells in you" (Rom 8:11, see also 1 Cor 15:12–28). The Christian hope then is for more than "going to heaven." It is for the transformation of our identities as human persons in God's new work of creation, and all of this within the transformed context of the new heaven and new earth in which righteousness dwells.

The question does, however, remain: short of the second coming and the resurrection, what happens to those who die in Christ? Although our bodies die, do our identities perish? In one sense, we need to affirm at this point that death is death and we should not pretend otherwise. Death is the cessation of earthly life and needs to be accepted as such. And yet God is stronger than death and is able to keep us in, through, and beyond death. God neither forgets nor lets go of us. Death itself is a mystery, but for the

Christian it is a safe mystery. Although death is rightly called "the last enemy" (1 Cor 15:26), it is an enemy that has been subjugated and overcome. Its sting has been drawn: "When this perishable body puts on imperishability, and this mortal body puts on immortality, then the saying that is written will be fulfilled: 'Death has been swallowed up in victory.' 'Where, O death is your victory? Where O death, is your sting?' The sting of death is sin, and the power of sin is the law. But thanks be to God, who gives us the victory through our Lord Jesus Christ" (1 Cor 15:54–57).

The simplest way to characterize the so-called "intermediate state" between our death and the final resurrection is to say with the apostle Paul, "Yes, we do have confidence, and we would rather be away from the body and at home with the Lord" (2 Cor 5:8). Those who die in Christ go to be with Christ, and Christ is with the Father. This is perhaps as much as we properly need to know. However, questions do arise as to the nature of this intermediate state. Is it a conscious condition or is it more like peaceful sleeping, waiting for the day when we shall awake? (Dan 12:2). Scripture certainly speaks of "those who have fallen asleep" (1 Cor 15:6 margin; 1 Thess 4:14 margin), but this may be speaking from the human perspective—death looks like sleep. In other places there are suggestions of a conscious existence in the presence of God: "But you have come to Mount Zion and to the city of the living God, the heavenly Jerusalem, and to innumerable angels in festal gathering, and to the assembly of the firstborn who are enrolled in heaven, and to God the judge of all, and to the spirits of the righteous made perfect" (Heb 12:22–23). Most significantly, there are the words of Jesus to the dying thief on the cross, "Truly I tell you, today you will be with me in Paradise" (Luke 23:43). Although Hades is the realm of the dead, some at the time of Jesus began to differentiate it into two realms, the abode of the blessed which was called "Paradise," and that of the lost and alienated. Jesus seems to accept this idea. This is where the idea of "going to heaven" has its justification. But it should be noted that this is still an interim condition pending the last judgment, and that for all its blessedness it was still understood as incomplete precisely because it was existence without a body, and human beings are intended to be embodied creatures.

The apostle Paul referred to this future embodied existence in this way: "For while we are still in this tent [i.e. body], we groan under our burden, because we wish not to be unclothed but to be further clothed, so that what is mortal may be swallowed up by life" (2 Cor 5:4). Since this may be difficult to understand, he argues elsewhere that the body we are given by God is appropriate to the age in which we live, either this age or that which is to come: "So it is with the resurrection of the dead. What is sown is perishable, what is raised is imperishable. It is sown in dishonor, it is raised in glory. It is sown in weakness, it is raised in power. It is sown a physical body, it is raised a spiritual body. If there is a physical body, there is also a spiritual body" (1 Cor 15:42–44). The idea of a "spiritual body" may seem paradoxical, but if we take the resurrected body of Jesus as our pattern we are led to think of a glorified body that is not restricted by earthly limitations but can still have form and tangibility. This expansive, full-bodied existence is how we should imagine the future God has for us.

HELL

If the resurrection of the body and existence in the new heaven and new earth are the positive Christian hope, what are we to say about the opposite, the fate of the lost? We have already seen the distinction between Hades, the realm of the dead, and Gehenna, the place of final punishment and destruction. Again, it is as well to remember that these are symbols and images of spiritual realities of which as yet we have no direct experience, but that does not mean we can discard the images or the realities they represent. Jesus had a surprising amount to say about final judgment and was quite blunt in his language about its outcome: "And these will go away into eternal punishment, but the righteous into eternal life" (Matt 25:46); "And if your right hand causes you to sin, cut it off and throw it away; it is better for you to lose one of your members than for your whole body to go to hell [Gehenna]" (Matt 5:30); "I tell you, many will come from east and west and will eat with Abraham and Isaac and Jacob in the kingdom of heaven, while the heirs of the kingdom (that is, those who were supposed to have received the kingdom) will be thrown into the outer darkness, where there will be weeping and gnashing of teeth" (Matt 8:11–12—the phrase "weeping and gnashing of teeth" is recorded six times in the teaching of Jesus). Jesus taught the love, mercy, and compassion of God, but did not shrink from setting out the implications of the just wrath of God against those who do evil. He saw no incompatibility between these ideas. He confronted the people of his day with the reality of divine judgment, both in this age and the age to come (Matt 11:20–24). He foresaw the coming judgment on Jerusalem and wept as he did so (Luke 19:41–44; Matt 23:37–39). As Jesus foresaw and predicted, Jerusalem was destroyed by Roman legions (in AD 70); he saw this as a consequence of the city's rejection of himself and his message. For Jesus, divine judgment was a reality.

The word Gehenna in the New Testament is found exclusively on the lips of Jesus. It referred, in the first instance, to the Valley of Hinnom, or Tophet, to the southwest of Jerusalem and outside its walls. It was the rubbish dump for the city and was filled with the smell of putrefying flesh. It had once been the location for child sacrifice by King Ahaz who, "made his sons pass through the fire, according to the abominable practices of the nations whom the Lord drove out before the people of Israel" (2 Chr 28:3; 33:6). Gehenna contained among other noxious things the burning and rotting corpses of stillborn children, executed convicts, and suicides, all on public display. It was a place of horror. In Mark 9:47–48, having previously warned his hearers three times of the danger of being thrown into Gehenna, Jesus cites Isaiah 66:24 to the effect that in Gehenna "their worm never dies, and the fire is never quenched." In other words, the maggots of the town tip and its attendant and perpetual burning of rubbish were symbolic of an eternal rubbish tip, one which belongs to the "age to come," to which the enemies of God will be consigned in the final judgment. There is an eternal place of judgment and disintegration corresponding and like to the Hinnom valley, and it is a place of rejection and exclusion, of "outer darkness," because it is removed from the light of God's presence. This is a truly terrifying image, and so it is intended to be, because the fate of which it speaks is one that is to be avoided, that of losing God and the blessings of knowing God.

No one goes to hell accidentally. If it is true in this life that God can say, "Have I any pleasure in the death of the wicked, says the Lord God, and not rather that they should turn from their ways and live?" (Ezek 18:23), and that God, "is patient with you, not wanting any to perish, but all to come to repentance" (2 Pet 3:9), then only those go to Gehenna who choose to do so, having resisted through life all that God has done and continues to do to win them to a better way. Those who share in eternal life are those who say to God, "Your will be done." Those who are on their way to eternal death, or the "the second death" (Rev 20:14), are those to whom *God* says, "*Your* will be done." Disintegration in Gehenna is the final outcome of a life lived in defiance and rejection of God, or perhaps simply indifference towards God. We reap what we sow: "Do not be deceived; God is not mocked, for you reap whatever you sow. If you sow to your own flesh, you will reap corruption from the flesh; but if you sow to the Spirit, your will reap eternal life from the Spirit" (Gal 6:7–8). The images of fire and burning are frightening to us and are used precisely as a warning. "I tell you my friends, do not fear those who kill the body, and after that can do nothing more. But I will warn you whom to fear: fear him who, after he has killed, has authority to cast into hell [Gehenna]. Yes, I tell you, fear him!" (Luke 12:4–5). Fire consumes and destroys; it also cleanses. God is described by means of fire: "Indeed our God is a consuming fire" (Heb 12:29). At the end of it all, however, the image of fire is still just an image. The reality we have to deal with is an encounter in the final judgment with God's own self, the God who is "the first and the last," and there is nothing that the human imagination can conceive that surpasses the tragedy of at the last gazing upon the glory and beauty of God and realizing what has been lost. This is rightly described as hell, the hell of God-forsakenness. But hell has been endured in our place by God's own Son who has "descended into hell" on our behalf upon the cross in order that no other human being need undergo such God-forsakenness (2 Cor 5:21; Gal 3:13). It is only those who resist his gracious gift who consign themselves to final destruction.

Christians do not so much believe in eternal punishment as regret it. If there is any comfort to be gained, it is that the final judgment is not yet. There is still everything to play for. In the present age, the God of grace persists in pursuing the lost and no one is able to set a limit to how long that search will continue and the extent to which the lost will be pursued. What we see is only a small part of the divine quest for lost creatures and in all probability contains many surprises. We live in hope that all that is evil and cruel will one day be destroyed in Gehenna, otherwise depicted as the "lake of fire" (Rev 20:10, 13–15), and done away with forever. Even the thought of hell can provide grounds for hope. We also live in hope that the number of human beings who share that fate will be as few as is divinely possible, consistent with God's love and justice.

DEATH

The realities of "Death and Hades" are also to be thrown into the "lake of fire" (Rev 20:13), underlining the figurative nature of the language. Death, according to Paul, is the last enemy of God to be destroyed (1 Cor 15:26). "Death will be no more; mourning and crying and pain will be no more, for the first things have passed away" (Rev 21:4). Death is the negation of life, and from this derives its nature as an enemy. At the same time, within the cycles of life that belong to an organic, living-yet-mortal creation, death is part of the natural process. Creatures come into being, grow, flourish, fade, and then die, leaving room for yet other creatures to have their time and place. In a purely natural sense, death is part of life and reminds us that God alone "has immortality and dwells in unapproachable light" (1 Tim 6:16). In this natural sense, there is nothing to fear in death. We might imagine that human beings also belong to this order of coming and going, and that even in an unfallen world would come to the end of their lives as a matter of course. What are we to make then of the fundamental claim that death is the consequence of sin (Gen 2:17)? What is referred to here is addressed to human beings rather than the creation at large and is concerned with spiritual death. Since sin dislocates us, separating us from the source of life that is God's own self, when we turn away from God we are like a brand that is withdrawn from the fire and loses energy, fading and eventually being extinguished. Unfallen human beings would no doubt have come to the end of their lives only to give those lives back to God in the transition from this mortal life into the immortality that comes from communion with God. Communion with God transforms everything and can turn what might otherwise be an anxiety-provoking experience into an occasion of blessedness. As it is, death for human beings has become death-in-alienation, with all the attendant uncertainties and fears that this brings.

What is indicated here, as previously discussed, is that human beings, who are embodied souls or "ensouled" bodies, are not inherently immortal. Their hope of immortality derives solely and completely from their relationship with the eternal God and not from within themselves. They are born with the possibility of not dying, but of entering into eternal life. In the story of the Garden of Eden this is symbolized by the presence in the midst of the garden of the tree of life from which they were freely able to eat (Gen 2:9, 16). The tree stands before them and is available to them, but they have to take from it and eat. The fall away from God means that access to the tree of life is no longer so readily possible (Gen 3:22–24). The way is blocked. Human beings have forfeited their destiny and from now on stand in need of restoration and salvation. This is provided for them through Christ whose death on a cross (interestingly, on a "tree"—1 Pet 2:24 margin), meant that "he might taste death for everyone" (Heb 2:9) and so become "the source of eternal salvation for all who obey him" (Heb 5:9). The final vision the New Testament offers is of the river of the water of life flowing from "the throne of God and of the Lamb"; "On either side of the river is the tree of life with its twelve kinds of fruit, producing its fruit each month; and the leaves of the tree are for the healing of the nations" (Rev 22:1–2). In the new creation that God is bringing to pass, therefore, death has no place and there is much, much more than the *possibility of not dying*. Now there is *no possibility of dying*. Death has been swallowed up in life.

For those who refuse the divine invitation to life, however, there is a different and terrible kind of logic. The spiritual death that derives from alienation from God, the ground of our being and the source of all life, if not remedied through turning to God, becomes in the age to come eternal death, final and absolute separation from God without the possibility of remission. This is described as "the second death" (Rev 20:14), the death that lies beyond death, and represents the cessation of existence accompanied by the regrets, remorse, and accusations of conscience that seem to be indicated when Jesus makes his references to "weeping and gnashing of teeth" (Matt 8:12; 13:42, 50, etc.). This is the "eternal punishment" referred to by Jesus in Matthew 25:46, and it is eternal not in the sense that it goes on happening throughout all eternity without ever ceasing (though some believe this), but that it belongs to the eternal age that is to come and that it is final and irreversible. "Eternal" is a qualitative rather than a quantitative adjective.

The picture painted indicates why we should be glad that the last enemy has been overcome, "so that what is mortal may be swallowed up by life" (2 Cor 5:4). Although we still have to "walk though the valley of the shadow of death," we are not on our own, "for you are with me, your rod and your staff—they comfort me" (Ps 23:4 margin). Christ has already made the journey into death and has subdued it, so that when we die we tread a path he has already negotiated. He can guide us through. We must come to the end of our lives, yet we need no longer die in alienation from God but in communion with the Father, through Christ, and in the Holy Spirit. Death has been transformed from being an enemy to being a friend. "For to me, living is Christ and dying is gain" (Phil 1:21).

JUDGMENT

Death represents the judgment of God on everything that stands opposed to God's will and purpose. Only that which accords with the nature and being of the world's creator has a future. In past chapters we have distinguished between vindictive wrath and just wrath and have expressed the conviction that there is nothing in the wrath of God that is vindictive; rather the divine wrath, God's settled opposition to what vandalizes and distorts the good creation, is entirely just. In this sense, both the love and wrath of God are fundamental to Christian hope since they indicate that evil will not finally be allowed to triumph. God's wrath is the guarantee of the final triumph of justice. When human beings set themselves against God they set themselves against the very grain of the universe and therefore are liable to receive in their own persons the "due penalty for their error" (Rom 1:27). Although our observation of the evolution of nature yields many examples of conflict and depredation, there is at a more fundamental level a cooperation, mutual dependence, and synergy to the natural world that speaks of how life should be. It is God-given. When human beings violate this and seek instead for dominance and wanton exploitation, they damage themselves and reap the results of their actions. In this process we see the divine judgment that decrees we reap what we sow. Judgment may thus be described as "intrinsic," in the sense that wrong actions open up negative consequences.

We see already in this the just wrath of God, God's settled opposition to sin, as surely as in the processes of nature and its bounty we see the love of God (Matt 5:45). Judgment, then, is not something that happens only at the end of history, but rather accompanies us through life as we endure the deserved consequences of our own wrong actions. This is the truth in the otherwise somewhat generalized biblical claim that the righteous prosper and the unrighteous do not: "Happy are those who do not follow the advice of the wicked. . . . In all that they do, they prosper. The wicked are not so, but are like chaff that the wind drives away" (Ps 1:1–4). Moreover, because human beings are irreducibly social and communal beings and are bound up with each other in the bundle of life, we cannot avoid the consequences of both the good and the bad that others do.

In the biblical perspective God's judgment is exercised primarily by allowing us to experience the consequences of our own actions. God gives us over to the way we have chosen in order that we might learn to do differently. This was true in the experience of Israel and Judah when they were exiled into foreign nations. After centuries of the covenant people yearning to be like the other nations and even to worship their gods, God gave them what they wanted, only for them to discover how bitter this was. Yet, against the odds, it was the forced deportation of a large proportion of the Jews into exile that became the point at which Judaism's character began to be formed, in the absence of a temple and of a land, around the Scriptures they took with them and the synagogues they established as places of gathering and of study. God's judgment was intended as a discipline, as a provocation to return to obedience to the covenant (Deut 8:5, 19–20). So even the judgment of God was part of God's mercy, not allowing the people to live in delusions of their own imagination, but bringing them up short by confronting them with the truth about themselves. Three times in Romans 1, the apostle Paul asserts that God "gave them up" (vv. 24, 26, 28) to the consequences of their own actions when people refused the truth and turned from God. Although there are other, more immediate and direct ways, in which God might be said to judge, this seems to be God's primary and preferred way of doing so.

The judgment of God, however, is not supremely about punishment and condemnation. These inevitably play a part, and it would be superficial to claim otherwise. Judgment involves God's responses to our deliberate and chosen actions and therefore inevitably has a retributive, though never arbitrary, character. It is related to what we choose to do and must in that sense be retributive. But all of this is in the service of a higher goal and greater good. A judge, after all, in any righteous practice of law, is called to preside over a process in which the truth is allowed to emerge. This is the primary sense in which God is the Judge of all the earth (Ps 94:2). God judges the earth with righteousness and equity (Ps 96:10–13). Under God's sovereign rule over history, the truth will finally emerge about every human action, and the end of the process will be that transparent justice triumphs. This Judge is therefore one in whom we may trust, and God's judgment something we should welcome. Although it is a temptation for any legal system to defend the status quo and guard the interests of the powerful, this Judge is one who has particular regard to the victims. God, although entirely just, is not a neutral judge, but works actively to deliver justice for the poor: "The Lord sets the prisoners free; the Lord opens the eyes of the blind. The Lord lifts up those who are bowed down; the Lord loves the righteous. The Lord watches over the strangers, he upholds the orphan and the widow, but the way of the wicked he brings to ruin" (Ps 146:7–9). When the biblical witnesses contemplate a final judgment and a last day (John 12:48), it is the day of final encounter with God and with truth, when all is seen for what it truly is, when the victims will be vindicated and evildoers condemned. God "has fixed a day on which he will have the world judged in righteousness by a man whom he has appointed, and of this he has given assurance to all by raising him from the dead" (Acts 17:31).

The biblical witness is unanimous that human beings will be judged by God on the basis of the works they have done or failed to do (Matt 25:31–46). This means that it will not be on the basis of what people claim that they will be judged, but on the evidence of their lives. "Not everyone who says to me 'Lord, Lord,' will enter the kingdom of heaven, but only one who does the will of my Father in heaven" (Matt 7:21). We have already established that we are not justified by works, but by grace through faith in Christ. Yet faith is not mere lip-service but the turning of our whole lives towards God, and therefore will inevitably issue in the transformation of our living. Faith without works is therefore dead (Jas 2:18–26). Jesus taught that only those will stand in the judgment who have truly heard the word of God and obeyed what they have heard (Matt 7:24–27). Hearing alone is not enough. It is important therefore for those who believe to "be all the more eager to confirm your call and election, for if you do this you will never stumble" (2 Pet 1:10). Yet the believer faces final judgment with confidence since for him or her judgment is something they have already undergone in Christ: "There is therefore now no condemnation for those who are in Christ Jesus" (Rom 8:1) and, "We know that we have passed from death to life because we love one another" (1 John 3:14). When the apostle Peter proclaimed that Christ is "the one ordained by God as judge of the living and the dead" (Acts 10:42), he probably had two things in mind. The first is that Christ is the measure of what it is to be a true human being and therefore it is against the standard he sets that we ourselves are to be judged. The second is that as the one whom God has sent to "seek out and to save the lost" (Luke 19:10), our attitude and relationship to Christ determines our future destiny: "Whoever believes in the Son has eternal life; whoever disobeys the Son will not see life, but must endure God's wrath" (John 3:36).

We return to the idea that the role of a judge is to preside over a process in which the truth is enabled to emerge. So it is with God. The Judge of all the earth will surely only do that which is just (Gen 18:25). For this reason the judgment of God is not something to fear but to celebrate. To a fallen and suffering world, the judgment of God cannot come soon enough. When it does come, the word of God will be, "See, I am making all things new" (Rev 21:5). This is a stupendous promise, especially if it is taken at its maximum value. For surely "all things" can be taken to mean not only all things that will be in existence at the end but also all things that have ever existed. We are presented then with a vision of all things that exist and all things that have ever existed being judged, redeemed, healed, and renewed. For the avoidance of doubt, however, the same chapter does on to say concerning the new heaven and new earth, "But nothing unclean will enter it, nor anyone who practices abomination and falsehood, but only those who are written in the Lamb's book of life" (Rev 21:27). Such is the purifying judgment of God. God is the ultimate "last thing" with which any of us has to do.

15

The Way of Jesus Christ

BEFORE THE FIRST DISCIPLES of Jesus attracted the title "Christian" (Acts 11:26), they were frequently known as those who belonged to the "Way" (Acts 9:2; 19:9, 23; 22:4). This is an appropriate term, not only because they belonged to one who called himself the "way" (John 14:6), but also because he called them to a distinctive way of life as his followers. "Then Jesus told his disciples, 'If any want to become my followers, let them deny themselves and take up their cross and follow me. For those who want to save their life will lose it, and those who lose their life for my sake will find it'" (Matt 16:24–25).

THE SHAPE OF DISCIPLESHIP

There are ways in which we can take up the cross and follow Jesus and there are ways in which we cannot. Jesus alone was able to offer himself on the cross in our place and on our behalf as an atoning sacrifice. This is his saving work and he alone was qualified so to act as our representative. For this reason we cannot do what Jesus did but can only accept with faith and gratitude as a gift that which has been done for us. Christ acted here as our savior and it is foolish to imagine that we can do anything other than look to him and place our whole reliance not on what we can do but on his saving work. On the other hand, there may be ways in which we can indeed "take up our cross" in the way Jesus did.

The ambitious mother of two of the disciples, James and John, the sons of Zebedee, once made a foolish request to Jesus,

> "Declare that these two sons of mine will sit, one at your right hand and one at your left, in your kingdom." But Jesus answered, "You do not know what you are asking. Are you able to drink the cup that I am about to drink?" They said to him, "We are able." He said to them, "You will indeed drink my cup, but to sit at my right hand and at my left, this is not mine to grant, but it is for those for whom it has been prepared by my Father."
> —Matt 20:20–23

Jesus here indicated that James and John could in fact "drink the cup" that he was about to drink. Probably he had in mind that they were able to give themselves to a martyr's death for the sake of the one in whom they believed. This was certainly to happen to James within a relatively few years (Acts 12:2). But are there other ways in which the followers of Jesus are able to imitate his self-giving upon the cross? The answer to this must be a definite Yes. The whole life of Christian discipleship is one in which the life of Jesus and his way to death can become the guiding pattern for our own lives. We "take up our cross" in the sense that we tread in Jesus' footsteps. With the help of his Spirit we seek to be as he was and to do as he did. In this sense, Simon of Cyrene, who carried the cross-piece after Jesus as he stepped towards Golgotha, is an example of what it means to be a Christian (Mark 15:21).

The Gospels tells us a remarkable amount of what Jesus did and taught. They are powerful and revolutionary documents whose influence upon the world has been beyond calculation. They are primary documents for believers in Jesus since they are the source of our knowledge of him and are designed to shape us in our discipleship. The Gospel of Matthew is set out in five sections that are reminiscent of the five Books of Moses, the books that set out the basic teaching of the faith of Israel. Jesus, even more than Moses, is our teacher and guide in how to please God and live as God's faithful people. It is strange therefore that the basic creeds of the Christian faith, such as the Apostles' Creed (see Appendix 1), actually say so little about the life of Jesus. His whole ministry is reduced to a comma in between "born of the Virgin Mary" and "suffered under Pontius Pilate." Whereas we are grateful for what the creeds teach us *about* Jesus, they have little to say about the teaching *of* Jesus, and so all the more at this point we need the Gospels to inspire and guide us. Christ's saving work is directed towards reconciling us both to God and to ourselves as God's children. It is in order that we might be "conformed to the image of God's Son" (Rom 8:29) that we have been brought out of darkness into light. Christ himself represents the restoration of the image of God in humanity and so likeness to Christ is our goal and purpose. We are being "transformed into the same image from one degree of glory to another" (2 Cor 3:18). Yet how are we to understand this?

It is striking that in a whole series of ways the New Testament does not require us to be like Christ. The imitation of Christ does not mean following the customs of dress or the incidental details of lifestyle of a first-century Jewish male. For gentiles it does not even require adherence to the customs of Jesus' own religious practice. Gentiles are not required to be outwardly circumcised or to observe Jewish dietary practices, holy days, or festivals, although if we in good conscience freely choose to be or do so there is no objection to be raised (Rom 14:1–6). In following after Jesus the concentration is firmly on the fundamental shape and pattern of Jesus' life, on his humble self-giving and the outpouring of his life upon the cross. This is the shape of discipleship and it is clearly set before us: "Let the same mind be in you that was in Christ Jesus who, though he was in the form of God, did not regard equality with God as something to be exploited, but emptied himself, taking the form of a slave, being born in human likeness. And being found in human form, he humbled himself and became obedient to the point of death—even death on a cross" (Phil 2:5–8). The apostle Peter makes it even more explicit: "For to this you have been called, because Christ also suffered for you, leaving you an example, so that you should follow in his steps. . . . When he was abused, he did not return abuse; when he suffered, he did not threaten; but he entrusted himself to the one who judges justly" (1 Pet 2:21–23).

It is in the essential shape of the incarnation and redeeming work of Christ that we discern the fundamental pattern of Christian discipleship. In so far as we participate in this self-giving pattern of life our own lives have the power to become redemptive. This quality of life, transcending the perennial conflicts and self-seeking of ordinary human living, has the power to transform. It is no surprise then that on the occasion when Jesus washed the feet of his disciples, itself an illustration of his whole lifestyle, he also went on to say, "So if I, your Lord and Teacher, have washed your feet, you also ought to wash one another's feet. For I have set you an example, that you also should do as I have done to you" (John 13:1–17). Such a way of life requires us to "deny ourselves" by turning away from our preferred path of selfish love, to "take up our cross" as a deliberate choice to follow after Jesus and make him the determinative centre of our lives, and a willingness to yield control of our own lives and destinies in order to abandon ourselves to the Father of Jesus Christ in whom true life is to be found. It is this fundamental pattern to life that we are called upon to follow, rather than the incidentals of time, place, and culture that were of necessity true of Jesus.

THE LIFESTYLE OF JESUS

Jesus was unambiguously Jewish. The Judaism of his day was very diverse and it is hard to claim that there was anything at that time resembling an "orthodox" Judaism. For this reason it is mistaken to imagine that Jesus was in any sense against Judaism. Instead, he occupied positions that were shared by some in the Jewish spectrum around him and rejected by others. Inevitably his views were in conflict with some of the Jewish parties of his day, but this was a question of advocating particular views *within* contemporary Judaism, not of arguing against Judaism itself. In particular, Jesus at times came into contention with the party of the Pharisees, with whom he otherwise would have had much in common. It is sometimes the case that the people we argue with most are those who are most closely related to us. There is evidence that some at least of the Pharisees found their way into the Jesus movement after the resurrection (Acts, 15:5; 21:20. The apostle Paul was a Pharisee: Acts 26:5). They were a devout group who attempted to extend the purity laws of their religion into areas where the Scriptures did not apply them. In the eyes of many, therefore, they were guilty of going beyond the teaching of Scripture, a view that Jesus appeared to have shared (Matt 15:1–9). They were also aggressive in converting other Jews to their point of view (Matt 23:15). Jesus was insistent on the priority of the Scriptures themselves and resisted their being rendered void by the addition of new traditions (Matt 5:17–20). For Jesus, it was clear that love for God was the first and greatest commandment and that it was swiftly followed by love of neighbor.

> When the Pharisees heard that he had silenced the Sadducees, they gathered together, and one of them, a lawyer, asked him a question to test him. "Teacher, which commandment in the law is the greatest?" He said to him, "'You shall love the Lord your God with all your heart, and with all your soul, and with all your mind.' This is the greatest and first commandment. And a second is like it: 'You shall love your neighbor as yourself.' On these commandments hang all the law and the prophets"
> —Matt 22:34–40

In citing these two commandments Jesus was doing nothing new. The first is taken from Moses' teaching to the Israelites before entering the promised land (Deut 6:4–9), and the second from the book of Leviticus (19:18). The Deuteronomy commandment became a significant part of Jewish liturgy. Known as the *Shema* (from the Hebrew imperative meaning "hear"), it was to be recited by devout Jews each morning and evening. Jesus was, therefore, reiterating a fundamental component of Jewish faith and worship. It indicates that Jewish religion was not primarily about law but about love, love for the God of Israel. Obedience to the laws given by God was to be an expression of love for this God, and if this was true for Israel, it was also true for Jesus, and it is true for his followers in the expanded Israel of the church. Love for God is the highest priority and it renders all other aspects of Christian discipleship possible. "For my yoke is easy," said Jesus, "and my burden is light" (Matt 11:30). Love for God is closely followed by love for neighbor, since to love God is to be nourished by the love of God for God's creation and those made in God's image. On another occasion Jesus amplified love for neighbor by adding, "In everything do to others as you would have them do to you; for this is the law and the prophets" (Matt 7:12). Loving one's neighbor as oneself and only doing to others what you would have them do to you counts as one of the guiding principles for human behavior and ethics. Similar statements are made both in Jewish sources and those of other religions, and this only serves to underline these principles as a primary source for Christian living. As true love for God is nourished, so the fruit of a loving life conforming to these principles becomes a reality. The opposite is also true: where the reality of these principles is lacking then a person's religion is unlikely to be founded on love for God. Following in the way of Jesus, therefore, involves nurturing these attitudes within our own hearts: "Those who say, 'I love God,' and hate their brothers and sisters, are liars; for those who do not love a brother or sister whom they have seen, cannot love God whom they have not seen" (1 John 4:20).

The way of Jesus means practicing love for God and for neighbor, but it raises natural questions. The question, "And who is my neighbor?" was once put to Jesus by a lawyer (meaning an expert in the law of Moses) who had entered into dialog with him about inheriting eternal life. It became the occasion for one of Jesus' greatest parables, the story of the Good Samaritan, who, unlike a priest and a Levite, who passed by on the other side of the road, came to the help of a traveler who had been beaten and left for dead by robbers. The Samaritan, who nominally was supposed to be a person despised by the Jews, rescued the man, applied first aid to him, delivered him to an innkeeper, paid for his care, and then promised to return (Luke 10:25–37). Characteristically, Jesus then added a twist in the question he posed to the lawyer: "Which of these three, do you think, was a neighbor to the man who fell into the hands of the robbers?" Unwilling to use the word "Samaritan," the lawyer replied, "The one who showed him mercy" (v. 37). The question, "Who is my neighbor?" is an attempt to delimit those whom I am called to love as myself. If I can persuade myself that a given person does not come into the category of "neighbor," I can release myself from the obligation to love. By contrast Jesus' question, "To whom can I show myself to be a neighbor?" excludes no one since the answer is, "anybody in need who comes across my path, however much of an outsider or enemy I consider them to be." Jesus was compassionate and humane, both in what he taught and what he did, and this is the way along which he directs us.

LOVE FOR ENEMIES

What we have seen of the way of Jesus is of outstanding value and it is paralleled at points both in the best of the Jewish teaching that was behind Jesus and in other religious traditions. Yet there comes a point at which Jesus goes beyond anything that has preceded him, and that is in his call to love our enemies.

> You have heard that it was said, "You shall love your neighbor and hate your enemy." But I say to you, Love your enemies and pray for those who persecute you, so that you may be children of your Father in heaven; for he makes his sun rise on the evil and on the good, and he sends rain on the righteous and on the unrighteous. For if you love those who love you, what reward do you have? Do not even the tax-collectors do the same? And if you greet only your brothers and sisters, what more are you doing than others? Do not even the Gentiles do the same? Be perfect, therefore, as your heavenly Father is perfect.
> —Matt 5:43–48

As a matter of detail, nowhere in Scripture does it tell us to love our neighbor but hate our enemy. This is why Jesus says, "You have heard it *said*," rather than "written." As we have noted, some interpreted love for neighbor in restrictive, rather than expansive, terms and considered there was every reason to hate enemies, particularly, no doubt, the brutal and oppressive Romans. Jesus offered an alternative and better way, though one that is exceedingly difficult, the way of love even for enemies. If any form of behavior is likely properly to be called "Christian," then this is it. This point appears to have been well understood in the rest of the New Testament. Jesus set the example when from the cross he prayed, "Father, forgive them; for they do not know what they are doing" (Luke 23:34). The response of Jesus to being ill-used was not to return hatred for hatred but to absorb the wrongdoing and return it with forgiveness and love. The apostle Paul captured this fundamental attitude when he said, "Beloved, never avenge yourselves, but leave room for the wrath of God; for it is written, 'Vengeance is mine, I will repay, says the Lord.' No, if your enemies are hungry, feed them; if they are thirsty, give them something to drink; for by doing this you will heap burning coals on their heads.' Do not be overcome by evil, but overcome evil with good" (Rom 12:19–21, citing Prov 25:21–22).

Ultimately it is God's work to judge people's actions and reward them appropriately, not ours. We can be assured that God will certainly set the record straight in the fullness of time. In the meantime, as Jesus saw and taught, there is great redemptive power in interrupting the vicious cycle of recrimination that is such a stubborn aspect of human behavior and, instead of trading insult for insult and hurt for hurt, absorbing the wrong that is done to us and responding to it with the willingness to forgive. This is how God responded to human hostility on the cross. The cross is not to be understood as the Father punishing the Son for sins he has not committed. Rather, in the cross we see the heart of the Father whereby in and through the Son the Father absorbs human hostility and himself endures the consequences of human sin by taking them upon God's own self. In this way, God overcomes human sin, interrupts the vicious cycle of recrimination, and calls a halt to it. There are other dimensions of Christ's atoning work, as we have seen, but this is certainly one of them. We are able to imitate this aspect of the cross, to "take up our cross" and follow Jesus in this regard. When we follow in this way we are sharing in God's redeeming work because this kind of behavior has the power to change relationships and societies. The Christian community is called to overcome evil with good, not to deepen the problem of human evil by the old strategy of returning evil for evil.

JESUS AND THE WAY OF PEACE

There can be no doubt that Jesus rejected any use of violence in the fulfillment of his mission. Violence was a genuine option for him because he came from Galilee, which was the breeding ground for the violent insurrectionists known as the "Zealots." Jesus had a least one former Zealot in his band of disciples (Luke 6:14–16), and in addition, Judas Iscariot may have had Zealot sympathies. The Zealots were later to rise against the Romans, giving them a pretext to destroy Jerusalem in AD 70. Jesus clearly foresaw that this would happen, predicted it, and understood that it was a consequence of the rejection of his own non-violent way (Luke 13:34–35; 21:20): "Put your sword back into its place; for all who take the sword will perish by the sword" (Matt 26:52). The way of Jesus is sometimes called "non-resistance" because of his words, "But I say to you, Do not resist an evildoer" (Matt 5:39), but a fuller understanding of his teaching suggests that "non-violent resistance" might be a more accurate term.

Jesus gave examples of how it might be possible to respond to wrongs done to one's own person. He was speaking to Jewish people who were under the control of an alien power, the Romans, who ruled in Israel by means of Jewish or semi-Jewish collaborators. Such people were used to being ill-treated by their oppressors and were often faced with the dilemma of offering resistance, in which respect they did not stand a chance, or of accepting the status of victim, in which case their humanity would be degraded. Jesus offered a way of responding that avoided both returning evil for evil, and so proving almost as bad as the perpetrator, or accepting victim status. One example was as follows: "You have heard that it was said, 'An eye for an eye and a tooth for a tooth.' But I say to you, Do not resist an evildoer. But if anyone strikes you on the right cheek, turn the other also" (Matt 5:38–39). On the surface, this sounds as though Jesus was advocating passive endurance of ill-treatment, but there is more to it than that. To strike someone's right cheek you would use the back of your right hand. This was a standard way of reinforcing inferiority. Those who considered themselves superior to others, like the soldiers of an occupying force, would assert that superiority with a back-handed slap. In these circumstances, Jesus says, offer to them the left cheek. This would require them to use the palm of the right hand and would be a way of saying to them: "you have to treat me as an equal, not as an inferior." In this way, violence is not returned for violence, yet at the same time the status of victim is declined in a peaceful but effective form of protest. Moreover, the teaching of Jesus at this point was more than a contradiction of the "eye for an eye, tooth for a tooth" principle. (Lev 24:19–20). This was never about revenge, but about justice and proportionality, and so about the limitation of punishment to no more than was equitable. Jesus was extending this limitation by following its trajectory to the point of non-return of evil for evil.

In a further illustration Jesus says, "And if anyone forces you to go one mile, go also the second mile. Give to everyone who begs from you, and do not refuse anyone who wants to borrow from you" (Matt 5:41–42). According to Roman military law, a soldier could lay hold of a person in an occupied territory and compel them to carry his pack for the length of a mile. After that, however, they were strictly forbidden, under pain of punishment, to force them to carry it any further. Jesus therefore describes a situation in which an Israelite is forced to carry the pack for a mile and after that insists on carrying it a further mile, thus putting the soldier at risk of punishment and consequently throwing him into confusion. Both the illustrations given here have an element of humor to them, but they help us understand that Jesus is not advocating passivity, rather, he is offering a third way, one of non-violent resistance, between recycling hatred and wrongdoing and accepting ill-treatment without protest. It should be stressed here that in giving these illustrations Jesus was not enunciating a new law. There are certainly situations in which it would not be appropriate to turn the other cheek. What Jesus offered was illustrative of how the creative imagination can negotiate inspired ways for overcoming evil with good. To treat them as laws to be rigidly applied in all situations would be to lose their prophetic value. However, those who wish to follow in Jesus' way and have inwardly resolved that they will avoid resisting evil by means of evil should pray for the kind of creative imagination that Jesus had.

The commitment of Jesus to the way of non-violence raises many questions for those who live in societies that depend on the legitimate and legal use of force through policing to curb the criminal violence of the few. Some of these questions are referred to in the last chapter. At this point, it can clearly be stated that, whatever may be necessary for the social order, the good news of the kingdom of God can never be and should never be promoted through the use of violence or compulsion. This would be entirely against the way of Christ and would, in fact, undermine it. The gospel of Christ can only ever be effective where it is freely accepted and embraced. Any element of compulsion or threat can only hinder the work of Christ. Jesus was never willing to shed blood or to expect others to do so in his name, but only to give up his life and shed his own blood for the sake of the world. This is his redeeming action, and the closer we come to it, the more redemptive our own lives are likely to be, that is to say, the more likely they are to set limits to evil and to promote the good.

JESUS AND JUSTICE

Jesus saw himself as a prophet and as being in the prophetic tradition of the people of Israel. As Jerusalem stoned the prophets and messengers of God (Matt 23:37), Jesus expected the leaders of Israel to reject him (Mark 8:31; 9:12). In the history of Israel, the prophets spoke in the name of God to the people, reminding them of the obligations of the covenant from which they had departed. They reminded the people of the need for righteousness and fairness in their dealings with each other and especially with the poor and the disadvantaged, often referred to as the "widows and orphans," those who in the circumstances of the time lacked a productive male to provide for them. Unlike some modern ideas of social justice, the responsibility to act was not seen as lying primarily with governments, which in biblical times had no welfare function, but with persons. There are many inequalities in the world, some caused by human actions, such as corruption and indolence, and others by failed harvests, extreme weather conditions, and lack of resources. In such a world the prophets called upon the people of the covenant for righteousness, for treating people fairly, paying proper wages, rejecting exploitation, and showing mercy and generosity towards the poor. As God was merciful, so those who looked to God were called to show mercy. All of this was carried through into the ministry of Jesus who demonstrated particular empathy towards the poor, so much so that the first of the beatitudes is, "Blessed are you who are poor, for yours is the kingdom of God" (Luke 6:20). His concern for the poor and oppressed was also in evidence at the beginning of his ministry when Jesus announced his understanding of his mission. "The Spirit of the Lord is upon me, because he has anointed me to bring good news to the poor. He has sent me to proclaim release to the captives and recovery of sight to the blind, to let the oppressed go free, to proclaim the year of the Lord's favor" (Luke 4:18–20, quoting Isa 61).

Some of the most stringent of Jesus' words were directed at the rich. On one occasion, a "certain ruler" approached Jesus to ask what he needed to do to inherit eternal life. Jesus recited the commandments (though omitting the tenth commandment, to do with "coveting") and the man claimed to have kept them all. Jesus then said to him, "There is still one thing lacking. Sell all that you own and distribute the money to the poor, and you will have treasure in heaven; then come, follow me." When the young man turned away Jesus said, "How hard it is for those who have wealth to enter the kingdom of God! Indeed, it is easier for a camel to go through the eye of a needle than for someone who is rich to enter the kingdom of God" (Luke 18:18–25). Wealth is, apparently, a major obstacle to the spiritual life and entry into the kingdom. For this reason God favors the poor: "He has filled the hungry with good things, and sent the rich away empty" (Luke 1:53). Jesus described money as "mammon" (Matt 6:24 RSV) or as "the unrighteous mammon" (Luke 16:9 RSV), suggesting that wealth was like an idolatrous power with an inherent bias towards covetousness and unrighteousness. As such, it draws people away from the true God. It has to be tamed and made use of, not to accumulate even more wealth, but to make friends of people (Luke 16:9). Jesus' own example was of a simple, modest lifestyle without any form of ostentation or luxury. In this way he was able to be alongside and to identify with the poor: "Foxes have holes, and birds of the air have nests; but the Son of Man has nowhere to lay his head" (Matt 8:20). "For you know the generous act of our Lord Jesus Christ, that though he was rich, yet for your sakes he became poor, so that by his poverty you might become rich" (2 Cor 8:9).

With all this said, there were characters in the Gospels who did possess wealth and used it to enhance the ministry of Jesus. Jesus' mission and that of his disciples was funded by wealthy and well-connected women: there were "Joanna, the wife of Herod's steward Chuza, and Susanna, and many others, who provided for them out of their resources" (Luke 8:3). In his death Jesus was provided for by two wealthy but secret disciples, Joseph of Arimathea and Nicodemus (John 19:38–42). The whole ministry of Jesus would have been very different were it not for such people prepared to invest their wealth in Jesus. This gives a somewhat different, perhaps complementary, perspective on Jesus' very trenchant critique of wealth and its uses. But it does not mean that we can evade the challenge of his words and example when it comes to our own attitudes to wealth and possessions: "Take care! Be on your guard against all kinds of greed; for one's life does not consist in the abundance of possessions" (Luke 12:15).

JESUS AND PRAYER

This chapter began by affirming that those who follow the way of Jesus are following its basic shape as a way of humble, self-giving, self-sacrificing love. It is participating in this self-giving, generous movement that counts, rather than following a strict rules-based morality (though this may at times have its place). It is only in reliance on God's gracious love that it becomes possible to live in such a way, and this is a fact that we find in the life of Jesus himself. Jesus lived in dependence on the Father. From the beginning he wanted to be "about my Father's interests" (Luke 2:49 margin). When addressed on one occasion as "good teacher," he responded by saying, "Why do you call me good? No one is good but God alone" (Luke 18:18–19). This does not indicate that Jesus was not good, only that he was not conscious of his own goodness, though overwhelmingly conscious of the goodness of God. As displayed throughout his ministry, and most clearly of all in the Garden of Gethsemane, Jesus knew an intimate relation with the Father whom he constantly called "Abba" (Luke 10:21–23; Mark 14:36). It was this relationship that gave him assurance that he was indeed the Son of God, an assurance that was deepened in the moments of his baptism at the outset of his ministry: "And a voice from heaven said, 'This is my Son, the Beloved, with whom I am well pleased'" (Matt 3:16–17).

Jesus was sustained in his ministry because he drew his strength from the Father to whom he prayed. We read that Jesus would withdraw from the crowds at times when he was being drained of spiritual energy, and often go up a mountain or to a deserted place, in order to pray (Mark 1:35;

Luke 5:15-16). He prayed in times of specific need or opportunity (John 17:1), and in times of crisis and distress (Matt 26:39, 42, 44). He prayed on the cross (Luke 23:34). He taught his disciples that if they were to ask anything in his name then it would be done for them (John 14:13-14). God was to be understood as a warm, welcoming Father (Luke 15:11-32) who would certainly give good things and the Holy Spirit to those who ask (Luke 11:13). For this reason disciples should go on asking, searching, and knocking at the door in their prayers to God in the assurance that they would find. They should ask simple prayers without too many words, since God already knows what they need (Matt 6:7-8; 7:7). They should not harbor resentment or lack of forgiveness in their hearts since this is a hindrance to prayer (Matt 6:14-15). Nor should they parade their prayers before other people in order to gain their admiration, but should rather play down their piety (Matt 6:16-18). They should be prepared to persist in prayer until they received an answer (Luke 18:1-8). And to illustrate his teaching Jesus offered the disciples a particular prayer that has since become known as "the Lord's Prayer" and is an established part of Christian liturgies (Matt 6:7-13).

The way of Jesus Christ cannot be lived out without the resource of prayer in communion with the Father through the Son and in the Holy Spirit. It is not a way that can be imitated in our own strength, nor a series of laws that we are able to fulfill without divine assistance. It becomes possible only when we participate in the life of Christ and are formed by his spirit of self-giving love and compassion. It involves a commitment to pathways of peace and a willingness to absorb rather than recycle the wrongs that are done to us and the negative actions and emotions that may be directed to us. To do this successfully requires that, like Christ, we should have a strong and secure sense of our identity and mission as children of God and followers of Christ. It requires a resilient and prayerful spirituality that can creatively inform our imaginations and enable us to rise above stock reactions and responses. The way of Christ is not easy—it led him to a cross. But the resurrection is the confirmation that this is a way that both reflects the ways of God with sinful human beings and pleases God when it is put into practice. It also has the power to bring about change and achieve redemption in human lives and societies.

16

The Word of God and the Words of God

ALL THE CONVICTIONS OF the Christian community that we have so far described are drawn from and are dependent upon the testimony of the Scriptures of Israel and of the church. The former we have consistently described as the "Hebrew Scriptures," because they are for the most part written in the Hebrew language and deal with the story of the people of Israel. The latter we have referred to, following tradition, as the "New Testament," because they represent the belief that in Christ, God's covenant has been both renewed and extended to those from all nations who are gathered into the Christian community. These Scriptures were written in the Greek language that had been the common speech of the ancient world since the time of Alexander the Great. The fact that there is a New Testament in turn gave rise to referring to the Hebrew Scriptures as the "Old Testament." Though these writings are indeed ancient, Jewish believers are uncomfortable with the notion of their being called "old," lest this be taken to mean that they are no longer of value and lest this in turn be taken to mean that the Jewish people themselves no longer have a place in God's purpose. Here we assert that the New Testament grew out of the Old and cannot be understood apart from it, so those Scriptures continue to be essential for the church, even though the way to interpret them has changed.

Although all these writings are now known collectively as "the Bible" (which is Greek for "book") and are generally made available in a single volume, it would be more accurate to understand the Bible as a library of writings or a series of books. The "Old Testament," as generally understood by Christians, contains thirty-nine books and follows the Jewish canon (that is, the content of the Old Testament as generally recognized among Jews), although it is ordered differently. The Jews divide their Scriptures into three sections: Torah (Law), Prophets, and Writings, of which the Torah is given priority. Some Bibles include in the Old Testament a further section known as the "Apocrypha" (which means "hidden"), and this contains a number of secondary writings regarded as authoritative for teaching by Roman Catholics, but not by Protestants or Jews. The New Testament contains twenty-seven writings, including the four Gospels, the book of Acts, the letters ascribed to Paul, Peter, and John, the book of Hebrews (of which the author is unknown), and the book of Revelation.

This explanation of Christian convictions could well have started with a chapter on the Bible since all of them are dependent on its testimony. However, we are primarily concerned with the authority and truth of the Bible's content rather than with a theory about the Bible. Those who believe in the Bible do so because, having heard the message it proclaims, they have become persuaded of its authenticity, truth, and power and have become "captured" by it. The Bible's testimony has a self-authenticating power that carries weight. The writings themselves are the vehicle through which this truth is conveyed to us. Having explored this truth, it is now appropriate to give more specific attention to the vehicle itself.

REVELATION

The Bible is well understood as the record of a cumulative process of events and their interpretation through which divine revelation has come to human beings. It is well to start with the simple conviction that God is unknowable. God surpasses human knowledge and lies beyond both the intellect and imagination of human beings. Human forms of inquiry work at their own level, and so we might have a degree of confidence in human attempts to explore the physical creation that is accessible to us and can be explored by means of the senses. We might have a lesser degree of confidence in human investigation of human beings themselves, their psychology and sociology. When it comes to matters of philosophy we are entering into a more speculative zone in which objective criteria as to what is true or false are less obvious. By extension, knowledge of those things that are spiritual and ultimate, of the divine, eludes our best attempts at discovery and we are driven to agnosticism and the acknowledgement of mystery.

We do not know, because we cannot know, that which lies so far beyond our meager powers. We may indeed be able to formulate a range of questions about where we come from, whether there is a purpose to life, how life is to be lived, whether there is life beyond this life, and so on, but asking questions and offering assured answers are different things. Moreover our problem is not only that we are finite, we are also, in a Christian understanding, fallen. Our minds are darkened by both ignorance and sin. There may indeed be clear signs of the existence of God in the things that have been made (Rom 1:18–23), but being willing to draw this obvious conclusion is another matter altogether. The truth can be inconvenient and we may not be willing to face it. Especially if we prize above all things our independence and autonomy, to acknowledge that there is a God who might make legitimate claims upon us may be more than we wish to believe. The temptation then is to avoid such a belief or, expressed in biblical terms, "all who do evil hate the light and do not come to the light, so that their deeds may not be exposed" (John 3:20). Much that passes as "reason" is in fact nothing more than "rationalization," finding reasons not to believe, in order to escape the potential moral implications of believing in God. It is because human intellect is limited and human motivation corrupted that we stand in need of divine revelation.

Revelation is that initiative of God whereby God chooses to make God's own self known. God enters into human affairs in order to communicate God's own self to finite and fallen human beings. Without this experience of revelation we would remain forever in ignorance An early example of this is God speaking to Abram (later Abraham) and telling him to leave his own country and go to the land God would show him (Gen 12:1–3). This primal act was the beginning of the story of the people of Israel, and of human restoration, out of which the rest of the biblical revelation was to grow. How God "spoke" here to Abram is not specified, though we are later told that "the word of the LORD came to Abram in a vision" (Gen 15:1). We are to think then of some form of visionary experience accompanied by words of promise, challenge, and guidance. Again, whether the words were heard out loud or simply deeply impressed on mind and heart is not known to us, nor need it be. This was a sufficiently clear and definitive act to achieve its purpose and was the first of many such experiences to be recorded in the Bible. Even apart from the Bible, it is well established that human beings have mystical and visionary experiences, though the question of their authenticity is one that will always remain open.

To say that the Bible is the record of a cumulative process of acts and their interpretation through which divine revelation is made known is to claim that Abraham's experience, repeated on a number of occasions, was the first of many such moments and that they were more than random. They had a direction and a purpose and amounted to a story, the story of Israel, and that of Christ, whose story grew out of Israel's. The story is recited as a connected narrative at a number of points, but particularly clearly so in Nehemiah 9, in which Ezra the scribe, a significant contributor to the development of the Hebrew Scriptures, reviews the story of Israel up to his day. It is in summaries such as this, and in the general sweep of the Scriptures, that the people of Israel expressed and rehearsed their understanding of their own identity and their place in God's purposes. The writings they produced for this purpose are remarkable from a literary point of view as well as from a theological perspective.

GOD AND THE PEOPLE OF ISRAEL

The story of Israel stretched back to Abraham and the patriarchs, who flourished in the Middle East in the first half of the second millennium BC. The Scriptures relate the ways in which, having chosen Abraham for his historic role as the father of the nation, God then guided and preserved his posterity through times of plenty and of trouble. Along with many others, Abraham's descendants took shelter in Egypt in a time of famine and eventually were made slaves. The most significant events in their history came with the emergence of Moses (which is an Egyptian name) as their military and religious leader and their deliverance from captivity, their rescue from Pharaoh's armies at the Red Sea, their journeying in the wilderness, where they experienced the further revelation of God at Mount Sinai, and their eventual conquest of the land that had been promised to them, the land of Canaan. These were the formative events of Israel's history and they are related in the Scriptures in such a way as to make it clear that in all these things God was with them. It is in the emerging faith and religious practice of Israel that we discover their uniqueness, one that was, however insignificant they were numerically, to shape the world. They called God "Yahweh" and looked upon God as a great king who had delivered them from Egypt and was their savior (Exod 20:2). The idols of the nations were nothing more than chunks of wood and stone (Isa 37:18–19; 41:22–24). God had no rivals and was the only true God (Isa 44:6; 45:18, 22), the Lord of nature who ruled over the people that had been delivered and made a covenant with them, one that required them to respond to their salvation by obeying the law they were given. They believed themselves chosen by God for this purpose, to be a holy nation and a priestly kingdom (Exod 19:1–6). They looked for the blessing of God upon their earthly lives. As God could not be portrayed in images, they were forbidden to make idols or images of God and understood that the sovereign God was not to be manipulated (which was part of what lay behind the idea of idols). They thought and spoke of God in intensely personal and anthropomorphic terms. Unlike the surrounding nations they did not see their God as a nature deity, though God was powerful over nature, but as the one who rules over history and is able to do unrepeatable historical acts, like the exodus. God was willing to answer the prayers of the people and could be called upon in times of distress (2 Chr 7:14).

It is in the light of these basic beliefs that the rest of the Hebrew Scriptures unfold. Through the period of the judges and of the kings, there was no concealment of the fact that Israel was at times cowardly, ungrateful, and rebellious. Although God was believed to fight for the people he had called in order to preserve them, when they were disobedient this same God could also turn against them and become their enemy: "The Lord has become like an enemy; he has destroyed Israel" (Lam 2:5). This is how they came to understand the deportation and exile of a large part of the people, including its elites, to Babylon in the sixth century BC; yet even this came to be seen as God's discipline and as a time for Israel to be re-established and renewed as a truly obedient people. The people were returned to their own land, but spent much of their subsequent history under foreign domination, out of which emerged the hope for a future deliverer, a Messiah who would return to them their full dignity as a people.

In many ways, the Bible resembles a travelogue, tracing the history of the people and their physical and spiritual wanderings. Along the way the cumulative process of divine acts and their interpretation continued with increasing insights, not least through Israel's prophets, as to the true nature and purpose of the one God in whom they believed, and, most of all, of the faithfulness of God to the covenant that had been made with this people. The emphasis on divine acts should be noted since God was deemed to act on behalf of the people, providing for them and protecting them. Yet acts on their own require interpretation, and this cannot be done without words. The prophetic interpretations of God's activity and the insights displayed by the biblical writers are therefore crucial in the formation of Scripture. God acted in history, so the Bible is unambiguously an historical book; but the words of the prophets and writers gave and recorded the meaning of those acts in a way that was itself believed to be inspired by God. "First of all you must understand this, that no prophecy of Scripture is a matter of one's own interpretation, because no prophecy ever came by human will, but men and women moved by the Holy Spirit spoke from God" (2 Pet 1:21).

CHRISTIANS AND THE OLD TESTAMENT

A Christian perspective on the Hebrew Scriptures is gained by the apostle Paul's use of the word "guardian" to describe them (Gal 3:23–25 NIV). The "guardian" or guide supervised the education of a Greek child until the child became of age. It is as though the faith and history of Israel provide us with the alphabet, the thought forms, and the concepts that we needed to understand the Christ when he came. Without the Old Testament, the New Testament writings would make little sense to us, but as it is they are full of meaning, because they draw on the rich history and faith of the Law, the Prophets, and the Writings. The Christian is convinced that all the writings that have gone before, with their accumulated acts and interpretations, have prepared the way for the coming of God's Son. And all the writings that have followed on by way of testimony to that event look back to that coming as the decisive act of God in human history. The inspired words that have preceded the coming of the Christ, and those that have followed on, have pointed forwards or backwards to the coming of the Word, who is God's clearest and greatest communication to humankind: "Long ago God spoke to our ancestors in many and various ways by the prophets, but in these last days he has spoken to us by a Son, whom he appointed heir of all things, through whom he also created the worlds" (Heb 1:1–2).

The word "scripture" simply means "writing," but it has come to have the added sense of a writing that is particularly important, inspired, sacred, or holy. It can safely be claimed that however the words or the Word of God have come to us, without something having been written to record those words, their impact would have been lost. Words are very common. We use them on a daily, even moment-by-moment basis. They can be very powerful when spoken, either as blessing or curse. They enter into our soul and live with us, but unless they are written, when we die they also pass away with us. The value of a writing is that it can endure to perpetuate the memory and the impact of what has been done and said. The cumulative process of God's acts and inspired words being transformed into writing (or "inscripturated") means that they can endure for all time and become universally accessible. They can also exist as an objective and permanent record, remaining available for reference and consultation for all people for all time. Jesus said, "Heaven and earth will pass away, but my words will not pass away" (Matt 24:35).

God's acts in history have been interpreted for us in words, and those interpretations have been written down and recorded in what we now value as the holy Scriptures, the classic and inspired writings first of all of the people of Israel and then of the Christian community. Through them we have access to the words that bear witness to the Word, which is Jesus Christ. Through them that Word is able to speak to us. The Scriptures are rooted in history, in events that have happened in which the presence of God has particularly been discerned: the calling of Abraham, the raising up of Moses, the exodus, the giving of the Law and the covenant, the exile in Babylon, the coming of the Christ, and the coming of the Spirit. According to 2 Timothy 3:16, "All scripture is inspired by God and is useful for teaching, for reproof, for correction, and for training in righteousness, so that everyone who belongs to God may be proficient, equipped for every good work." The Scriptures here are "the sacred writings that are able to instruct you for salvation through faith in Christ Jesus" (v. 15). These verses summarize the convictions the Christian community has about the Bible, Old and New Testaments. The word translated "inspired" here literally means "God-breathed," and so has more the sense of *"ex*pired" rather than *"in*spired." The Scriptures come to us from God through a variety of witnesses and writers who have been moved and guided by God to write down their testimony and give an account of their interpretation of the acts and doings of God. In this sense, the Scriptures are both human and divine, bearing all the hallmarks of the full humanity of the writers, while at the same time possessing a quality and an authority that marks them out as divinely given.

INSPIRATION

One way to illustrate the nature of inspiration is to imagine a teacher who has a class full of pupils. The teacher is very inspiring and engages each pupil to the full. As a consequence, each pupil shows the influence of the teacher in the work he or she produces, but each one also does so in a way that bears all the characteristics of his or her own personality and understanding. An observer would be able to detect the marks of the teacher's inspiration in the perspectives and approach of each pupil, but would also recognize their own individuality and distinctiveness. In a similar way, each of the biblical writers has been taken hold of by a common theme that runs through the Bible, but all tell their story in a way that is true to themselves. The outcome is an unfolding narrative that cumulatively bears testimony to the revelatory work of God. For all its humanity, the fact that the Scriptures are inspired by God means that God has enabled the biblical writers to render their own witness to the work of God and to do so in ways that are truthful, reliable, and sufficient.

According to the Timothy texts, the primary purpose of these Scriptures is "to instruct you for salvation through faith in Jesus Christ" and, secondarily, to equip the believer for righteous living and godly service. The Scriptures, then, bear witness to the reality of God as the creator of the world and to God's work of salvation from the time of Abraham and culminating in the coming of the Messiah whose name is Jesus. Although the author of the Fourth Gospel was speaking of his own Gospel, the explanation of his purpose in writing can be applied to the whole body of biblical writings: "Now Jesus did many other signs in the presence of his disciples, which are not written in this book. But these are written so that you may come to believe that Jesus is the Messiah, the Son of God, and that through believing you may have life in his name" (John 20:30–31). In pursuing this goal, the Scriptures are certainly reliable, and they are also sufficient: they tell us as much as we need to know to achieve their purpose. They do not tell us everything about everything, and many questions are left open and mysterious, perhaps to be addressed through the adventure of theological reflection and discussion. But they are enough to be, "a lamp to my feet and a light to my path" (Ps 119:105). Through the many words of Scripture emerges the Word, which is the self-communication of God's own self and which is supremely given in Jesus Christ, who is God's presence in person in the midst of human beings.

    The word "inspiration" both says something about how the Scriptures have come to us from God and also about the experience of reading them. When read with an open heart and a degree of faith, the Scriptures possess a kind of divine energy or spirituality that has a way of working upon the reader. They possess the power to illuminate, to open our eyes to new realities. They can pierce into our hearts and are sometimes likened to a "sword": "Indeed, the word of God is living and active, sharper than any two-edged sword, piercing until it divides soul from spirit, joints from marrow; it is able to judge the thoughts and intentions of the heart. And before him no creature is hidden, but all are naked and laid bare to the eyes of the one to whom we must render an account" (Heb 4:12–13). We attribute this effect to the Holy Spirit, whose presence in and through the Scriptures is implied in the word "inspired," the Spirit being the breath of God. The Spirit enables the Scriptures to become a word from God that illuminates our hearts and minds: "I pray that the God of our Lord Jesus Christ, the Father of glory, may give you a spirit of wisdom and revelation as you come to know him, so that, with the eyes of your heart enlightened, you may know what is the hope to which he has called you, what are the riches of his glorious inheritance among the saints" (Eph 1:18). The role of the words of holy Scripture is to open us up to the one who is the very Word of God, Christ "in whom are hidden all the treasures of wisdom and knowledge" (Col 2:3).

INTERPRETING THE BIBLE

It should be clear from what has been said that the Bible is a book that is central to the life of the church and that it should be read, marked, learnt, and inwardly digested. As believers study the Scriptures and listen to its message, as they follow its various plots and sub-plots, as they reflect upon its many characters and their doings, as they take on board its positive witness, as they wrestle with its more difficult passages and presentations, so they absorb its truths and are shaped by what they read. Sometimes this is achieved through the questions it provokes as much as through the affirmations it invites. The Bible should be read systematically in gatherings for worship; it should be studied and pondered in the company of other Christians and in private. Believers should aim both for a broad knowledge of the whole biblical landscape and also for a detailed grasp of individual books and passages. It will quickly become clear that the Bible is a long and complex book and that it does not yield up its witness easily at every point. This is all the more reason to engage with it in depth. Listening to the Bible is a lifetime's work. And the challenges the Bible poses to a reader through its more obscure, difficult, and troubling passages are an invitation to think and study more profoundly, to seek to understand why they have been included in the text.

In the provision of inspired writings as the primary and classical record of God's revelation we cannot avoid the conclusion that God has taken a great risk. By placing the Bible in human hands the risk of mistranslation, misinterpretation, and misuse has been opened up. There is the risk that the manuscripts on which our Bibles are based are themselves faulty and have been corrupted. Fortunately, and unlike most other ancient texts, we possess so many of these ancient manuscripts, especially of the New Testament, that it becomes possible by a scientific process of careful and scholarly comparison to reconstruct the originals with high levels of accuracy. Even so, it is well known that any translation work runs the constant danger of betraying the original meaning of a text. At this point, the existence of many translations allows for contrast and comparison in opening up the full meaning of the original languages. More risky still is the possibility of misinterpretation such that we impose our own meaning on the biblical text and then proclaim our faulty interpretation to be the authoritative Word of God. It becomes clear that it is one thing to have the Bible, truthful, reliable, and sufficient as it is, and another to understand its witness accurately and interpret it faithfully. On some matters, a range of interpretations could enrich rather than distort our understanding of the Bible, but there are some areas where the very nature of Christianity depends upon an agreed and shared interpretation. The Bible cannot mean everything and anything we want it to, and so the way we approach it needs to be guided by reliable principles.

We have already indicated that the Bible records and interprets the acts of God in human history: it is an historical book and the Christian faith is an historical religion, rather than, say, a nature religion or a form of timeless philosophy. At its core, therefore, the Bible is historical and certain events, supremely the life, death, and resurrection of Jesus, must be historically grounded in order for the Christian faith to be true. If they did not happen then the faith must fall. But the Bible is historical in a further sense in that it reflects at every point the language, culture, imagery, assumptions, and levels of understanding of the ages in which it was written. The historical events at the Bible's core are therefore described and interpreted in ways that reflect the contexts out of which they emerged. To take the Bible seriously means taking it on its own terms and not imposing upon it the assumptions of our present age and society. The biblical writers rendered their witness in the only ways they knew how, and these are not necessarily identical with our own approaches, conventions, and preferences. All of this needs to be borne in mind when we interpret the Scriptures and the following principles are relevant to this task.

The Bible is a diverse book. It is not unrelentingly one kind of literature, but comes to us in many literary forms and genres. Each book, and each part of each book, needs to be understood with reference to the kind of literature it is. As Hebrews 1:1 puts it: "Long ago God spoke to our ancestors in many and various ways by the prophets." The "many and various ways" includes writings that contain history, poetry, liturgy, laws, statutes, ordinances, legend, saga, apocalyptic, proverbs, parables, letters, gospels, songs and hymns, laments, story, allegories, metaphor, eye-witness accounts, figures of speech, and myth. None of these forms should be seen as judgments on the truth of the content of what is being communicated but as descriptions of the literary forms in which that truth comes. Reference has been made previously, for instance, to the category of "myth," concerning which there are particular misunderstandings. Despite its popular usage to mean something that is not true, in literary terms it refers to a form of story in which we are symbolically presented with what is persistently true about ourselves. It helps us understand the Bible to recognize that not everything in it should be taken literally and factually. Either we take the Bible literally at every point or we take it seriously as a truly historical book. As an example, and as has been noted, to read the book of Revelation literally is completely to misunderstand what its message is in the context of its times.

Each part of the Bible, therefore, needs to be read according to the literary form that is in play.

The Bible is a book with many contexts. Reference to the Bible's "timeless truths" is not true to the nature of the Bible itself. The Bible is very much "in time." Certainly there are truths that endure and that are true for all contexts and places, the commands to love God and neighbor are examples. But these are truths that have been spoken into particular contexts and that derive their expression from them. The very nature of prophecy, for instance, is not to announce high truths that are abstracted from any concrete situation but to speak a word from God into particular times and places. To understand them fully we must grasp the context. We might then also see that they have relevance in part or whole for other contexts and places, but equally their relevance might change according to the new context. The length of a man's or a woman's hair, or whether or not their head is to be covered (discussed in 1 Cor 11:13–16) was an issue in first-century Jewish and Greek culture, and still would be in some Islamic contexts, in a way that is not the case in Western societies. Yet the underlying issues of propriety, modesty, and not bringing the faith into disrepute are matters of enduring concern, even if they are to be expressed differently. Not every biblical stipulation needs to be made universal.

The Bible is a book of unfolding revelation. Revelation expands over time so that the will and purpose of God becomes clearer and more comprehensible as the light shines more brightly. The implication of this is that although all Scripture is inspired by God, not every part of it possesses the same degree of luminous relevance or authority. Some biblical passages are one-offs and unique, never to be repeated, such as the problematic passages in which God is said to require the merciless eradication of the Canaanite tribes (Deut 7:1–6). Such passages do not constitute norms for behavior but are regarded as "sealed" to the particular contexts from which they derive. Other commands are of limited duration and fall away as the mercy of God is more fully understood, such as the severe forms of punishment for some misdemeanors (Lev 20:10–16). Other themes and practices are transcended as a fuller understanding of God's will and purpose progressively becomes known.

The technical term for this process of interpretation is "sublation," and a good grasp of it is necessary for a proper interpretation of Scripture. A biblical theme can be "sublated" when it is taken up into a higher level of teaching or understanding and both rendered unnecessary in its present form and yet fulfilled by means of the new form it assumes. Jesus intended something like this when he said, "Do not think I have come to abolish the law or the prophets; I have come not to abolish but to fulfill" (Matt 5:17).

Jesus was warning his disciples not to believe that he had come to lessen the moral demand of Israel's law but rather to intensify that demand by bringing it to fulfillment. The supreme example of sublation is the way in which animal sacrifices were rendered unnecessary by the unique and once-for-all self-sacrifice of Christ on the cross (Heb 9:11–14, 25–28). Having made atonement, the perpetual offering of the blood of animals as prescribed in Hebrew religion no longer needed to happen, indeed these were seen to be mainly provisional pending the work of atonement by Christ. The power of sacrifice was taken up into Christ's own sacrifice and rendered unnecessary in its old form. Nonetheless, all the concepts that lie behind the idea of atoning sacrifices, and all the detailed instructions that are contained for Israel's benefit in the Hebrew Scriptures, might still have meaning for the Christian in illuminating and illustrating what it is that Christ has done. The same process of sublation can be seen in the practice of circumcision (which now becomes a matter of the heart rather than the body—Rom 2:29), the role of the temple (it is now the people of God who are understood as God's temple—Eph 2:21), and the Sabbath (which becomes a symbol of the rest we find in God—Heb 4:9). The principle of sublation means that the Christian reading the Old Testament can find it profitable for growing in wisdom and understanding without being obliged to put into practice all that it requires.

The Bible is to be interpreted through Christ. It should be clear then that the coming of Christ has made a considerable difference to the way we read the Hebrew Scriptures and relate them to ourselves. Once more we understand that the Christian faith is the interpretation of the faith of Israel and its Scriptures through the lens of a Messiah who was crucified and then raised. For the Christian, the Scriptures of the ancient covenant build up to Christ and enable us to interpret who he is and what he has done. Those of the new covenant bear witness to the fuller revelation of God in him. Christ is like the sun shining at its brightest. The Scriptures record for us God's acts and their interpretation in words. They are full of words from God and inspired wisdom, all of which carries weight and has spiritual power for the reader. But Christ is the Word of God, the one to whom the words point and who is in the fullest sense God's self-revelation. He is our final reference-point, the lens through which the rest of the Scriptures is to be viewed. No one point of Scripture should be taken as independent or as comprehensible without reference to Christ. The role of Scripture is to lead us to Christ and to offer obedience to him. Sadly, it is possible to read the Bible yet miss this point: "You search the Scriptures because you think that in them you have eternal life; and it is they that testify on my behalf. Yet you refuse to come to me to have life" (John 5:39–40). For the Christian, Christ-less readings of the Scriptures are no longer possible.

RESPONSIBLE INTERPRETATION

The Bible to be understood has to be interpreted and that means entering into its thought forms and unique perspectives. One helpful and imaginative analogy that has been suggested is to liken the Bible to a Shakespearean play in five acts of which the final act has yet to be written. The decision is made to gather a cast of skilled actors to improvise the fifth act. To do this they must immerse themselves in the first four acts, becoming acquainted with its plots, its characters, its predictions, its trajectories and thought-forms, and to pick up the hints and suggestions it makes as to how the play is destined to end. Above all, the actors are seeking to go beyond the mere text in order to enter into the mind of the author. They are formed and shaped by what they discover. In their improvisation they must stay true to the four acts already given, refusing to depart from them, but to maintain continuity with them, yet moving the narrative forward to its conclusion. To do this they need creative imagination, each other's assistance and a degree of inspiration.

Applied to the Bible we might imagine that there are four acts already written and they are about creation, fall, Israel, and Jesus. In addition, the first scenes of the final act are also written and they constitute the rest of the New Testament. Christian churches are communities of Bible readers and interpreters who are intentional about living "under the Word of God," letting it exert its life-giving authority among them. They have to live in the time of the fifth act, the present age in which God's purposes are being carried forward. They have the help and perspectives of each other in this task and most of all that of God's Spirit who continues to inspire and illuminate their understanding. Being true to biblical authority does not mean slavishly repeating what is there but rather becoming people who, because of their engagement with the Word, the words and the Spirit, truly know God, can discern God's mind and can faithfully live out God's purposes for today. They value the tradition of the Christian church, since it represents the ways in which previous generations of disciples have themselves heard the Word of God speaking to them. They also value the insights that come to them through reason, science, and the various branches of human inquiry. But all of these approaches are, for them, subject to the prior authority of God's Word as it comes to them through the Scriptures, and it is this that makes them different, lends them spiritual life and motivation, and gives them a cutting edge in the world. It is by such spiritual transformation that they become people shaped by divine revelation and able to serve the purpose of God for their generation. Supremely it is their commitment not to use the words of the Bible against people but to interpret them in love with a view to becoming complete and mature as followers of the Christ. This is their objective as they study and interpret the Scriptures—to first hear the Word of God for themselves and then to bear witness to it in the world: "Do not be conformed to this world, but be transformed by the renewing of your minds, so that you may discern what is the will of God—what is good and acceptable and perfect" (Rom 12:2); "Those who are spiritual discern all things, and they are themselves subject to no-one's scrutiny. 'For who has known the mind of the Lord so as to instruct him?' But we have the mind of Christ" (1 Cor 2:15–16).

17

The Goodness of God and the World's Suffering

PERHAPS THE GREATEST CHALLENGE to the Christian faith and its resolute belief in the goodness of God is the presence of pain in the world. How can a compassionate God and a suffering world be reconciled? It was in response to such questions that one of the Bible's most outstanding examples of literature came to be written, the book of Job (see the reference in Ezek 14:14). This is an early human writing that seeks to deal with the question of undeserved suffering. In itself, pain can be understood to be one of the mechanisms essential for protection in life; a signal that harm is being done, but the problem consists in the amount of pain that the world endures and its often apparently pointless nature. The conviction of the Christian community is that despite the seemingly overwhelming amount of human and animal suffering, it remains true that the world is God's good creation and that God is unambiguously good. Although, for the present, this must be an unprovable statement of faith, it is one that will in the fullness of God's time finally be shown to be true.

THE GOODNESS OF GOD

How we interpret the world depends upon where we are standing. For the moment, each and every human being is caught up in the events of life and occupies a very limited vantage point. It is no surprise therefore that there should be many questions that we struggle to answer since we cannot grasp the world and events within it in their full context. The point is that interpretation depends upon perspective, and we struggle to achieve perspective. Where we are standing inevitably shapes the ways in which we understand the world around us. Events, to be understood, need a degree of distance from beyond themselves to see how they relate to the whole. This is true of the wider world, whose events are often perplexing and confusing. It is also true of our own lives. All of us are time bound, contextually limited. Inevitably we see things from a self-interested and parochial perspective. Our evaluation of events, their apparent "goodness" or otherwise, accords with whether or not they contribute immediately to our perceived benefit. Sometimes, given distance and time, we begin to glimpse how experiences that at one time were unwelcome and unwanted actually shaped and formed us in ways we have come to value. At other times we see the "meaning" of things not at all. And human beings are inevitably wedded to the short term, rather than the long run. What we are able to consider "good" has, therefore, a rather limited scope. But the goodness of God is related to God's wisdom, the divine capacity to see things within the context not just of the long term but of the final goal of all things, and the divine patience, the capacity of God to endure in ways that we cannot until God's own purpose is fulfilled.

In the narrative of biblical revelation God is consistently understood to be good and to be the creator of a world that is itself structurally good. In Israel's psalms this is repeated time and time again: "O give thanks to the LORD, for he is good; for his steadfast love endures forever" (Ps 107:1). As we have seen, this point is significantly made in the first chapter of the Bible with its repeated statement, "And God saw that it was good," culminating with the final affirmation after the creation of humanity, "God saw everything that he had made, and indeed, it was very good" (Gen 1:12, 18, 21, 25, 31.). A good God created a good world, a world that is fit for purpose, for the growth and flourishing of all created things. God turns towards the creation with good will and wills its well-being and its peace. Whatever else needs to be said subsequent to this, it remains true that Christians hold to a doctrine of "original goodness."

This goodness of God is so frequently stressed in the Hebrew Scriptures as arguably to have the status of an interpretative key to the whole. The goodness, grace, and compassion of God, God's forgiving nature and his steadfast love are expressed in the strongest of terms. But this does not mean that the divine purity and holiness are lessened. God's love is holy love. God does not pass over sin and wrongdoing. Goodness is neither weakness nor indulgence. The Scriptures leave us in no doubt as to the passionate nature of the God of Israel and of the supremacy of the loving goodness that is God's own being. Whatever other images of God are employed in the

Hebrew Scriptures, and it is to be confessed that some of them are perplexing, this supreme vision of the goodness of God is Israel's understanding at its most mature and complete. It is one that is fully endorsed in the ministry of Jesus and in the New Testament.

A WORLD AT RISK

Given the kind of world we inhabit it is not surprising that the goodness of God should be contested, and with it the reality of God in any meaningful, certainly any Christian, sense of the word. Despite living lives more secure and more prosperous than at any point in history, we in the modern world are seemingly and paradoxically more aware of the world's suffering than at any time in the past. Human intellectual life has taken a turn to the self-obsessed in such a way as to be more preoccupied with God giving an account of God's own self to human beings than with the accountability of sinners before God. We also are more aware of the vastness of the scale on which the universe operates than can ever have been possible in the past. Whereas traditional theology was able to trace suffering in the creation back to the moral failure and culpability of Adam and Eve, this is now much more difficult, to the point of needing severe qualification. Whereas it was once maintained that Adam by his original sin perverted the whole order of nature in heaven and on earth, modern minds are much more aware of the age of the earth and the long processes of evolutionary history that preceded the appearance of the human race on earth, a history shot through with dying, death, struggle, conflict, and pain. How do we think of the goodness of the creator in the light of what has actually been created?

By any accounts, God has created a vulnerable, threatened world. Having ordered the primeval chaos out of which the structured world we know has emerged, it seems yet to be the case that the well-being of this creation is threatened by non-being, by a threatening chaos that has never fully been overcome. The chaos persists. To focus for a moment solely on the human dimension, humanity is *biologically* at risk. The processes of genetic reproduction lie open to misfiring in such a way as to give rise to minds and bodies that are not only less than fully able-bodied but sometimes tragically disabled. Humanity is *environmentally* at risk, in that we inhabit an ecology that is subject to catastrophe, to floods and hurricanes, to volcanoes and earthquakes, to fires, epidemics, diseases, viruses, strange mutations, and wild beasts that are significantly beyond our powers to order. Humanity is *historically* at risk in that we are held in the grip of forces over which ordinary people, and even powerful rulers, have as often as not no control, the aberrations of war and conflict, of power-seeking and power-keeping, of the oppression of the weak by the strong. History is a risky business and it has numerous victims, of whom the majority suffer innocently. Humanity is *morally* at risk with a seeming inability to resist the overwhelming power of temptation to do wrong and the ability not proper to any other creature to destroy ourselves, other species and our environment. And may we add that in the normative Christian vision human beings are *ultimately* at risk if it is indeed true that there are destinies that await us, that human potential is not exhausted by the experience of the present age, but that there are ages to come in which for good or ill we reap the harvest we have sown in the few short years, for some *very* few years, in this age.

Enough has been said to make the point, and the point is well enough known anyway. How can belief in the goodness of God be maintained in the face of the tragic risks to which human beings have been exposed and on account of which they suffer? Are we not verging on the incoherent when we continue to believe in such goodness? Can this really be done?

THE FREE-WILL DEFENSE

Many of Christianity's cultured despisers are clear that indeed it cannot. The established argument to this effect is still considered to be a powerful refutation of Christian belief: "Is God willing to prevent evil, but not able? Then he is impotent. Is he able, but not willing? Then he is malevolent. Is he both able and willing? Whence then is evil?" The classical Christian response to this proposed dilemma is the free-will defense, according to which even the omnipotence of God is circumscribed by the responsible and misusable freedom that a good creator has bestowed on creatures. On this account, it is precisely because of the goodness of God that humans are made with the capacity to respond to God and to do so freely, a capacity that implies the possibility also of withholding free response and so of participating in creation's deviation from the divine purpose. Here it may rightly be claimed that though embodied, earthly existence has its own fair share of suffering and pain, the worst forms of suffering come about through human agency, when human beings behave violently and rapaciously, without empathy and thought for others. It is at this point that we might rightly distinguish between *suffering* and *evil*. Evil causes suffering, but not all suffering comes from what is evil, since for there to be evil there must be malicious intent. At this point the Christian analysis of sin—which understands human beings as fallen, corrupted, and depraved creatures—rings true and is corroborated by the witness of history. Human beings can act like wild dogs and should be held responsible for their deeds.

Strong though the free-will defense continues to be, and cogently argued though it has been, it does not yet embrace all aspects of the dilemma. Human beings are already late arrivals on the evolutionary scene and emerged within a world that had already learnt to embed within itself patterns of conflict and predation for which human moral failure cannot be held responsible. Humans are culpable in their apparent unwillingness to rise above those patterns, but it is not they who have created them. To cater for this critique, the free-will defense might further be applied at a transcendent level to creatures, like the angels, that have allegedly preceded humans in rebelling against God. Such a doctrine of an "angelic catastrophe" has a long history in Christian doctrine, as we have already noted. The fall of "Lucifer" is therefore said to account for creation's bondage to decay before ever human beings emerged. On this reading, the one who "subjected creation to futility," as mentioned in Romans 8:20, was Lucifer. The sin of humans is that they join with the existing resistance to divine rule rather than reversing it.

Such a theory, although widely believed and with a long pedigree, labors both under the difficulty of being mythical in language and minimal within the biblical testimony, such that it can hardly count as a biblical doctrine (as we have previously discussed). Yet it may point us in a fruitful direction in that it locates the origins of sin in aberrations within the created sphere arising from the misuse of freedoms that not only human beings but the creation itself has. This is theologically significant in that it allows for the affirmation that God has created a good world whilst recognizing that in this good world things are not at all the way they are supposed to be. Rather than choose the mythic approach of a fall of angels to explain this, an alternative is to recognize that nature itself, having been granted its own kinds of freedom to develop and grow, has the power to deviate from the divine intention, to explore avenues of development that are in conflict with the divine nature and that constitute a world in which, even before human beings emerged, the natural world was already "fallen," tending towards the chaos over against which it is called to exist. This is the reality towards which the mythic account of a fall of angels points. Creation as a whole has its own freedoms and its own forms of resistance to God and so stands in need of redemption.

THE WISDOM OF GOD

The free-will defense has stood the tests of time and is indispensable within this discussion. But there are other ways of approaching the subject, and these can be found in the idea of the wisdom of God, which is closely aligned to that of the goodness of God. There is that which defies explanation. God is not a human being who can be spoken of as though God were one of us, explicable in terms we apply to ourselves. God is infinite wisdom and we should not expect that the divine ways will be readily comprehensible to us. "For my thoughts are not your thoughts, nor are my ways your ways, says the LORD. For as the heavens are higher than the earth, so are my ways higher than your ways and my thoughts than your thoughts" (Isa 55:8-9). This should perhaps prepare us to live with mystery and the unknown. It is possible to live with unresolved questions, and unresolved pain, by trusting to the wisdom of God, which passes understanding. And belief in the goodness of God may be maintained in the face of realities that may seem ostensibly to be contrary to it.

The approach adopted in this chapter looks for the resolution of the mystery of divine goodness and creation's suffering to the promised future, the ultimate horizon of human hope, when universal history reaches its goal and at last we creatures gain the perspective to see for ourselves the meaning of things. This is a fully biblical perspective. In the words of Paul the apostle, "I consider that the sufferings of this present time are not worth comparing with the glory that is to be revealed to us. For the creation waits with eager longing for the revealing of the children of God" (Rom 8:19). Or, "For now we see in a mirror, dimly, but then we shall see face to face. Now I know only in part; then I will know fully, even as I have been fully known" (1 Cor 13:12). Why it has to be this way is a mystery hidden in the wisdom of God. What we have is not an explanation but a confidence, a hope that enables us to endure and to believe. Yet this is not a hope without substantiation. Behind it there lies the general witness of the Hebrew and Christian Scriptures, which themselves grow out of experience of God that has endured through time, the experience born through difficulty and adversity that nonetheless God's heart is wonderfully kind. "Although he causes grief, he will have compassion according to the abundance of his steadfast love; for he does not willingly afflict or grieve anyone" (Lam 3:32-33).

Even more significant, from a Christian perspective, are the events that are definitional for understanding the ways of God, namely the cross and resurrection of Christ. If the cross is an indication of God's willingness to identify with, even to embrace, the depths of human pain in its many manifestations, the resurrection is the sign of God's power to transform even this into glory and blessedness. The cross and resurrection are not simply events, they are *signature* events, indications of the way God chooses to work in the world and bring to pass a gracious purpose. The providence of God does not exclude the possibilities of tragedy, loss, and suffering, but contains the capacity to absorb, overcome, and transform them into a greater, ultimate purpose the full consequences of which we have yet to see, but concerning which we may hope with confidence. The wisdom of God has not excluded the possibility of a world that can become bound to death and decay, but to the contrary has determined that it is just through such a world that God's own glory and goodness might finally be displayed, to the infinite benefit of creatures.

DIVINE PROVIDENCE AND THE FREEDOM OF CREATURES

How then are we to imagine this providential purpose? In what follows there is one approach that is rejected and another that is advocated. The position rejected is that which is sometimes known as the doctrine of "meticulous providence," namely the belief that because God's will is supreme everything that happens in the world is ordained and willed by God. Such a doctrine seeks to glorify God by attributing all events to the divine will. On this account, if there is any real randomness or uncertainty in nature or history then God is not God. Rather, everything that happens in nature and in human history is foreordained by God. Yet crucially, this should not be seen as compromising divine goodness since what counts is intention. What God determines is determined with good intention, whereas human beings who sin do so with bad intention and this constitutes their actions as evil. Advocates of this view therefore seek to preserve the goodness of God by an assertion: God is good, period, whatever God does. It appears that evil is ordained by God, yet paradoxically God is not its author. When the coherence of this statement is questioned appeal is made both to divine mystery and sovereignty. Who are we to question God?

This account of providence is surely problematic. If God actively wills what is evil, it requires considerable mental gymnastics to preserve the divine goodness. In the face of this criticism we are left with a bare assertion that divine goodness is not compromised. Yet it is one thing to attribute evil to wrongful creaturely choices and quite another to assert that the many destructive and disastrous events that happen, apparently randomly, in the world and that catch up the innocent in their happening are in fact deliberately willed and planned by God for our good. At the same time, it is surely right to assert that everything that happens must in some way be related to the will of God if God is to be God. If God *wills to permit*, for instance, it is still God who does the willing since God is not a victim of circumstance. Yet there are alternative ways of construing the matter that better safeguard both the sovereign will and the goodness of God. Here is one possible way.

God has willed to create a world that contains agents that are free. To be sure, any freedom granted to creatures can only be freedom if exercised within a world of existing constraints and necessities. This is such a world. Freedom is constrained within limits. The granting of freedom to creatures is itself part of the work of creation and results in a world of massive variety and fruitfulness, of diversity and difference. It is itself a creative mechanism. God's creation involves calling things into being, constructing entities out of what has been made and enabling creatures also to make themselves, to realize the potential with which they are imbued. God creates by "letting be," as is implied in the blessing upon creation in the Genesis narrative and the imperative to "be fruitful and multiply" (Gen 1:22, 28). In being dependent upon God, the creation has its own divinely willed responsiveness and freedom over against God. It possesses agency. In the act of willing creation God foreknows all things, including all that created agents will do and how the personal God will respond in the light of such actions. The divine omnipotence is therefore also well conceived as *divine omnicompetence*, the capacity of the unfathomable creator to respond to creatures' actions, to redeem them, fashion them, and comprehend them within an over-riding purpose. God does not therefore actively will all that happens, but God lets creation be so that it too has agency, the capacity, even if a limited one within the constraints of necessity, to direct itself. At the level of the animal creation this may be understood as randomness and variation, but at the human level it has the character of choice, of responsiveness or its lack. The project of creation is not well thought of as an enactment of what has been already decided from eternity but as in itself an act of creation, a process of unfolding, the living of a story. And God's purpose is to work through all things "for good for those who love God, who are called according to his purpose" (Rom 8:28). Such an approach does not necessarily answer all the questions, but it does offer a way of living hopefully with that which we do not and cannot truly understand until God's project of creation is complete.

LIFE AS A "VALE OF SOUL-MAKING"

At this point it may be worth saying that the goodness of God and the goodness of creation need not be taken to mean that earthly existence was ever intended to be easy. One common approach imagines a world of perfection from which we have fallen by reason of human sin. We have lost out on paradise. Indeed, Christians frequently speak as though prior to the fall the world was perfect, as God intended it to be. By contrast, an alternative approach views paradise as a future reality to be attained and the world as a "vale of soul-making." The condition of human beings arises not from a fall from perfection but from a *failure to rise* to the vocation of living in the image of God. It is a falling short of a destiny (Rom 3:23). In this account the first human beings were not perfect but only at the beginning of a journey that would bring them to perfection in the fullness of time. They were given a good beginning, but the beginning is not the destination. The world they inhabited was one in which they would encounter difficulty, danger, and struggle, but within it they were called to learn how to trust in God as dependent creatures. It was intended as a place in which, through facing and overcoming life's challenges, people might achieve depth and character. Their very vulnerability was the spur for trust and faith in their creator in communion with whom all of life's obstacles could be addressed. When this world was pronounced "very good" by its creator (Gen 1:31), what was implied is not that creation was already perfect but that it was "fit for purpose," and the purpose intended was that of soul-making, the growth of humans through struggle, adventure, and exploration to maturity and completeness. The approach favored in the present chapter follows this second approach.

GOD'S ULTIMATE PURPOSE

Much of what we have so far considered is still within the framework of the free-will defense, the justification of the goodness of God by reference to the freedom of the creature, a freedom that is itself a higher good that is worth the "risk" it inherently involves. Our attention now turns more decisively to the dimension of the ultimate divine purpose that undergirds the world and its history, the assertion that the world's sufferings need to be seen against the future purposed by God, which is itself unimaginably beautiful in its goodness. Given the weight of the world's suffering, what future hope might possibly justify the cost involved?

Once more there are two approaches worth comparing and in so doing we revisit material that has already been explored. There is a strong and persistent pattern of thought amongst Christians that reasons as follows: it is clear from the Scriptures that history has a double outcome, heaven or hell, eternal life or eternal damnation, a final divorce of the redeemed and the lost. We can account for this double outcome in one of two ways: (1) it is a consequence of human free will and choice. Salvation is offered to all and those who decline it doom themselves to eternal loss; or (2) it is a consequence of the divine choice. God wills that it be so in order to reveal both divine mercy and divine justice. History reveals what has in fact been the divine intention from the beginning, to save some and to damn others. This doctrine is known as "double predestination" and claims to be a logical and necessary deduction from the evidence. The issue at stake is the priority and supremacy of the divine will. If human beings determine the double outcome then human beings and their choices are finally sovereign in creation, and not God. To safeguard the sovereignty of God, the double outcome has to be ascribed to God's own will and decision. Yet the cost of this position is high, since the notion that God creates some with the intention and purpose of damning them for all eternity inevitably casts a shadow over the nature of God's goodness. Traditionally it is countered by the retreat into assertion and mystery: God is good despite the way it may seem to us. By definition what God chooses must be good. It is our human perceptions of goodness that are skewed, not God's. As Paul says in a relevant passage, "But who are you, a human being, to argue with God?" (Rom 9:20).

Some Christians have clearly found this to be a satisfactory way of thinking about the eternal purposes of God, others that such theological logics seriously undermine a doctrine of God's goodness. On the other hand, neither is the alternative resolution of the difficulty that puts destiny in the hands of human beings altogether persuasive. Christian theology is about confidence in God, and God's ability to achieve that which God purposes. It is possible to justify the reality of evil in the world only if we also conceive that it is massively outweighed by a final purpose that God has the power and patience to bring to pass. Suffering remains agonizing suffering, but awareness of the divine presence on the journey towards the ultimate triumph of God's good purpose does at least give some sense of hope and meaning. Yet for this assurance properly to outweigh the weight of human suffering it becomes necessary to think of the final and abundant salvation of God's creatures—if not a universal salvation then certainly one that includes the majority of creatures and insists that God's love can save us all. The impetus towards this is *moral*. God surely has the power not to allow the divine purposes to be frustrated, but rather to prevent creatures rejecting their own good by persisting in the pursuit of the lost.

It is possible to hold an understanding of universal salvation without of necessity embracing "universalism" as some kind of forgone conclusion. Life is indeed risky, the human heart obdurate and the power of human decision a reality. God is debtor to no human being and the final number of the redeemed is God's alone to decide. We cannot presume upon the grace of God nor settle down into any kind of complacency, since this would be a lack of reverence towards the Holy One. Yet the reference to a "great multitude that no one could count" (Rev 7:9) leads us to think adventurously. The goodness and wisdom of God can be defended more coherently within an ultimate vision congruent with the biblical hope that the end towards which all things are tending is one in which all things visible and invisible experience redemption (Col 1:19–20). To affirm that the almighty God loves all begs the question of why an all-powerful God should be unable finally to save all, should God so choose. In relation to our particular topic, the greater the scope of salvation, the more the goodness of God can be asserted in the face of the world's suffering and pain.

The biblical vision carries our gaze in the direction of a greater hope more wonderful than any of us can currently predict or imagine. And this surely bears upon the question of God's goodness. If the final outcome is in any sense close to what the New Testament images for the creation then the sufferings of this present age can indeed be seen in a different perspective. This perspective does not make pain less painful, or cruelty less cruel, but it may help us to live with the mystery in the confidence that God is not only good, but also wise, infinitely wiser than ourselves, and that God is also patient in ways that we are not, patient with the creation and the final bringing about of the day when the earth will be filled with the knowledge, the glory, and the goodness of God.

What therefore matters is how we live in the present, how we respond to events good or ill that come our way, how we learn to live with resilience as people of faith, hope, and love in a world replete with overwhelming experiences in the face of which we are sometimes powerless. Believing that God is indeed good, wise, and patient has the potential to make us also good, wise, and patient, and so in this valley of soul-making to become people of depth, of resilience, and of compassion. It is true that the problem of human suffering causes people, believers and unbelievers alike, to question the goodness of God. There is a form of atheism that is so distressed by the presence of pain and suffering that it abolishes any idea of God in order to protest against it. A God who permits this kind of thing is not worth believing in, so it claims. However satisfying this may feel to the outraged mind or the wounded heart, it is difficult to see how it in any way alters or changes the situation. If there is no God, then suffering, death, and final extinction are all there is, and the dying of the light all there can be to look forward to. Such a view permits no hope of healing or renewal or restoration of the world. By contrast, belief in a God who has an ultimate purpose of redemption is the true protest against such a dying and pointless world. It is an affirmation of life that in spite of all enables us to live with hope, trust, and joy. It is the confidence that the last word to be spoken of is one of life and not death. God is the guarantee that these things shall be.

18

Humanity's Spiritual Quest

ACCORDING TO THE APOSTLE Paul, speaking to the Athenians in Acts 17:26–27, "From one ancestor [God] made all nations to inhabit the whole earth, and he allotted the times of their existence and the boundaries of the places where they would live, so that they would search for God and perhaps grope for him and find him—though indeed he is not far from each one of us. For 'in him we live and move and have our being,' as even some of your own poets have said." It is a profound human intuition that the physical, material creation is bounded by a world of spiritual, transcendent reality. There are indeed more things in heaven and earth than are dreamt of in human philosophies. Humanity's religious and spiritual quest is a universal phenomenon because humanity's deepest needs are spiritual in nature. As long as there have been human beings, there has been religion in some shape or form, to the point that a religious sense can be identified as a fundamental aspect of human nature. It appears now to be an established fact that human beings are hard-wired to be religious, to give allegiance to some power or powers beyond themselves, and to see purpose in things. Religious thinking and practice of some kind appears, then, in the evolution of human beings, as a defining aspect of the *humanum*, the essential quality of what it means to be human. It represents the human quest to find meaning outside and beyond themselves in a spiritual reality that impinges upon them, even if it is not clearly understood. Such attempts may be clumsy and ill-informed, as the use of the word "grope" to translate Paul's words implies, but the fact that they exist at all tells us something significant about humanity and, potentially, about the world we inhabit.

THE BENEFITS OF RELIGION

Why human beings are hard-wired to be religious is worth considering. According to one theory, religion belongs to the survival mechanisms thrown up by the evolutionary process. So, in order to ensure the likelihood of the survival of their own species, human beings have developed ways of giving themselves and each other extra value by asserting that there is some special relationship between humans and the realm of the divine, such as the notion that humans are made in the image of God. Killing one another, or at least killing members of one's own tribe, is therefore forbidden as a sacrilegious act; and although this does not prevent it happening, it does inhibit it. Religion, therefore, is a survival mechanism. Some would go on to assert that since it has done its job it is no longer needed. A second approach links religion with morality. If we have a sense that we are being observed by God or gods, even when we are on our own, we are more likely to behave well than not. A sense of God inhibits bad behavior and encourages the good, and here we can locate the beginnings of morality. A third suggestion is that groups and individuals that are religious tend to be healthier and to live longer than those that are not, and so, once more, human survival and evolution are enhanced. There is now considerable hard evidence to suggest that this is true: religious beliefs provide a sense of our place within the universe, prayer opens us to resources beyond ourselves, belief in God helps us to endure in hard times, rituals and rites of passage mark our progress through life, and congregations, mosques and synagogues and their equivalents, provide communities of assistance and belonging that enhance life and promote health.

Cumulatively, therefore, the benefits of religion are of marked significance that can be objectively demonstrated. Whereas there is no reason to deny the truth in any of these approaches, and good reason to celebrate them, a fourth approach might simply claim that human beings are religiously responsive because there is in fact something to respond to. Religious experiences are signals of a greater reality, and, as such, are of profound importance. The spiritual world is real and presses in upon us in a way that we cannot ignore but must make some kind of sense of. If life is indeed about development and adaptation to the environment in which we are placed, then part of that environment is the spiritual realm that exists precisely because, "God is not far from each one of us" and, "in him we live and move and have our being."

THE DANGERS OF RELIGION

All this having been said, Christian conviction does not give unqualified support to religion and even finds grievous fault with it. Many Christians would claim not to be religious but simply to be devoted to Jesus. For a start, judged by Christianity's own standards of truth, most religion is simply wrong. It does not convey the truth about God as Christians believe it to have been revealed in Jesus Christ, but rather represents limited human attempts to imagine and portray the divine, attempts that, though they may contain a grain of truth, are misdirected, and even at times profoundly dangerous. Cruel and abominable practices, such as human sacrifice, have been perpetrated in the name and for the sake of false gods. According to Paul, "there are many gods and many lords" (1 Cor 8:5), but none of them are true. They are human fabrications. Furthermore, religion is often implicated in many of the conflicts that tear the human race apart and render its divisions so hard to overcome. Religious differences are often a pretext for persecution and hatred. Religious conviction can itself become ideological, being used to over-ride human empathy and kindness in the name of an inflexible higher principle. It is regrettable, but not totally unjustifiable, that people of religious conviction are often portrayed as judgmental and unsympathetic.

Human religion is, self-evidently, a human creation and as such is bound to reflect the ambiguity of the human race itself, both its dignities and its depravities. There is good religion and there is bad religion in the same way that there are good politics and bad politics. Yet just as it is impossible for humans collectively to live without some forms of politics (though individuals may refuse to have anything to do with them) so they cannot live without some form of religion. The proper and realistic issue is not whether religion should be abolished altogether because of its potential dangers (as some would like to see happen, but are doomed to be disappointed), but how good and true religion can be made to triumph over the bad.

CHRISTIAN CONVICTION AND THE WORLD RELIGIONS

It is, and always has been, a clear Christian conviction that the resurrection of Jesus Christ from the dead constitutes him as a unique and supreme figure in humanity's quest for God. It is true that, in one sense, any religious figure, indeed any individual person, can be called "unique." Each person is what he or she is, and just as fingerprints are unique, so is the person who bears them. When we speak of Christ as "unique," however, we have more than this in mind. We mean that in him God was present in the world in a way that God has not been present in any other person. God was incarnate personally in Christ and not in the same way anywhere else, although God is indeed "not far from each one of us." In turn, this means that the work of atonement and reconciliation that God has wrought in Christ is both unique and once-for-all. The testimony to this in the New Testament is clear, and the following verses will recur in this chapter: "All things have been handed over to me by my Father; and no one knows who the Son is except the Father, or who the Father is except the Son, and anyone to whom the Son chooses to reveal him" (Luke 10:22); "I am the way, the truth, and the life. No one comes to the Father except through me" (John 14:6); "There is salvation in no one else, for there is no other name under heaven given among mortals by which we must be saved" (Acts 4:12). "Therefore God also highly exalted him and gave him the name that is above every name, so that at the name of Jesus every knee should bend, in heaven and on earth and under the earth, and every tongue should confess that Jesus Christ is Lord, to the glory of God the Father" (Phil 2:9–11). The fact that Jesus was raised from the dead is both the ground on which this claim to uniqueness is made and the confirmation that it is true. No other religious or spiritual teacher has been raised from the dead, nor even such a claim made about them. The resurrection is part of the uniqueness of Christ. To deny this uniqueness is, in effect, to deny the truth of the Christian faith and to reduce Christian conviction to simply one among a range of possible options for the religiously minded. In effect, it becomes no longer a conviction at all, but simply a preference. Moreover, the claim is much more than a subjective statement along the lines that the name of Jesus is the only name "for me," as one might state a preference for a football team. Rather, it is objective: Christ is the unique Savior for the whole world. His name is the highest, period.

Yet it must be freely admitted that the Christian claim is problematic as well as dramatic. It is no surprise to learn that it was both "a stumbling-block to Jews and foolishness to Gentiles." It remains so for very many people and is a great cause of offense. Yet to those who believe, it has shown itself to be "the power of God and the wisdom of God. For God's foolishness is wiser than human wisdom, and God's weakness is stronger than human strength" (1 Cor 1:22–25). It is scandalous to suggest that a particular human being and the particular events of his life hold within themselves the key to human destiny in a way that the grand sweeps and concepts of human religions do not. People would be more comfortable with a religion that claimed less for its founding figure and was content to see other pathways as equally valid for those who choose them. This is particularly so when the Christian claim is interpreted in terms of power. Does the claim to Christ's pre-eminence and supremacy mean that he and his followers have the right to dominate and control because they alone have the truth? This logic is certainly sometimes pursued in Christian circles and begins to sound like a form of religious tyranny. Yet it is worth remembering that the one who is declared to be supreme by the resurrection is the humble Savior who gave his life in sacrifice and who washed the feet of his disciples in love. Tyranny is the last word to be applied to his way. The resurrection is therefore sanctifying not coercive power over others but the power of such self-giving, non-violent love finally to overcome evil, despite all assumptions to the contrary. It is certainly the case that Christian conviction makes a truth claim concerning Christ, but then so does every other religion and ideology in its own way, including those that claim that all religions lead to the same end. Even atheism and agnosticism constitute claims to the truth, namely that God does not exist or God cannot be known, and there has been no shortage of powerful figures (in the twentieth century in particular) who have wanted to impose these claims to negative truth upon their societies.

The genuine difficulty for Christian conviction is how to reconcile God's particular, saving activity in the unique and only Christ with God's universal will to save, springing out of the love of God for all creatures and the atonement made by Christ for all people. The coming of Christ was of necessity located in a particular time and place. It is through belief in and knowledge of this very particular Christ that people are reconciled to God and enter into their true humanity. The good news of Jesus Christ was preached beginning in Jerusalem and moving out first into the Mediterranean world and then to the four corners of the earth. Hearing and believing the good news is essential for personal salvation: "But how are they to call on one in whom they have not believed? And how are they to believe in one of whom they have never heard? And how are they to hear without someone to proclaim him?" (Rom 10:14). Yet high though communication is on the agenda of Christian communities, it must be conceded that of the estimated 60–100 billion human souls that have so far existed, the majority have probably never heard the good news of Christ, and even fewer have understood it. This may be because they did not live long enough to do so, or lived their lives prior to his coming or beyond the reach of any possible knowledge of him. God's strategy of coming to this world in the very particular reality of Christ would seem, on this measure, as much a means of excluding people from salvation as of including them. Yet this would contradict the message of John 3:17: "Indeed, God did not send the Son into the world to condemn the world, but in order that the world might be saved through him." Reconciling the particular and the universal and showing how the life, death, and resurrection of Christ can be the means by which every human being that ever lived might be saved are tasks to which we shall return once we have explored further some other religious traditions.

THE RELIGIONS AS HUMAN RESPONSES TO THE DIVINE

On the face of it, the world of human religions is chaotic, with every conceivable belief or practice being represented within it. Human religious responses to the mysteries of existence are a mixture of creativity and confused ignorance. Within them we may find that which is God-given since through general revelation—that is, the witness to God that is given in the created world (Rom 1:19)—there is an awareness and form of knowledge that every human being instinctively possesses or can acquire. Glimpses of divine truth are therefore to be found in the works of sages, philosophers, and religious thinkers alike. Alongside this are elements of distortion, since humans misuse and suppress even the truth that is available to them (Rom 1:18). Because of the power of evil that is loose in the world we are also entitled to claim that there are de-humanizing, deluded, and dangerous, even specifically evil, elements to some religious thought and practice. As we have indicated, human religions are thoroughly mixed and ambiguous and need to come under divine judgment just as much as any other activity. This claim about the fallen nature of religion can even be applied to Christianity as a religious phenomenon, which has at times become prey to ways and means that do not belong among those who are followers of the crucified. Crusades, inquisitions, and religious wars have no place in authentic Christianity, as should always have been clear. For Christians, it is *Christ* who is supreme, not Christianity as a complex religious system. Christ judges even those movements that give allegiance to him.

Recognizing this, it might be claimed that the main religious traditions that can be traced in human societies do indeed represent explorations of the spiritual life and of response to the divine. In seeking to explain life they explore the logically possible sets of answers to the fundamental existential human questions. The great world religions therefore, which represent the religious quest in its most mature form, follow different pathways of explanation that include idealism (the belief that ultimately only the spiritual exists), dualism (spirit and matter exist in independent spheres), theism (the material exists in complete dependence on the spiritual), and monism (there is one reality, of which spirit and matter are different aspects). Judaism, Christianity, Islam, and some other religions are located in the theistic tradition by reason of their belief in one ultimate creator from whom all other things have their being. Other major religions can be placed within the other categories.

Whatever the confusions and corruptions of religion therefore, underneath them there is a serious exploration taking place as to the nature of reality, with a testing out of viable possibilities as to how to understand it. This is not to say that all of them are necessarily correct (the Christian believes they are not), but that at their best they can be taken as honest searches for the truth and as serious conversation partners for Christians. In conversation there is that which may be learnt and that which may be imparted. However, in that they propose different answers to the basic existential questions, it cannot be claimed that they are all ultimately offering different pathways to the same reality. Actually what they offer is different pathways leading to different ends. To pretend otherwise is to fail to respect their stark differences and to deny to them their own integrity. Serious examination of the religions actually uncovers the incompatibility of their answers and warns against prematurely finding a spurious unity between them. If there is a unity to be celebrated it is not to be found in the answers given but in the questions asked, the fact that human beings have been made "to search for God and perhaps grope for him and find him." Christian can respect the quest on which others are engaged precisely because it corresponds to their own quest. In the process their own convictions may be tested, and in all probability strengthened. However, there is every reason why they should hold to their own commitment to the uniqueness of the Christ, especially when they do so in the loving and gracious spirit of Christ himself. If they wish to commend their unique Savior, it will be through a combination of positive affirmation of the truth about him and Spirit-led embodiment of his kindness.

GOD'S PROVIDENCE AND THE WORLD'S RELIGIONS

It should be seen from what has been said that it is not enough for Christians simply to deny the validity of other religious traditions. Although they may disagree with them, there are points of agreement that can form the basis for positive conversation. This would be most fully true of Judaism, which is related to Christianity as a sibling descended from the same parents, namely biblical faith. We may argue about the inheritance but cannot deny a common parentage. It would also be true of other theistic traditions. It is not only shared belief that we may have in common but a recognizable piety and devotion that can command respect. Yet the Christian may be able to go further than this and trace in the world's religions a divine purpose, even while maintaining the areas of disagreement with them.

It is clear that religious faith and practice, whatever their sometime distortions, provide for millions of people a context within which they may live their lives and find both purpose and meaning. They are ways of creating a symbolic universe that staves off what could otherwise be an abyss of emptiness and meaninglessness. Human beings are above all concerned with living efficiently, getting on with their lives and facing life's necessary challenges. To do this they need some kind of reference point in relation to which they can orientate themselves in the confusing flux of existence. They also need role models that will be exemplars of how life needs to be navigated; and they need resources of hope, faith, and love that will sustain them through joy and suffering. For vast numbers of people it is their religious faith that provides one or all of these things. Moreover, life has to be lived communally and the bonds and ties that unite people are often religious in nature—the word "religion" actually comes from a word meaning "to bind." Religious festivals and celebrations provide opportunities for feasting and fasting that punctuate the passage of time and provide scope for changes of tempo and remission from work. If we add to this the fact that human beings have religious feelings and are capable of expressing awe and worship, we might conclude that the practice of religion provides a medium through which people might find a degree of spiritual satisfaction. They look to their religious traditions to provide the narratives within which morality may be informed and practiced. Even if the Christian believes that much of the time such energies are misdirected and that they are in need of more accurate understanding of the true nature of God, the fact is that the world religions provide something highly significant that preserves and sustains communities and individuals. We are entitled to see in this, therefore, something providential, the work of God in preserving human life, even as it waits for its full redemption, or at least its progression into a fuller understanding of the truth. And the Christian can respect the roles that religion plays at its best, even while seeking to witness to a Christ who, he or she believes, can fulfill the longings of the human heart more completely than any other possibility.

Negatively, religion may be seen as a hindrance to receiving the truth as it is in Jesus, a power that promotes spiritual blindness, and sometimes it has this effect. But positively, the world's religions may be seen as provisional, capable of something better and fuller, and also as preparatory, laying the foundations, though each in different ways, for the true vision of God. If this be thought to be a bold statement then it is worth reflecting again that Christianity also, as a human system of religion, stands in need of purification, reform, and improvement in the light of the very Christ to whom it bears witness. The well-established idea that the church always needs to be undergoing reformation in the light of the Word of God applies to the Christian religion as a whole, until it becomes what it is truly supposed to be. If Christian convictions are shaped by the hope that there is a coming day in which God has "a plan for the fullness of time, to gather up all things in [Christ], things in heaven and things on earth" (Eph 1:10), then the idea that the religions themselves will one day be judged, purified, completed, and redeemed in Christ and for Christ's glory may be bold, but it is not unimaginable. The Hebrew Scriptures paint startling pictures on a number of occasions of the turning of the nations to Israel's God in the fullness of time (Isa 2:1-4; 45:14-16; 56:1-8; Zech 2:11; 8:22-23). And the God who is at work within us, "is able to accomplish abundantly far more than all we can ask or imagine" (Eph 3:20).

SALVATION AND THE WORLD RELIGIONS

What then can we say about God's work of salvation and the world's religions? History and experience reveal that people do not change their religion easily. Only a small percentage of people move from one religion to another in the course of a lifetime, and the reasons for this should be clear from the ways we have described the benefits that religion offers. For personal and communal reasons people become embedded in their religious tradition such that to break away from it is likely to mean that they forfeit the very things, such as family, friends, and community, that make life bearable. It is certainly the case that in the course of missionary work individuals may come to faith in Christ and make the change. It is also the case that sometimes there are movements of whole groups of people in the direction of Christian faith and commitment. Often this is against the background of previous religious ways, such as the caste system, they have found demeaning and abusive. In Christ they find dignity and freedom, and this can motivate a corporate shift. All of these transitions are to be welcomed and expanded, but added together they still mean that vast swathes of people are outside the knowledge of Christ. Here we return again to the tension in the Christian faith between the particular and the universal. Does the very particularity of Christian conviction, with its claims about Christ and his cross, in effect exclude the multitudes that lie beyond contact with it?

To resolve this tension, there are those who assert that since God will admit all people to eternal life anyway the tension hardly matters. This does not accord with the conviction that justification through personal faith in Christ and his saving work is necessary for salvation (John 3:16). Others propose that all the religions are but varying pathways to the same goal and that they all therefore have saving power. Christ is simply one way of finding salvation, but others are available. In the previous section it was argued that a better way of understanding the religions is in terms of divine providence: God uses them to preserve humankind pending the day when salvation will come. Besides, each religion has a different end or goal in view and so to insist that they all lead to the same outcome is to violate the integrity of their claims. It is better to recognize the irreconcilable nature of their differences rather than to make bland claims about them. The resolution we propose here is rather that through the particularities of Christ and his cross, God has done something for the whole of humankind that enables God to bring salvation to all people. The particular has universal significance. We might say that through the cross and resurrection of Christ, God has qualified God's own self to be the Savior of the world. In Christ, the Word of God through whom all things were made has become incarnate and by taking the sins of the world upon himself in reconciling atonement, the Word of God has transformed the situation of the whole world. Everybody is affected by it. The church is commissioned to preach this good news to the ends of the earth. But even as it does this, God is not confined to the church and its proclamation but is able to reach into people and places where the church is not. The particular is therefore the means and accompaniment of universal outreach.

GOD'S WAY TO US

It is often asserted that there are many ways to God and that Christians are arrogant and exclusive when they claim that Christ is the only way, as John 14:6 declares. It usually escapes notice, even on the part of Christians who quote it, that in this verse Jesus actually says, "No-one comes to *the Father* except through me." Knowledge of God as Father very much reflects the way Jesus himself understood his own relationship to *Abba*, the God of Israel. This is a distinctively Christian way of thinking and names the intimacy that through Christ all people may now have with the creator. There are certainly many ways of seeking after God and there may be many ways of being conscious of God, but personal knowledge of God *as Father* does seem to be distinctively, perhaps uniquely, Christian. There are also many ways of coming to Christ. But what do we make of the claim that there are many ways to God, just as there are many ways up a mountain?

From a Christian point of view, the claim that there are many ways to God labors under a misconception. The whole point of the Christian message is that God has made a way to us, rather than us to God. Salvation is from the Lord. People may be prompted to search for God, but the search will never be complete until God takes the initiative and comes to them, allowing them to find. Salvation is a gift that comes to us freely and in grace. The God in whom Christians believe is not one to whom we can attain even by our own religious efforts or pathways. But this God seeks the lost by coming to them where they are and encountering them as the God who saves. This simple insight cuts through many of the questions that arise. Instead of asking, "do the religions all lead to God?" the question becomes, "Is God able to seek for people and find them, even despite the religions in which they are embedded?" The answer to this must surely be Yes, since "for God all things are possible" (Mark 10:27). No one can gainsay this. The famous verse at the centre of this discussion is therefore capable of being read in several ways. John 14:6 certainly affirms the unique place of Jesus as the one through whom and because of whose work we are able to come to the Father, and to this end there is no one else on whom we or anybody else may rely. But if in the course of our mission, as sometimes happens, we encounter people who seem to know the Father already, independently of any preaching by the church, we are entitled to say that though we know not how, because this person knows the Father, it can only be through Christ, the Christ who reaches into places we cannot. Furthermore, if it is Christ who is the way, the truth, and the life, then the knowledge of who truly belongs to him is his alone, and he is not confined to the community of the church nor are the religions any insuperable barrier to his working. Christ goes where he chooses and we cannot impede him: "No one knows who the Son is except the Father; and no one knows who the Father is except the Son and anyone to whom the Son chooses to reveal him" (Luke 10:22). This in no way negates the responsibility of the church to preach and bear witness, but it is a healthy reminder that the responsibility for bringing salvation to people does not by any means rest solely on the shoulders of the church.

If we pay close attention to the testimony of Scripture we find there clear evidence of God's saving work outside the line of Abraham and beyond the covenant communities of Israel and the church. There is a scriptural tradition of the "noble pagan," sincere believers in God who were embedded in their pagan contexts and yet who were acceptable to God. In the history of Israel these included Job (Jas 5:11), Melchizedek (Gen 14:17-24), Abimelech, king of Gerar (Gen 20:1-18), and the queen of Sheba (Matt 12:42). The prophet Amos pointed out that the belief that God was at work in Israel did not exclude the work of God in other nations, though in ways hidden from

Israel herself: "Are you not like the Ethiopians to me, O people of Israel? says the LORD. Did I not bring Israel up from the land of Egypt, and the Philistines from Caphtor and the Arameans from Kir?' (Amos 9:7). In the New Testament the noble pagans include the magi who came from afar to worship Jesus at his birth (Matt 2:1–12). A particular example is Cornelius, the Roman centurion in Caesarea, who is described as "an upright and God-fearing man, who is well spoken of by the whole Jewish nation" (Acts 10:22). Cornelius' case led the apostle Peter to say, "I truly understand that God shows no partiality, but in every nation anyone who fears him and does what is right is acceptable to him" (Acts 10:34–35). Cornelius and his household accepted Christ, received the Holy Spirit, and were incorporated into the messianic community of the church. But even before this, he was acceptable to God, and evidence of the work of God in drawing people into faith and trust outside the line of Abraham and the church. Although up to the point of hearing of Christ they did not know his name, what God did in Christ included those we have mentioned and the saints of the past within its scope, and such reconciling forgiveness was conveyed to them by the God to whom they drew near.

Christian conviction is able to affirm the unique significance of Christ's incarnation and atonement while at the same time believing that what Christ did, he did for all, and that the benefits of his salvation can be imparted by God universally as God chooses and purposes. It is able to recognize that God works in people regardless of their creed and even when they do not acknowledge Christ with their lips. This does not lessen the need for the Christian community to bear its witness to Christ, as it has been commissioned to do, and to seek the lost. Neither does it diminish the Christian insistence that Christ remains the true witness to God and that he is the one against whom all claims to revelation should be measured. As with Peter preaching to Cornelius, there will be moments when the witness of the church and the workings of God beyond its boundaries collide and become evident. But it does mean that that same Christian community can fulfill its mission with a hope and optimism rooted in God about the people it is unable to reach and the places it is unable to go.

19

The Credibility of Christianity
Advocates and Apologists

THIS EXPLANATION OF CHRISTIAN convictions took its starting point from the resurrection. The belief that Jesus Christ was raised from the dead determines and shapes the Christian community's way of understanding and explaining the world. All further convictions proceed from this point. Although the reality of the resurrection as an event within history can be defended and supported through intellectual argument, it cannot be definitively proven other than to the satisfaction of each individual who takes time to look into it. This should not surprise us since there are very few things, outside the world of mathematics (and some might question even that), that can in fact be proven beyond doubt, especially in relation to history, which contains many uncertainties. Reasonable and plausible grounds for believing claims to truth may be given, but for a person to commit themselves to those claims, there must always remain a disposition on the part of the interpreter to accept these grounds as persuasive. Closed minds do not learn anything. The believer finds the Christian version of reality coherent and convincing and is prepared to risk his or her life on its truth. This is the meaning of faith. But this would not be the case were it so much at variance with what we think we know from other areas of human inquiry that it became intellectually unsustainable.

Although the Christian faith cannot be proved by reason alone, it could be falsified, that is, shown to be so far adrift from what we otherwise think we know that its truth cannot be upheld. Faith is not the ability to believe anything and everything, however implausible or nonsensical it might be.

Neither is it blind. Rather it is *reasonable trust*, trust consistent with evidence and argument. Faith is the willingness to entrust one's life to something and someone because they have shown themselves to be sufficiently worthy of such trust that reliance may be placed upon them. Inevitably therefore, in every generation the Christian faith confronts new intellectual challenges. It has to defend itself against contradictions. This is to be welcomed precisely because the challenges help to test Christian claims and where necessary to stimulate their clarification and refinement. However distinctive they may be, and however dependent upon revelation, they do not exist apart from the general market of ideas.

It may freely be admitted that no one by the exercise of reason alone would have invented the Christian faith. The idea that the salvation of the world depends upon a particular human being and the event of his death upon a Roman instrument of execution is hardly common sense. This does not mean it is not true, only that it is not the kind of claim human beings would advance if they were looking to invent a plausible new religion. Yet this very claim is the one that for two thousand years has seized the imagination and engaged the intellect of billions of human beings from all epochs, cultures, races, and strata of human society, and continues still to do so with extraordinary energy. It is profoundly revolutionary. It represents the overturning of conventional ways of thinking and the revaluation of all values. From the beginning it has been contested on multiple grounds, and yet thus far has managed to outthink, outlast, and out-love all its rivals, consigning many of them to the obscurity of history. Whether it can continue to do this in the face of today's intellectual challenges has yet to be seen and is where this chapter focuses.

The Christian community must face the task of making God real for the contemporary world. The follower of Jesus does well to accept that there is not one inch of Christian ground that has not been contested along the way. The struggle for the truth of the faith is to be waged on many fronts simultaneously and requires constant reflection and thought to stay abreast of the challenges. The objections raised have come from philosophical, religious, moral, historical, scientific, and political perspectives. The Christian discipline of responding to these objections is called "apologetics," which has nothing to do with apologizing, but everything to do with mounting a defense of Christian belief (1 Pet 3:15). It has aimed at removing them as obstacles to faith while recognizing that argument alone cannot awaken faith in a person. At the heart of the Christian message there is what the apostle Paul described as a "stumbling block" or, more literally, a "scandal." "For Jews demand signs and Greeks desire wisdom, but we proclaim Christ crucified, a stumbling block to Jews and foolishness to Gentiles, but to those who are called, both Jews and Greeks, Christ the power of God and the wisdom of God. For God's foolishness is wiser than human wisdom, and God's weakness is stronger than human strength" (1 Cor 1:22–25). Many objections to Christianity are based upon false understanding or faulty assumptions and so can be removed. But God's "stumbling-block" is intentional: it requires people to think differently and begin the process of renewing the mind.

As indicated, objections to Christian faith are multi-dimensional. In this section the aim is to identify those dimensions so as to be aware of the breadth of the intellectual task Christians must face in maintaining its defense.

PHILOSOPHICAL PERSPECTIVES

Those people who embrace Christian convictions do not typically do so because they have reviewed all the philosophical arguments and decided Christianity is the most credible option. Some do, but for most people their faith in Christ is more intuitive and immediate, the result, for instance, of an experience of conversion, divine providence, worship, or inward persuasion. Yet it is unlikely that a person's faith will endure through time if it encounters questions to which they can find no satisfactory answer. Philosophy is the discipline of thinking deeply and clearly about the world and how we understand it. It might be described as "thinking about thinking," and aims at sorting out sense from nonsense. It subjects claims to truth to radical scrutiny. Not least, philosophy is concerned about justifying any claims to truth and so is about "epistemology," the science of human knowing. Can religious beliefs be justified and defended on philosophical grounds or do they simply represent a preference, what some people choose to believe? To what extent do they make sense in the light of what human beings think they otherwise know about the world? At this point apologetics comes very close to another area called "philosophy of religion," which is also a well developed and lively intellectual discipline.

Much philosophical energy has gone into debating arguments for the existence of God. These have included the "cosmological argument," which reasons from a contingent universe that does not explain its own existence to the reality of an uncreated creator of all things. God has no beginning and is not caused, and so can be the cause and origin of all things. The "teleological" argument reasons from the fact that things appear to have an end or purpose to a creator who determines what that purpose is and gives an overall purpose to existence. The "moral" argument reasons that the human sense that some behaviors are absolutely wrong implies an ultimate and objective moral law, which is impossible without a God; and the "ontological" argument, which moves from the idea of God to the existence of God on the grounds that God is that than which nothing greater can be thought. But God can only be this if God actually does exist (because existing is greater than not existing), and so God must of necessity exist.

Given the arguments in its favor, the existence of God is at the very least a probability and not only a possibility.

The nature of these arguments has changed over the years as they have been challenged through debate. Critics are right to claim that they do not amount to *proofs* since none of them can demonstrate the existence of God in an uncontested way. Yet they do remain as arguments and indicators. They capture the sense that this world is dependent upon something or someone for its existence and is not self-creating. They provide an explanation for the world's existence without which any search for ultimate meaning would need to be abandoned. They are still compelling and reasonable pointers to the probability of God's existence, especially when taken cumulatively and together, and they continue to exercise the minds of critics and defenders alike. For the Christian they establish the fact that belief in an eternal, infinite, personal creator is warranted and sustainable. God cannot be subjected to empirical verification, nor can God's existence be demonstrated by argument; but belief in the reality of God is instinctive and basic, reasonable and logical, and involves no less of intellectual integrity.

RELIGIOUS PERSPECTIVES

It is a mistake to imagine that objections to Christianity come only from the world of unbelief. Christianity has been contested also by those who hold firm religious convictions, but of a different order from those of Christians. For instance, some of the core ideas of the Christian faith are held by Muslims to be irreverent towards God since they speak of God becoming a human being, an idea that is believed to reduce God's sublime majesty. Claiming that God has a Son is for them an example of such attempts to undermine the singularity and supremacy of the divine. Both Judaism and Islam question Christianity's claim to be monotheistic. The doctrine of the Trinity, which can be described as the most radical and distinctive of all Christian doctrines, is contested in the name of the unity of God. They represent it as a form of polytheism. In addition, Judaism takes issue with the New Testament interpretation of verses from the Hebrew Scriptures and with what it regards as a Christian make-over of Jesus, transforming him from being an identifiable Jewish teacher into a divine (and so non-Hebraic) figure. Some Jewish scholars, however, deny this and point to the ways in which Jesus identified himself as "the Son of Man," thus rooting his own calling in what is anticipated in Daniel 7. To them, everything that Christianity claims has its origins and parallels in the Judaism of Jesus' own day. Islam, which came some centuries after the birth of Christianity, might accurately be understood as an attempt both to correct and replace it with many of its primary assertions about God, Jesus, human beings, and salvation. Its beliefs were consciously fashioned in disagreement with Christian teachings. By contrast, Buddhism finds the idea that God is personal inferior to its own aspiration to merge with an impersonal ultimate reality.

Apologetics in relation to other religions therefore involves the justification of orthodox Christian beliefs (the claim that God's unity is to be understood as communion not singularity, for instance). It also shows how Christian ideas about God, such as redemption and divine fatherhood, exceed in value the beliefs of other traditions. Although the Christian faith is at variance with much that is believed in other faith traditions, there is also, of course, that which is held in common. Christians may therefore find themselves talking to each other *about* other religions (clarifying the differences and the issues), talking in debate and dialog *with* other religions, and sometimes debating *alongside* other religions over against atheists and secularists. Apologetically, therefore, Christians might find themselves agreeing with people of other faiths in a form of what is sometimes called "co-belligerence." All of these forms of conversation require apologetic knowledge and skills, but of different kinds.

MORAL PERSPECTIVES

Whereas it is still possible to hear people say, "I don't believe in Christian doctrines but I do believe in Christian ethics," it is also becoming increasingly common to hear Christianity denounced as immoral. In part this comes from the militant belief that all religion is harmful in that it causes good people to do evil things in its name. In part it comes from the alleged association of Christian faith (and the other Abrahamic religions, Islam and Judaism) with patriarchy, "homophobia," and environmental destruction. In other respects it comes from rejection of a Christian "meta-narrative" that allegedly has the effect of marginalizing and victimizing those who do not conform to its conceptions of what is both normal and normative. Belief in an afterlife is seen as potentially immoral because it inspires people who believe in it to sacrifice themselves (sometimes deliberately as in radical Islamic suicide bombings) in the belief that they will be received into paradise. In liberal and permissive cultures, Christianity can be seen as anti-progressive and retardant of human development towards a more "civilized" society because of its strict moral beliefs. History is then interpreted to show that the church has resisted all supposedly positive moral developments (women's rights, birth-control, divorce, abortion, gay rights, animal rights, euthanasia). These re-interpretations come to assume the nature of secular and unquestioned myths. In response, apologetics calls into question the validity of these claims and at the same time exposes the track record of anti-Christian ideologies, such as fascism and atheistic communism. Whereas there are abundant evidences of religion being dangerous, the same is true of politics or science, and yet neither activity can be dispensed with. The need is to distinguish the good from the bad, true religion from false religion. Belief in God does not corrupt human nature; but human nature can corrupt even belief in God. In responding to the moral charge, it is of enormous assistance to Christians that they appeal to the character and example of Jesus of Nazareth and that Jesus stands the test of time, despite the failures of those who have confessed faith in him. The life and teaching of Jesus are very constructive starting-points in advocating the faith.

Where there is an unbridgeable gulf in moral debate between the Christian faith and secular humanism is in the belief that human beings exist for a purpose and that purpose is determined by their creator. The good life therefore consists, for Christians, in living according to what God has made us to be, to conform to the divine purpose for life. Christians see their life as being subject to the will and pleasure of God, and they therefore seek to live their lives in harmony with that purpose. They do not believe human beings should regard themselves as independent from God but accountable to God. They are stewards of a God-given existence and their happiness depends not upon overthrowing the divine order but on embracing it and living within it. This stands in contrast to the idea that we can choose to be whatever we want to be, that human beings themselves are the arbitrators of what is right and wrong and that any interference with human autonomy is a form of oppression.

HISTORICAL PERSPECTIVES

The Christian faith is historically rooted and depends for its truth upon the existence in history of a person called Jesus of Nazareth bearing a credible likeness to the Christ of Christian faith. It is not surprising that the history that underlies Christian witness should be scrutinized and questioned by the use of contemporary historical methodologies. It has been claimed on historical grounds (by a small minority) that Christ never existed. The prejudice and bias behind such a claim is normally clear. More commonly it is claimed that what we can know of the historical Christ is very limited and that the truth about Jesus has been distorted by subsequent Christian thinkers so that the original religion of Jesus bears only the smallest resemblance to the Christ of later Christian devotion and doctrine. The apostle Paul is usually identified as the first and most major culprit in this process. The apologetic task in relation to this enterprise is to show how the skeptical starting points of some of the historians involved already dictate the conclusions they arrive at. Of course, it is the duty of scholars to be skeptical, but it is also appropriate to be skeptical about skepticism. In the academy doctorates are achieved and reputations made by overthrowing received opinions and coming up with novel and unprecedented ideas, and this then creates an unwarranted bias towards ideas that have not previously been advanced. What poses as objective history is often ideologically determined, reflecting the biases of the researcher rather than any sober reading of the historical record. A fair reading of the history, treating Jesus as we would other figures in history, as discussed in the first chapter, confirms rather than undermines a Christian interpretation of him and raises tantalizing questions about the events surrounding his death to which the claim that Jesus was raised from the dead is a credible response. Far from Christian belief being a distortion of who Jesus was, it can be compellingly shown to have developed organically from the events and teaching of his life.

SCIENTIFIC PERSPECTIVES

It is, of course, widely assumed that "science" has disproved the existence of God, or, at the least, rendered God a construct of which we no longer have need in order to arrive at satisfactory explanations of the universe. God is seen as unnecessary, perhaps even a distraction. For this reason, it is a common perception that major threats to Christian belief are posed by science, despite the facts that the scientific enterprise has arisen from within a Christian context that has stimulated free exploration of nature, that many of history's leading scientists have been deeply committed believers and that many eminent scientists today are practicing Christians or believers from other religious traditions. Particularly by referring to evolutionary theory as a way of explaining the way things are, religious faith of any kind is relegated to the past, to the time when people could have been forgiven for their superstitions in a way that, in the light of increased knowledge, is no longer excusable. Paradoxically, non-theistic scientists have proceeded, having abolished God, to construct new deities in the form of "Evolution" and "Nature" and ascribed to them both purpose and agency in a way that substitutes for the God they have abolished.

Apologists will respond to this by being respectful of science as a noble discipline, while criticizing "scientism" as itself predicated on an act of faith that cannot be scientifically demonstrated. They will point out that the "contradictions" between science and religion are overdrawn and that there is room for complementary interpretations of the reality we all inhabit. In particular, they will show that the appeal to evolution as a necessary and sufficient way of "explaining" the world is itself an act of faith that is not based upon evidence but is a product of wishful thinking. The issue here is not whether some appeal to the evolutionary development of the world is a *necessary* dimension for understanding (it is), but whether it is *sufficient* to account for "life, the universe, and everything."

In reality, although there may on the surface be a conflict between science and religion, the claimed conflict is apparent rather than real, and superficial. It may, as an example, exist between certain minority interpretations within religion (for instance, the idea of a creation in six twenty-four hour days a few thousand years ago—so-called "young earth creationism") and tested scientific ideas of evolution. But these are ideas that are not intrinsic to Christian faith and that are held by a relatively small (albeit enthusiastic) number, some of whom come to see in time that they are unwarranted. God is certainly to be confessed as creator, but the means of creation are open to discussion. That such minority issues attract attention altogether out of proportion is a fault both of vociferous Christian groupings and enraged scientists who oppose them. Actually, at a deeper level there exists a convergence between the scientific method and Christian faith that is quite striking, since both in their own ways are concerned with knowledge gained through experiment (in the Christian case the experiment of knowing God through Christ), and with growth in confidence by a process of on-going testing about the ways that experienced reality might be described and articulated. Science and religious discourse, properly understood, have complementary not conflicting roles since each approaches the world of reality from a different perspective. The scientist is concerned with how things work, how they have become the way they are. The theologian is concerned with why things exist and what purpose they fulfill, in other words, with questions of meaning. There are certain questions the theologian cannot determine in advance but must leave to scientists to uncover by observation and experiment in their own field. Science must be allowed its own integrity. But there are areas in which the scientist exceeds his or her competence when moving beyond the empirical world of things into the more profound realm of meaning and morality. Of course, the scientist and the theologian might well be the same person, or the same communities, adopting two different approaches and fully aware of the difference between the two. This should be a great and enriching partnership. Yet true and wholesome knowledge of the world cannot be gained by the scientific method alone, just as, as has been previously indicated, "I-It" knowledge needs to be complemented by the "I-Thou" knowledge of human relationships, love, and personal engagement. Knowledge is a matrix of different ways of knowing and cannot be reduced to the merely scientific without immeasurable loss, even if the scientific is a valid way of illuminating our knowledge of many of its aspects. Religion, science, and the arts in that sense are all part of the overall human quest for understanding.

Properly understood, science is a methodology, a tried and tested way of gaining reliable knowledge about the observable world. It goes astray when it becomes an ideology, that is, when it claims that it is the only arbitrator between what can be deemed to be true and what false. This is the distinction between science as a progressive, open-minded discipline and "scientism" as an alternative, closed-faith position. As an ideology, it becomes, in effect, a kind of religion, since its claim to be the only way of knowing the truth is a statement of faith, an unprovable assumption that cannot be tested by its own criteria, and so not the kind of claim that can be rationally or scientifically substantiated. It is an existential position that is assumed to be true, not so demonstrated. Similarly "reason" is not the sole possession of one type of thinker, but takes various forms within diverse bodies of knowledge, all of which, including science, are based upon certain unproven and unprovable preferences. With the new religion there goes the new priesthood of the scientific commentator. It is not surprising therefore when science-as-ideology declares itself to be the enemy of spiritual or religious approaches to life since it sees them as rivals not partners. In effect, scientism is using the prestige of the scientific method to mask its own pretensions. Wise and temperate scientists know that this is a false path and that true science does not close its mind to new possibilities, ways of thinking, or paradigms. And the scientific methodology is all the time uncovering the wonders and mysteries of the universe and the fact that the more we know about it the more we know we do not know.

From within science itself questions arise as to whether our current materialist paradigms of reality are sufficient to explain the mysteries of life. Experiment is dependent upon phenomena being repeatable and replicable within a controlled environment. But human experience shows evidence of realities that cannot be fitted into this model: the mystical, singular, spiritual, transpersonal, and supranormal. Current models of science are ill-suited to pursue this realm, but that is not to say that it does not exist. The next scientific paradigm shift, that some scientists themselves are calling for, could well be into a vision of reality that recognizes there to be more than the merely material. None of this proves Christian convictions, but it does create an environment in which claims to engagement with a spiritual world can be held to be more credible.

POLITICAL PERSPECTIVES

Part of the work accomplished by Christian apologists of the past was that of deflecting those attacks on Christianity which led to the persecution of believers and their exclusion from mainstream society. The articulation of Christian perspectives in the public realm continues to be part of the apologetic task and borders on the similar role of "advocacy," the constructive setting forth of Christian-inspired policies and perspectives in society. If the Christian faith accurately describes what it means to live in truly human ways before the face of God, then its insights and commitments should be heard in the public realm and be part of the debates taking place in the public square. This runs contrary to the view that religious beliefs belong exclusively in the private realm. Learning to express Christian insights appropriately and intelligently in the public or common realm is itself a skill to be learnt. With the advance of medical technology, the discipline of bioethics has particularly come to the fore, and presents delicate issues for debate in the public arena. In many of these areas there are not necessarily any straightforwardly Christian points of view, but there will often be perspectives informed by Christian faith and conviction. However, when it comes to matters of poverty, human trafficking, torture, human dignity, religious freedom, reconciliation and forgiveness, personal and social righteousness, and the common good, Christians have much both to say and contribute that comes from the very heart of their convictions.

PARTNERS IN CONVERSATION

The perspectives identified here demonstrate a breadth of engagement to which responsible Christian advocates might potentially contribute in both defending and promoting Christian convictions. To be involved effectively requires considerable amounts of knowledge, at least about the spheres in which one has particular interests, and wisdom in knowing how to argue without alienating, and how to be assertive without being aggressive. Yet different people find different things persuasive. Fine arguments do not of themselves necessarily persuade, because the real struggle to accept Christian convictions is often actually happening on other than the intellectual level. In addition, it should never be overlooked that part of the apologetic task is to confirm the Christian community in the coherence and credibility of its own convictions. In cultures that frequently raise questions about faith, Christians need to be aware that their personal commitments of faith are intellectually sustainable and have integrity. In the Christian understanding head and heart belong together in the enterprise of faith. Without such confidence in the justifiability of their beliefs, Christians will retreat into a private and tribal world that views faith as entirely subjective rather than as an act of reasonable trust for which there may be no knock-down proofs, but for which there are certainly good reasons. A church suffering from an inferiority complex is unlikely to do the world much good. By contrast, a church confident about its identity and its beliefs will make a difference.

With this in mind, it is possible to identify the kinds of conversations partners with whom Christian communities are likely to engage. Here we set out some examples.

SEEKERS AFTER GOD

If human beings are made in the image of God, it should not surprise us that they seek for spiritual meaning and direction to their lives. The seeker is already asking questions to which Christians believe the gospel has the answer. People consistently demonstrate an instinct to believe in transcendence, to seek for something beyond themselves. However, this will often find expression in ways that are muddled and uninformed. Although people are on a journey, the journey should take them somewhere it is worth going. If people are to come to an informed and genuine faith they will often need help in removing false understandings of the Christian way, or in overcoming negative experiences of Christianity they may have had in the past. Obstacles, real and imagined, need to be identified and tackled. This may often be done by offering people alternative ways of thinking about particular aspects of the faith, showing that previous models or interpretations have been distortions rather than proper expressions of that faith. To do this requires a degree of confidence in one's own grasp of Christian conviction and in interpreting it appropriately and faithfully.

OTHER RELIGIOUS TRADITIONS

Recent censuses have confirmed what is already well known through observation, that we are living in a multi-dimensional society that is at the same time Christian, secular, and religiously plural. Conversations with those of other faith traditions are therefore increasingly common and demonstrate the need to remove obstacles, often deep-seated, which prevent proper understanding of the gospel. There are new insights to be gained in such conversations, as much about one's own faith, seen through the eyes of another and in contrast and comparison to how they believe, as about that of other people. However, as those who are called to bear witness, Christians take seriously the engagement with those of other-faiths no less than those of no-faith, and it poses different challenges. Other faith traditions already accept the reality of God, or at least of a transcendent reality. The conversation centers round how to interpret that realm adequately, not whether it exists at all.

SECULARISTS AND MATERIALISTS

Secularism is the worldview that affirms there to be no spiritual reality and that all that exists is the material world. To see the world correctly, it claims, humans need to divest their understanding of the world of any trace of supernaturalism or transcendence. These are regarded as superstitious remnants of an outdated and unscientific worldview. This approach can also be called "materialism" or "naturalism" and is sometimes also associated with "rationalism" (though some types of rationalist are distinctly unreasonable). It is an ideology completely at variance with the Christian belief, shared by other religions and some philosophies, in an ultimate reality that is spiritual in nature. Secularism looks to evolution as an adequate and sufficient explanation of the world and argues that what appears to us to be design within the world, so suggesting a creator, is actually the product of random forces adapting to their environment and becoming more complex in so doing. While it claims to be rationalist in that only that which can be substantiated by reason is to be believed, it actually amounts, as has previously been argued, to a faith in its own right in that its fundamental tenets are themselves incapable of rational or empirical proof. It has faith in reason, in science, and in human nature. The apologetic task will therefore in part aim to show both that this "rationalism" is itself "faith-based" and that so-called "faith movements" are not necessarily irrational (although some may be), but can have their own form of rationality. Whereas most Christians in the West are inclined to believe that the influence of Christianity is in decline and is being marginalized, secularists believe that religion is resurging and is being allowed a disproportionate amount of influence in public affairs. They wish to draw a firm line between what is "public," and so non-religious, and what is "private," in which sphere people may believe whatever they choose.

In this context, it is well to draw attention to the contention that good apologetics should not only be able to defend Christian belief against criticisms (negative apologetics) but go on the offensive (positive apologetics). Negative apologetics seeks to remove objections to Christian faith whereas positive apologetics shows the inadequacies of other worldviews, presents a positive case for Christian truth claims and shows the advantages and gains of a Christian worldview. As an example, the problem of evil raises issues for Christian faith, but the very fact that we can speak of evil and that we find it offensive must be saying something about our innate human moral sense and a feeling that "things ought not to be this way." Why, in a godless, empty world, should we feel like this? This might be thought of as "the argument from evil" *to* God. As a further example, a test of a godless worldview is not only whether it makes reasonable sense but whether it is possible to live with its logical implications, which often leave no grounds for moral distinctions between good and evil.

POST-CHRISTIANS

A small but often well-informed audience towards which apologetics may need to be directed is that of people who once professed the Christian faith but who believe that they have grown beyond it. Sometimes these are former clergy who have become disillusioned with their beliefs and now believe that modern ways of thinking have exposed religious language as merely metaphorical or "non-realist," that is, it does not refer to any objective reality but to internal states of mind or experience. Others have been influenced by radical forms of feminism into the belief that the Christian religion in particular is inherently patriarchal and so hostile to the interests of women. Yet others in this group are what might be called "disillusioned fundamentalists" who are now as fervent in their non-belief as they may once have been in their belief. Post-Christians, having been "insiders," know what it is to experience Christian belief and worship from within. Having become disillusioned, they can be trenchant in their criticism. Yet the question will remain in each case as to whether they are reacting against the Christian faith as it is properly to be understood or against a caricature they have previously espoused. A clear grasp of well-understood convictions can help disentangle the confusion.

THE "NEW AGE"

The New Age movement represents a very varied cluster of spiritualities and interests. Those involved are not usually troubled with the same questions about rational verification that secularists may have, having little difficulty in believing in miracles, or angels, or spiritual powers of good and evil. Devotees of older nature religions, such as Wicca, will often feel that they have been misrepresented and demonized by the Christian church in the past. This is true particularly of the assumption Christians might make that "witchcraft" (Wicca) and Satanism are one and the same. Self-defining pagans, for instance, are usually clear that they are devotees of a nature religion, rather than of the powers of darkness, and, indeed, see Satanism as in some sense a Christian construct, Satan being a derivative from Christian rather than pagan thought. Yet many New Agers remain open and receptive to Christian experience. An apologetic response will be concerned to understand the distinctions within the New Age and to relate Christian testimony to it accurately and fairly. Although a good intellectual grasp of Christian teaching must help this, an attractive and authentic experience of God's grace is likely to be the crucial factor.

It can be seen that to engage intelligently with all of these contemporary audiences requires a wide range of knowledge and understanding. Those who see themselves as advocates and apologists, while having a broad grasp of their task, will have to make choices about where they specialize. Behind all these conversations there stands the question of authenticity: do Christian communities of faith demonstrate a spiritual experience and conviction that conveys genuine spiritual energy and power that is able to attract and convert those who are looking for answers? Earlier in this book we identified the criteria of coherence, correspondence, and congruence in testing the credibility of Christian beliefs. Christian convictions need to hold together or cohere persuasively; they need to correspond to the way things actually are and relate to the real world; and they need to demonstrate a congruence with Christ himself as the one who is the way, the truth, and the life. Together these make a powerful case. True spiritual community is compelling and Christian convictions lack persuasive power if they are not supported and embodied in communities of thoughtful, spiritually intelligent believers. This is the final subject to which we now turn.

20

Communities of Salt and Light

THE STARTING POINT FOR this book was the assertion that Jesus Christ has risen from the dead and that his living presence is still to be known in the communities of faith that believe in him and gather around him. Having explored the range of Christian convictions it is now possible to return to those communities of faith to consider their mission and role.

As already indicated, the New Testament uses many images to describe the Christian community, but three are most dominant. They are the idea of *the people of God* (1 Pet 2:9), an image that connects the church with the history of Israel and God's purpose to call out for God's own self a covenant people obedient to the divine purpose (Exod 19:5–6); the idea of *the body of Christ* (1 Cor 12:12–31), an image that relates the church to Christ as the head of the body (Col 1:18) and stresses the variety-in-unity to be found within it; and the idea of *the temple of the Holy Spirit*, an image that stresses continuity with the tabernacle and temple of the history of Israel and sees that history being fulfilled in the community of Christian disciples in whom God's Spirit now abides (Eph 2:21–22). Together these images bestow great importance on the church and signify its centrality in God's purpose for creation. To be part of this community is to contribute to the well-being of all humanity by sharing decisively in the compassionate and gracious purposes of God.

SALT AND LIGHT

In an important passage Jesus taught that the community of his disciples was the "salt of the earth" and the "light of the world," and instructed them on the importance of maintaining the purity of their life together and the clarity with which they bore their witness in the world (Matt 5:13–16). If this is true, then active life within the Christian community is one of the greatest forms of service we can render humankind. The images of salt and light are themselves instructive since they point to the two modes of the Christian community's existence. Light gains its power from being intense and visible. It represents high energy, being focused in one particular place so that from there it might illuminate the darkness. By contrast, salt is intended to be scattered. When it is so, it is absorbed into food and loses its visibility while maintaining its impact. In the world of Jesus, salt was used both to season and to preserve against decay, and occasionally in certain forms it was also used to fertilize the ground. The images of light and salt point to the church's existence, first as a gathered community, focused in particular places and visible to the world; and also as a scattered community engaged in the life of the world and discretely making its impact as a range of individuals. It both serves as a preservative in resisting evil and as a stimulant in supporting that which is good. It is through the dynamic created by gathering and scattering and then re-gathering that the churches make their impact upon the world.

THE GATHERED COMMUNITY

Although there is only one church of Jesus Christ, it is to be found in a multiplicity of communities that are spread across the world. They take many forms and are the expressions of many different cultures. What they have in common is a devotion to Jesus Christ as Lord and a shared participation in God's Spirit. It is important for churches to gather since, "For where two or three are gathered in my name, I am there among them" (Matt 18:20). In effect, it is the presence of Christ in a community that makes it into a church. Without this it would be an assembly with either social or political intentions but not the spiritual community that is the church of Christ. To gather "in the name of Christ" implies that it is for knowledge and love of him that a church comes together. It does so to confess him as Lord (1 Cor 12:3), to worship him as the Son of God, and through him to draw near to the Father in the power of the Spirit (Eph 2:18). Such worship is the primary purpose of the churches. When we worship, we re-order our own world by returning to our fundamental relationship to God, and in so doing we maintain a presence in the world that runs counter to its own drift and holds open the possibility of its transformation. For Christ to indicate that he is present in such communities suggests that he is present in a way that is distinctive. Although the risen Christ may rightly be understood to be universally present through the Spirit, he is present in Christian communities to a degree and extent that is more intense. Christ is *savingly* present, restoring those who believe to their true being. In that he is present in believers (who are a temple of the Holy Spirit individually as well as corporately—1 Cor 3:16), he is present in Christian communities in the relationships and interactions between those believers, in the bonds and the love that are between them. Christ gains access to a community through the Word that is proclaimed and believed among them (1 Thess 1:6) and through its members who are bonded together. It should go without saying that although these communities may own and use buildings, it is the gathered people who are the church. Buildings are a place for them to meet and a base from which to engage in mission and service.

The gathered community of Christians comes together at regular intervals and can be recognized by the things that it does. The first Christian community established the norms and expectations for all subsequent communities: "They devoted themselves to the apostles' teaching and fellowship, to the breaking of bread and the prayers" (Acts 2:42). These components are fundamental to a church's life. The apostles, having been with Jesus from the beginning (Acts 1:21–22), were uniquely qualified, as Jesus intended, to teach about him, to recall and explain his teaching, and to be witnesses to his resurrection. They were the authoritative guardians of Christian conviction and their teaching was foundational (Eph 2:20). It would later be transmitted through the New Testament writings and still forms the normative basis of what is believed and lived in Christian communities. Added to this is fellowship between those who have come to believe so that they might share their experiences of God's grace, and encourage each other to hold fast to it. The "breaking of bread" refers both to the pleasure taken in eating together (Acts 2:46) and the enactment of the Lord's Supper that Jesus had ordained as a regular practice among his followers (1 Cor 11:23–26). "The prayers" suggests that the believers not only prayed spontaneously but maintained a rhythm of prayer on the pattern of the Jewish temple worship. The first Christians met in homes and in the precincts of the Jewish temple; they met on a daily basis and in particular on the first day of the week, the day on which Christ had risen (Acts 20:7; 1 Cor 16:2), and which was also the first day of God's original creation, according to Genesis 1. Together these fundamental elements of Christian worship constitute the primary activities of any Christian community and are the means by which its life is renewed, safeguarded, and sustained. A community that forsakes these things rejects its own identity. One that fosters them promotes, to the contrary, its own well-being and has the potential to be spiritually vibrant and transformative. It discovers, by God's grace, the energy to attract others into its life and to incorporate them into the worshiping community (Acts 2:43–47). In this way it establishes the kind of effective community that can act as a base for the transmission of its faith.

By gathering together, Christian communities establish their presence in a location and make themselves available to others. As a person's body makes that person identifiable to others, so the church as the body of Christ can be located and become available through its public and open gatherings. Christ can be found there. The invisible church of Christ is therefore always becoming a visible community of flesh and blood. Although persecution has sometimes required the church to meet in secret, it is not a secret society, but seeks to be transparent to others: "for this thing was not done in a corner" (Acts 26:26). The light of the Christian community that Jesus referred to is intended to be a reflection of the one who is the light of the world (John 8:12). By exalting him in its midst and by continually re-telling his story, a community allows his light to shine so that it becomes, as it was intended to, "a city built on a hill" that "cannot be hidden" (Matt 5:14). Although inevitably separated from each other in space and in time, and sometimes by disagreements and divisions, every Christian community can look forward to a future time when the whole church in heaven and on earth will be gathered in the presence of God: "After this I looked, and there was a great multitude that no one could count, from every nation, from all tribes and peoples and languages, standing before the Lamb, robed in white, with palm branches in their hands. They cried out with a loud voice, saying, 'Salvation belongs to our God who is seated on the throne, and to the Lamb!'" (Rev 7:9–10). This is the church of Christ in its ultimate expression. The church that the risen Christ is gathering is multi-cultural, multi-lingual, multi-ethnic, and multi-national. It is not defined by race or class or ethnicity but solely by a shared and humble faith in Jesus Christ as Lord and as savior of the world. In the light of the future vision towards which it is pressing, its responsibility is to foster that which makes for its unity in faith, its holiness in life, its engagement in mission, its faithfulness to Christ, and the teaching of his apostles, and its inclusion of all peoples voluntarily within its boundaries. This is traditionally expressed as the church being "one, holy, catholic, and apostolic."

DEFINING THE CHRISTIAN COMMUNITY

Although the Christian community is open to all who wish to share its convictions and its practices, it does have a clear identity and a non-negotiable central focus in Jesus Christ. It calls people to commitment to all that it stands for. Commitment to Christ is expressed, among other ways, in the practices of Baptism and Communion. Communion is also known as the "Lord's Supper" and the "Eucharist" (from the Greek word for "thanksgiving"). These are sometimes called "ordinances" since they were ordained as enduring practices for the church by Jesus himself (Matt 28:19–20; Mark 14:22–25). They are also called "sacraments" from the Latin word *sacramentum*, which means an oath or declaration of commitment (1 Pet 3:21), since those who practice them are affirming or reaffirming their devotion to Christ. They are further described as "dominical" since they trace their origin back to Jesus the Lord (Latin: *dominus*).

The "dominical sacraments" may be thought of as dramatic actions or "visible words" that portray the gospel of Christ in different but complementary ways, as will be explained. Both practices may be thought of as defining moments, events in time that shape and condition everything that follows on from them. These two ordinances are central to the church in ways that are not precisely true of other valuable Christian practices, such as the holy kiss (or kiss of love: 1 Cor 16:20; 1 Pet 5:14), the laying on of hands (Acts 8:17; 19:6), or the right hand of fellowship (Gal 2:9). This is so since both Baptism and Communion are direct references to the central acts of our salvation in the cross and resurrection of Christ. Baptism refers to these by the burying and rising involved in immersion; and Communion in that it is a fellowship meal with the risen Christ and his followers made possible through the sacrificial death symbolized by the bread and the wine. In this way, both actions constantly draw our attention to what is at the heart of the Christian faith. By so doing they safeguard the essential nature of that faith by sustaining a clear focus on the centralities. They serve to mark out the Christian community, to set it apart from society at large by indicating that something significant is happening among this group of people. The church is called to be different in that it makes God as revealed in Christ its reference point and seeks to follow God's will exemplified by Christ. Jesus warned that salt is only useful and good when it retains its saltiness (Matt 5:13). When, in his world, salt was collected by being scooped up from the ground around the Dead Sea, it was highly likely to become adulterated and impure, being rendered useless. Like good salt, the church needs to maintain its purity and quality if it is to do the work to which it is called.

BAPTISM

Baptism involves the immersion of a candidate in water in the name of the Father, Son, and Holy Spirit upon that person's confession of repentance towards God and faith in Jesus Christ as Lord. It might also be practiced by effusion, the pouring of water over the candidate as a symbol of God's Spirit coming upon them. It involves a promise to serve Christ forever within the fellowship of the church and to dedicate oneself to the life of discipleship within the Christian community. After Peter preached on the day of Pentecost, his hearers were convicted of their sins and cried out, what should we do? Peter's reply was, "Repent, and be baptized every one of you in the name of Jesus Christ so that your sins may be forgiven, and you will receive the gift of the Holy Spirit" (Acts 2:38). This remains the normative way in which a person declares him or herself to be a Christian and those who are so baptized are reckoned within the Christian community. They have "come out" as Christians. Peter's words point to three significant actions. There is what *we* do, which is to turn from lives without God to the living God in repentance, forsaking the forms of living that are contrary to God's will. This includes personal trust in Christ and his atoning work. It should be said that no one comes to this point unaided, it is a work of God that brings us to this moment, so that even the faith we possess should be seen as the gift of God (John 12:32; 1 Cor 4:7). There is what *the church* does, which is to baptize us, as it is commanded and authorized to do. This is an action we do not do for ourselves and it involves entrusting ourselves to others (in the act of immersion) in the same way that we place our reliance upon Jesus Christ and our trust in the community of his followers. Then there is what *God* does, which is to bestow the Holy Spirit upon us so that we enter into the age of fulfilled promises granted by the Spirit and are empowered to live as disciples of Christ. Baptism is to be forced on no one and is to be entered into entirely voluntarily. It should be the product of careful consideration and sober thought as well as of joyful thanksgiving and love for God.

The symbolism of Baptism and the truth it portrays is extensive. At the most obvious level it is an act of spiritual cleansing that is intended to wash away the guilt and shame of past deeds and lifestyles (1 Cor 6:11). It is an act of new birth such that, as a child is born through water when its mother's waters break, so a person may be born again to a new and wholesome life through the work of the Spirit (John 3:5–6). It is an act of burial and resurrection, connecting us with the death and resurrection of Christ that are the means of our reconciliation to God and because of which we end our old lives and begin a new one (Rom 6:1–4). And just as a person is plunged into the water, so in Baptism a candidate is baptized in the Holy

Spirit, being brought into a new and dynamic realm of God's life and activity in the world (John 1:29–34, Acts 1:1–5). Baptism is intended to be a powerful act, redefining our lives and enabling us to make a clean break with that which is neither good nor godly and to enter into a new and living way. Jesus himself was baptized by John the Baptist at the start of his earthly ministry. It was at that point that he received the outpouring of the Spirit that enabled him to enter into his messianic ministry (Matt 3:13–17). Immediately afterwards he entered upon his mission with intent and purpose. When we are baptized we are identifying ourselves with Christ and being incorporated into his community and empowered by the Spirit so that we also may share in his mission and ministry.

COMMUNION

Baptism may be thought of as the rite or practice that marks the beginning of the Christian life. It is appropriate for it to take place in close association with a person's decision to become a Christian and is part of that process, an outward declaration of an inward discovery and transformation. It is intended to happen only once and is like a foundation that is laid, upon which everything else may be built (Heb 6:1–2). It is an "initiating rite," a doorway into Christian faith and community. But faith and commitment demand to be reaffirmed and re-expressed on a regular basis. For this reason there is a "continuing rite" that is practiced in the church, the simple sharing of bread and wine in order to recall the reality of Christ's death and resurrection. In this way communion with God and God's people is entered into and enjoyed. Communion may be celebrated frequently and is essentially a community meal rather than a solitary discipline. The evidence suggests that the first Christian communities would come together to eat and as part of that would observe Communion. For various reasons it became convenient to separate out Communion as a distinctive and symbolic meal on its own (1 Cor 11:20–22).

Like Baptism, Communion is multi-dimensional. It contains past, future, and present levels of meaning. The Christian meal is an adaptation of the Jewish Passover meal. In the Passover the Jewish meal recalled the way in which they had been delivered from slavery in Egypt (Exod 12:1–27). It was celebrated by all Israel once a year in the spring and undertaken in such a way as to suggest that all subsequent generations of Israel had themselves been present in Egypt and were themselves the direct objects of God's salvation. In the newly adapted Christian meal there is also a backward reference. We are doing it in remembrance of Christ, his death and resurrection. We "proclaim the Lord's death until he comes" (1 Cor 11:26). The bread and the wine represent the fact that once God's only Son took human flesh and blood and shared with us our human life and fate. He did this for our salvation and to renew our life with his own. He offered himself as a sacrifice in our place, his body being broken and torn and his life poured out for us. He was raised from the dead and after his resurrection ate and drank with his disciples (Acts 10:41). These are the solid events in history that provide the basis for Christian conviction, and in Communion they are recalled not as bare history but as events that involve us, the benefits of which we share (1 Cor 10:16). In Communion we are giving thanks, so it is rightly described as a sacrifice, but a sacrifice of thanksgiving, rather than of atonement (Ps 116:12–19). Christ has atoned for sins once for all (Heb 9:28; 10:10). Our privilege is to go on receiving what he has done continually and to give thanks for it.

Communion also has a future dimension and anticipates the great feast that is to take place in the kingdom of God once it has come in all its fullness. Jesus spoke of a future day when, "many will come from east and west and will eat with Abraham and Isaac and Jacob in the kingdom of heaven" (Matt 8:11). At the Last Supper he indicated, "From now on I will not drink of the fruit of the vine until the kingdom of God comes" (Luke 22:18). The celebration of Communion is an anticipation of a day that has yet to dawn and that has been long awaited: "On this mountain the Lord of hosts will make for all peoples a feast of rich food, a feast of well-matured wines, of rich food filled with marrow, of well-matured wines strained clear. And he will destroy on this mountain the shroud that is cast over all peoples, the sheet that is spread over all nations: He will swallow up death for ever" (Isa 25:6–8). It means that the joy that will belong to all creation in the future kingdom can be experienced ahead of time and expressed in the present worship of the church: "Blessed are those who are invited to the marriage supper of the Lamb" (Rev 19:9).

Communion's third dimension is a present one. The Christ who once came in flesh and blood and who will come again in glory and power is the same Christ who comes now into our experience, to be encountered, known, and loved by those who believe him to be risen from the dead and who are his present disciples. It is for this reason that the word "Communion" is appropriate: believers hold communion with their Lord and in so doing with each other. They go back to basics. They become one body with Christ. As many grains of wheat become one in the making of a loaf, and many grapes are united as one in a cup of wine, so believers merge together and become one in Christ. Communion is a place of renewal, reconciliation, and realignment. One Aramaic word that has survived in our New

Testament (written in Greek) and that was used by the first Christians in their shared worship is the word "Maranatha," meaning "Our Lord, come!" Used at the end of a gathering, it could be a plea for the future coming of the Lord. Used at the beginning it could be a prayer that Christ would come to his people in the gathering itself. It can also be translated as "Our Lord has come!" Christ has come, Christ will come, and Christ does come.

Neither Baptism nor Communion is a magic event that produces effects irrespective of the attitude of those who receive them. They become effective only when they are received in faith and trust by those who accept them with sincerity and integrity. When this is the case, however, they become "means of grace," channels that God uses to bless and to nourish the community that has gathered in Christ's name. These practices that Christ has bequeathed to his church are to be seen as places of encounter, places of rendezvous, where the Christ who is able to meet us anywhere has promised in particular to be present. Yet they define and demarcate the Christian community.

MINISTRIES OF THE WORD

The community of salt and light gathers around the risen Christ who is in its midst. It also gathers because it has heard a summons to come to him. The good news of the gospel has been preached and made known, it has been believed and received and it has gathered a community of those who hear and live by its truth. This was so in the ministry of Jesus who preached and gathered disciples. It was so on the day of Pentecost when Peter and the apostles preached and several thousand came to believe and then "devoted themselves to the apostles' teaching" (Acts 2:42). It was true throughout the Acts of the Apostles and it is true now. It is true both chronologically and logically. The preaching of the gospel preceded the birth of the church. There would be no church without the preaching of the gospel because without it there would be no believers (Rom 10:14–15). Someone has to preach before the church can exist. Once a church has come into existence it continues to gather around Christ as Christ is made known through the Word. "So faith comes from what is heard, and what is heard comes through the word of Christ" (Rom 10:17). The Word makes us attentive to God. The Word may be proclaimed in various ways, through Scripture being read, studied individually or communally, explained, narrated, and proclaimed, but without the priority of the Word the church cannot endure, or at least not as a truly Christian community. For the benefit of that community the risen Lord, who is the head of the church, raises up servants from within it who will interpret, explain, proclaim, and communicate the Word for the benefit of those inside and outside the church alike: "The gifts he gave were that some would be apostles, some prophets, some evangelists, some pastors and teachers, to equip the saints for the work of ministry, for building up the body of Christ" (Eph 4:11–12). In one form or another, the nature of these ministries is shaped by the Word of God. Each form of ministry is a way of bearing the Word, either to those who have yet to believe or to those who do believe but need to live and die in the light of the Word they have received. It is not primarily that these ministries do the work of the church but that they enable the whole gathered community to achieve the potential that it has been given by God, with each part working in the way God has assigned to it within the body (Eph 4:16). Those who minister in this way deserve the respect, support, and cooperation of the people they serve (1 Thess 5:12–13), just as those so called should set an example and live according to the highest standards (1 Pet 5:1–5).

PURSUING A MORAL VISION

Both in the Old Testament and in the New it is clear that God seeks a people who will be holy and dedicated to the ways of the Lord. As the light of the world, the Christian community is called to be different. If it loses this capacity it becomes a mere reflection of surrounding societies and has nothing to offer. For the church to be the light of the world, Christ has first of all to be the light of the church. In the history of Israel God gave the people he had redeemed a series of laws to spell out for them how it was that they could respond to God in grateful obedience (Exod 20). These laws are still able to inform and instruct us about the life that pleases God and should be studied (1 Cor 10:11). However, Christians now have an embodiment of what pleases God in the life and person of Christ: "The law indeed was given through Moses; grace and truth came through Jesus Christ" (John 1:17). The Christian life should not be understood first of all as an attempt to keep the rules and to adhere to the laws without deviation. Rather, through meditation on Scripture and responsiveness to Christ, and in communion with him, we come into possession of a moral vision, a way of understanding and imagining what the good and godly life looks like. This moral vision is not forced upon us but formed within us as a disposition towards the good. It is a vision that concerns personal integrity and honesty, love for neighbor and enemy, compassion and generosity towards the suffering and the poor, faithful and life-long relationships in marriage and sexual integrity in singleness, care and tenderness towards children, simplicity and detachment from materialism, peace-making and peace-loving in place of conflict, responsible willingness to forego our own interests for the sake of others, forgiveness and kindness as a way of life, and a host of other virtues. In so far as Christian communities are able to attain to this vision, they are able to be light in the darkness. For the Christian, the first and most important commandment is to love God with heart, mind, soul, and strength. The second commandment follows from it and is to love our neighbor as ourselves (Matt 22:34-40; Mark 12: 28-34). These commandments are not forced upon us but inspired within us by the love of God. As we respond to God and internalize the love of God so love becomes our instinct and desire.

COMMUNITY ENGAGEMENT

If the image of light suggests that churches have a visible and intense presence in their communities, the idea that the disciples of Christ are the "salt of the earth" suggests that when they are scattered abroad, as most of the time they are, they can quietly exercise an influence out of proportion to their size. There are few people who do not have contact with at least one Christian, and Christians are present in virtually every sphere of life. Wherever they go Christians are witnesses. Whether they speak or remain silent they bear testimony by what they do to the one in whom they believe. When they gather together it is to worship God but also to prepare themselves for their witness in the world, to sharpen the edge of their Christian discipleship, to receive encouragement for the next leg of their journey. By living consistent and reliable lives, by committing acts of random kindness, by valuing people, working hard and well, and caring about the world, Christians can shape and influence the society in which they live. Christians are concerned to transmit their faith, to pass it on to others to share. They are concerned to incorporate others within their congregations, to be inclusive in the way they add to the church. The church is intended to be a redemptive community in which, by being brought into relationship with God, people find their true home. They are also concerned for the redemption of society, for improvement of the conditions in which people live. They are aware of the immense imbalances that exist across the globe and of the extremes of wealth and poverty that are found. Although they believe that the world's complete liberation and healing must await the final coming of God's kingdom, and although they are fully aware of the resistance of multiple powers to that kingdom, they also believe that the vision of the coming kingdom can inspire people to improve the present, to edge it gradually nearer a more equitable and compassionate world.

Engagement with the world as it is implies that the mission served by the Christian community involves the transmission of their faith through witness and church-based evangelization, the embodiment of the love of God through charitable and humanitarian action, and involvement at the political level to improve the legal and governmental frameworks within which people live. If the church belongs to the "order of redemption," in that it is a visible expression of the will of God to save, then the state belongs to the "order of preservation" in that its primary role under God is to preserve society from destruction by criminal and corrupt activity (Rom 13:1–7). In direct contrast to the order of redemption that follows (or should follow) the non-violent way of Jesus, the order of preservation has the power to compel and is able to use force to achieve its goals. The New Testament calls this the power of the "sword" (Rom 13:4). Whereas virtually all Christians would affirm the necessity for this, they might also differ as to the extent to which they can participate in this dimension, with a minority believing it lies beyond what Christians are called to. A majority are more inclined to believe that because the order of preservation is ordered, and in some sense ordained, by God, Christians might legitimately serve in its policing and enforcement functions as ways of preserving the peace.

Although they can never achieve a fully just and peaceful world, governments are called to provide a kind of peace and a semblance of justice in a fallen and broken world. They do their difficult work imperfectly and are themselves liable to fall prey to corruption and even criminality, with fateful consequences. All people have therefore a vested interest in stable societies in which justice is fairly and effectively delivered, prosperity promoted, and citizens enabled to flourish. Christians are rightly involved in these processes at every level, acting, as has been indicated, as salt that both helps to stem corruption and fertilizer that assists that which is healthy and nourishing to grow. Responsible citizenship is therefore a calling for all Christians (1 Pet 2:13–17), and active political service a vocation for those appropriately gifted and called.

THE PURSUIT OF THE GOOD

Christians do not need a reason to do good. Goodness is its own justification and reward. God is good, as the whole Bible attests on multiple occasions, and whoever pursues goodness in some sense pursues God. Jesus said, "Let your light shine before others, so that they may see your good works and give glory to your Father in heaven" (Matt 5:16). To resist the destructive acids that seek to erode Christian communities, it is necessary for those communities to be clear and resilient in their convictions. It is worth saying again that in Jesus Christ grace and truth belong inseparably together (John 1:17). Convictions unaccompanied by goodness and grace repel rather than attract. Convictions born in, inspired by, impregnated by God's goodness and grace, and leading to their ever deeper expression, are what the churches of Christ are capable of and what the world most of all needs of us.

> O the depth of the riches and wisdom and knowledge of God How unsearchable are his judgments and how inscrutable his ways! "For who has known the mind of the Lord? Or who has been his counselor?" "Or who has given a gift to him, to receive a gift in return?" For from him and through him and to him are all things. To him be the glory for ever. Amen (Rom 11:33–36).

Appendix 1

The Apostles' Creed

I believe in God, the Father Almighty, creator of heaven and earth.

I believe in Jesus Christ, his only Son, our Lord, who was conceived by the power of the Holy Spirit, born of the Virgin Mary, suffered under Pontius Pilate, was crucified, died, and was buried; he descended to the dead. On the third day he rose again; he ascended into heaven, he is seated at the right hand of the Father, and he will come again to judge the living and the dead.

I believe in the Holy Spirit, the holy catholic church, the communion of saints, the forgiveness of sins, the resurrection of the body, and the life everlasting. Amen.[1]

Despite its title, the Apostles' Creed was not produced by the apostles of Jesus, nor does it date back to when they were alive. It is, however, a statement of belief that attempts to be true to apostolic teaching and it goes back before 250 AD to the churches of Rome and Palestine. Its origins are in the "catechetical" process through which candidates would be prepared for Baptism in the early Christian communities. It was probably intended as a statement that they could make in the presence of the bishop to demonstrate their readiness to be baptized. The Apostles' Creed is a basic summary of essential Christian teachings. It has since become a regular part of church liturgies in which worshipers continue to confess their faith in God.

The Creed was never intended to be a full statement of Christian belief. It is worth commenting, however, that it takes a three-fold, trinitarian

---

1. Taken from *Common Worship*.

form and so reflects the structure of biblical teaching about the God of Jesus Christ who is acknowledged here as Father, Son, and Holy Spirit. Most concentration is given to the Son, with his career being briefly outlined. It should be noted however that little is said about his earthly ministry and this is one point where the Creed could be amplified. The concentration on the Son is not surprising, given that it is through Jesus that the Christian vision of God underwent such a significant and world-changing revolution. Lacking here are any attempts to explain the nature of the atonement and any reference to the Scriptures as such, though the whole is clearly based on Scripture. It may seem strange that such an unwholesome character as Pontius Pilate should regularly be remembered in Christian worship, and indeed it is. However, the presence of Pilate is a constant reminder that the Christian faith is historically rooted in the death of Christ under his governance. Perhaps also it is a reminder: "Do not put your trust in princes, in mortals, in whom there is no help" (Ps 146:3).

Appendix 2

The Nicene Creed

We believe in one God, the Father, the Almighty, maker of heaven and earth, of all that is, seen and unseen.

We believe in one Lord, Jesus Christ, the only Son of God, eternally begotten of the Father, God from God, Light from Light, true God from true God, begotten not made, of one Being with the Father, through whom all things were made. For us and for our salvation he came down from heaven, was incarnate from the Holy Spirit and the Virgin Mary, and was made man. For our sake he was crucified under Pontius Pilate; he suffered death and was buried. On the third day he rose again in accordance with the Scriptures; he ascended into heaven and is seated at the right hand of the Father. He will come again in glory to judge the living and the dead, and his kingdom will have no end.

We believe in the Holy Spirit, the Lord, the giver of life, who proceeds from the Father [and the Son], who with the Father and the Son is worshiped and glorified, who has spoken through the prophets. We believe in one holy catholic and apostolic church. We acknowledge one baptism for the forgiveness of sins. We look for the resurrection of the dead, and the life of the world to come. Amen.[1]

THE NICENE CREED WAS first promulgated in 325 AD at the Council of Nicaea, a gathering of Christian bishops meeting in Nicaea in Turkey to

---

1. Taken from *Common Worship*.

deliberate on the person of Christ. Controversy had been provoked through the teachings of Arius, a presbyter in Alexandria, who claimed that Christ was not fully God but rather a creature akin to an angel or a kind of secondary deity. The Arian controversy surrounded whether Christ's nature was to be described as *"like* God" or as *"the same as* God." In Greek there is only one letter, or "iota," of difference between these two descriptions, but a huge amount depended upon that one letter. The Council affirmed that Christ was the same as God in regard to his essential nature and so established firmly one of the most important of all Christian teachings.

The Nicene Creed can be seen to have a similar, trinitarian form to the Apostles' Creed, but the section dealing with Christ is considerably expanded to make it absolutely clear that he shares the divine nature. He is "eternally begotten of the Father" and "not made." To be "eternally begotten" means that what Christ is is derived from what the Father is. He is "of one Being with the Father" (the Greek here is *homoousios*, expressed in more Latin form as "consubstantial"). In other words, whatever the Father is, so is the Son. For this reason Christ can be said to be "God from God, Light from Light, true God from true God." Christ is as fully divine as is the Father. He is also fully human since he "came down from heaven" and "was incarnate," being "made man" of both the Holy Spirit and the Virgin Mary. This creed is equally emphatic in asserting the divinity of the Holy Spirit, who also is fully worthy of worship and honor. The logic is therefore clear: Christ is of one Being (consubstantial) with the Father and likewise the Spirit is of one Being (consubstantial) with the Father and the Son. God is both one and three without contradiction. Father, Son, and Spirit are to be worshiped.

The Nicene Creed is more fully known as the "Nicene-Constantinopolitan Creed" since it is believed to have undergone some changes at the Council of Constantinople in 381 AD. Its appearance in its present form was at the Council of Chalcedon in 451 AD. It has since become, more than any other creed or confession, the standard for discerning normative and authentic Christian belief. However, it does have certain limitations. The metaphysical language in which it is couched puts it at a remove from the more narrative language of the New Testament. In turn, this leads to potential neglect of the moral and ethical teachings of Jesus and of the call to discipleship, a tendency that is compounded by the fact that, like the Apostles' Creed, it says nothing about the life and ministry of Jesus between his birth and his death. The words "and the Son" that appear here in both creeds in square brackets (inserted by the author) were added at a later date and partly for this reason became the cause of further controversy between the Roman Catholic Church and the Churches of Eastern Orthodoxy leading to the Great Schism between them in 1054 AD.

Bibliography and Suggested Further Reading

Allison, Dale C. *Constructing Jesus: Memory, Imagination and History*. London: SPCK, 2010.
———. *Resurrecting Jesus: The Earliest Christian Tradition and Its Interpreters*. London: T. & T. Clark, 2005.
Badcock, Gary D. *The House Where God Lives: Renewing the Doctrine of the Church for Today*. Grand Rapids: Eerdmans, 2009.
Barbour, Ian. *Religion in an Age of Science*. London: SCM, 1990.
Bartholomew, Craig, and Michael Goheen. *The Drama of Scripture: Finding Our Place in the Biblical Story*. London: SPCK, 2006.
Boyarin, Daniel. *The Jewish Gospels: The Story of the Jewish Christ*. New York: New Press, 2012.
Brain, Peter. *Going the Distance: How to Stay Fit for a Lifetime of Ministry*. Kingsford, NSW: Mathias Media, 2004.
Buber, Martin. *I and Thou*. Reprint. New York: Continuum, 2004.
Church of England. *Common Worship: Services and Prayers for the Church of England*. London: Church House, 2000
Cottingham, John. *Why Believe?* London: Continuum, 2009.
Fergusson, David A. S. *The Cosmos and the Creator: An Introduction to the Theology of Creation*. London: SPCK, 1998.
Flusser, David, with Steven Notley. *The Sage from Galilee: Rediscovering Jesus' Genius*. Grand Rapids: Eerdmans, 2007.
Grenz, Stanley J. *Theology for the Community of God*. Grand Rapids: Eerdmans, 2000.
Gunton, Colin E. *The Christian Faith: An Introduction to Christian Doctrine*. Oxford: Blackwell, 2002.
Johnson, Luke Timothy. *The Creed: What Christians Believe and Why It Matters*. London: DLT, 2003.
König, Adrio. *The Eclipse of Christ in Eschatology: Toward a Christ-centered Approach*. Grand Rapids: Eerdmans, 1989.
Licona, Michael R. *The Resurrection of Jesus: A New Historiographical Approach*. Downers Grove, IL: IVP Academic, 2010.
MacDonald, Gregory. *The Evangelical Universalist*. Eugene, OR: Cascade, 2006.
Migliore, Daniel L. *Faith Seeking Understanding: An Introduction to Christian Theology*. Grand Rapids: Eerdmans, 1991.

Neufeld, Thomas R. Yoder. *Recovering Jesus: The Witness of the New Testament*. Grand Rapids: Brazos, 2007.
Olson, Roger. *The Mosaic of Christian Belief: Twenty Centuries of Unity and Diversity*. Leicester, UK: Apollos, 2002.
———. *The Story of Christian Theology: Twenty Centuries of Tradition & Reform*. Leicester, UK: Apollos, 1999.
Sanders, E. P. *The Historical Figure of Jesus*. London: Penguin, 1993.
Sinkinson, Chris. *Confident Christianity: Conversations That Lead to the Cross*. Nottingham, UK: IVP, 2012.
Stackhouse, John G. Jr. *Humble Apologetics: Defending the Faith Today*. Oxford: Oxford University Press, 2002.
Starkey, Mike. *What's Wrong? Understanding Sin Today*. Oxford: BRF, 2001.
Stott, John R. W. *The Cross of Christ*. Leicester, UK: IVP, 1986.
Vermes, Geza. *Jesus the Jew: A Historian's Reading of the Gospels*. Reprint. London: SCM, 1983.
Ward, Keith. *The Evidence for God: The Case for the Existence of the Spiritual Dimension*. London: DLT, 2014.
———. *What the Bible Really Teaches: A Challenge for Fundamentalists*. London: SPCK, 2004.
Wright, Nigel G. *God on the Inside: The Holy Spirit in Holy Scripture*. Oxford: BRF, 2006.
———. *A Theology of the Dark Side: Putting the Power of Darkness in Its Place*. 2002 Reprint. Eugene, OR: Wipf and Stock, 2010.
Wright, N. T. *Jesus and the Victory of God*. London: SPCK, 1996.
———. *The Resurrection of the Son of God*. London: SPCK, 2003.
———. *Surprised by Hope*. London: SPCK, 2007.

www.ingramcontent.com/pod-product-compliance
Lightning Source LLC
Chambersburg PA
CBHW030823230426
43667CB00008B/1342